MW01491356

The Tejano Diaspora

The TEJANO DIASPORA

Mexican Americanism & Ethnic Politics in Texas and Wisconsin

MARC SIMON RODRIGUEZ

PUBLISHED IN ASSOCIATION WITH

The William P. Clements Center for Southwest Studies, Southern Methodist University, by The University of North Carolina Press, Chapel Hill

Publication of this book has been made possible in part by support from
the Institute for Scholarship in the Liberal Arts, College of Arts and Letters,
University of Notre Dame.

Library of Congress Cataloging-in-Publication Data
Rodriguez, Marc Simon.
The tejano diaspora : Mexican Americanism and ethnic politics in Texas
and Wisconsin / Marc Simon Rodriguez.
p. cm. Includes bibliographical references and index.
ISBN 978-0-8078-3464-0 (cloth : alk. paper)
1. Mexicans—Texas. 2. Mexicans—Wisconsin. 3. Migrant labor—Texas.
4. Migrant labor—Wisconsin. 5. Citizenship—United States. I. Title.
F395.M5R57 2011
305.8968'720764—dc22 2010043605

15 14 13 12 11   5 4 3 2 1

FOR MOM AND DAD,
IN MEMORY OF GINGER

Contents

Illustrations and Maps

Illustrations

Maps

Acknowledgments

Much like the activists in this book, I grew up traveling by automobile between Wisconsin and Texas. My parents were witnesses to the activism of this era and participants in some of the main strands of social activism of the late 1960s. As the family of a former migrant worker, each December we would pack up my father's pickup truck and head down to Texas, moving south from Milwaukee, through Chicago, and joining an annual migration of cars south. If you are from a Tejano or Mexican family in the Midwest, this drive is a familiar one, resembling a mass exodus. When I was very young, we could identify the Tejanos and Mexicans by the many things they hauled south in their trucks or the celebratory Tejano or Mexicano bumper stickers or gothic lettering on the rear windows, and, as time passed, a creative array of vanity plates. Some brought washers, dryers, and other mysterious gifts under tarps. At rest stops, we talked to people from Texas and Mexico making the same annual trek. These migrants defined life by the industries that recruited them to the Midwest and the variety of agricultural products they helped plant, tend, harvest, and process across lives defined by migration and rooted in community. With so much in common, however, Tejano-origin and Mexican-origin families were different and considered each other distinct, and there was meaning for both in the different boundaries and borders they crossed. This book is an outgrowth of the very Tejano diaspora that it details.

My greatest debt is to the former migrant farmworkers, activists, and everyday people in Crystal City, Texas, and Wisconsin who talked to me about their lives across the diaspora. To the people from both the Tejano and Anglo communities in both states who took the time to meet with me, suggest others to talk to, and to all who shared memories, personal artifacts, and their own impressions of history in their homes and offices I will always be grateful. This is an archival study, yet the many oral histories I conducted and the vast number of conversations I had in Wisconsin and Texas shape and color its metaphorical and historical structure. Activists and migrants including Jesus Salas, Miguel Delgado, Salvador Sanchez, José Angel Gutiérrez, Arturo Gonzalez, Carlos Reyes, Mario Compean, Ezequiel Guzman, Juan Alvarez, Ernesto Chacon, David Giffey, Mark Erenburg, Bill Smith, Genevieve Medina, Lupe Martinez, and many others read parts of the book, offered suggestions and criticisms, or supported this project from the start by taking time to share their personal histories, scrapbooks, and family albums with me. Sadly, Amalia Aguillar, publisher of the *Zavala County Sentinel*, and Francisco Rodriguez, an important activist in Wisconsin and Texas, did not live to see the publication of this book.

Many people have helped me make this a better project. Michael Gordon and Joseph Rodriguez at the University of Wisconsin–Milwaukee encouraged me to consider historical research and graduate education. At Northwestern University, Henry Binford, Ed Muir, Josef Barton, James Oakes, James Campbell, T. H. Breen, Harold Perkin, and Nancy MacLean challenged my assumptions about history and supported me in my endeavors. Josef Barton spent hours talking to me about migration, ethnicity, and the variety of comparative movements of peoples across the globe and made me a better historian. His constant attention to the similarities between migrant streams and his vast knowledge of polyglot historical literatures made him the perfect mentor for a migration project. Aldon Morris and Jane Mansbridge, two leading social movement scholars, provided me with the first venue for sharing my work across disciplines, and Jane in particular, even after her move to Harvard, read and reread my materials and helped me refine my thinking on the nature and origins of social movement ideology among Tejano migrants. My graduate school classmates and friends in Chicago—Wallace Best, Michael Bailey, Patrick Griffin, and Christine Bradley—filled my days with fruitful discussion and more. Christine Bradley helped me prepare the first draft of this book, completed the bibliography, and transcribed hours of oral interviews, and I am grateful to her for making the process of researching and writing this book a less painful task. At the University of Wisconsin Law School, Arthur McEvoy and Carin

Clauss helped me to explore the subtle connections between law and society in my work and made this a better book. At Wisconsin, I also had the privilege of participating as a fellow in the J. Willard Hurst Summer Institute in Legal History, where I benefited from the input of leading legal historians. At Northwestern University and the University of Wisconsin Law School, I was fortunate enough to receive generous financial support for my studies and research.

Several organizations have supported my work by awarding me post-doctoral fellowships and other grants to complete the research for this book. In 2003, the Clements Center for Southwest Studies at Southern Methodist University awarded me the Bill and Rita Clements Fellowship for the Study of Southwestern America. The Clements Center provided me with significant research funding and a year to do research and revise my manuscript. The manuscript review seminar sponsored by the center enabled me to share my work with nearly a dozen leading scholars in the field of Mexican American history. The Woodrow Wilson National Fellowship Foundation's Career Enhancement Fellowship gave me a year free from my teaching responsibilities at the University of Notre Dame in which to complete the manuscript.

All books are the product of working relationships between professional library staff and scholars, and there are many librarians and archivists that helped make this book a reality. The librarians and archivists at Northwestern University, the University of Wisconsin, Madison and Milwaukee campuses, as well as librarians and interlibrary loan staff at Princeton University libraries and the University of Notre Dame libraries helped me track down and locate a great variety of resources. The staffs at the Wisconsin State Historical Society in Milwaukee and Madison, the Walter Reuther Labor Archives at Wayne State University, and the Center for American History, Benson Latin American Collections, at the University of Texas in particular all spent hours with me sifting through a great variety of materials. I would especially like to thank Princeton University Library for providing me with funding to help preserve over sixty years of the *Zavala County Sentinel*, and the Center for American History at the University of Texas for filming the thousands of brittle, time- and rodent-worn pages of this frontier newspaper that became a major news source for Mexican American and Chicano history.

Many scholars took time to read chapters or the entire manuscript and offered me helpful advice. For these labors, I am grateful to Stephen Pitti, Zaragosa Vargas, Dionicio Valdes, David Gutiérrez, Ramon Gutiérrez, Neil Foley, David Montejano, Lizabeth Cohen, Roberto Calderon, Jim Barrett, Mario Garcia, Daniel Rodgers, Jeremy Adelman, Kevin Kruse, Michael Bailey, Mark Brilliant, Sara Deutsch, Sherry Smith, Jim Gregory, George Sanchez, John Chavez, Benjamin Johnson, Richard White, Donna Gabbacia, Mae Ngai, Andrew Isenberg, Nell Painter, Matthew Garcia, Carlos Blanton, Devra Weber, Sherry Smith, David Weber, George Martinez, Jim Grossman, Bill Jordan, Christine Stansell, and Annelise Orleck, who each reviewed chapters or the entire manuscript. I owe a debt to Vicky Ruiz and Matthew Garcia for refining my thinking on the meaning of translocalism and culture. David Gutiérrez, Donna Gabaccia, Ramon Gutierrez, and Neil Foley constantly challenged me and argued with me about the meaning of migrant activism and Mexican American politics (we disagree still from time to time), yet these historians pushed me to constantly think and write more clearly—and for this and their friendship I thank them. Throughout my academic career, Dionicio Valdes and Zaragosa Vargas, two leading scholars of Tejano and Mexican ancestry life in the Midwest, have served as mentors, editors, and critics, and I am grateful to them for their longtime professional and personal input. The comments provided by all of these talented scholars helped me make this a much better book.

I have had the privilege of working at two of the most prestigious universities in the world, and the rich climate of scholarly discussion and debate has shaped my work as a historian. At Princeton University, I would like to thank Alejandro Portes, Anthony Grafton, Kevin Kruse, Andrew Isenberg, Kenneth Mills, Bill Jordan, Patricia Fernandez-Kelly, Nell Painter, Graham Burnett, Dan Rodgers, Jeremy Adelman, Dirk Hartog, Sean Wilentz, Colin Palmer, Christine Stansell, and Wallace Best for their collegiality and scholarly input. As executive secretary of the Shelby Cullom Davis Center at Princeton, I interacted daily with David Gutiérrez, Luca Einaudi, Hasia Diner, David Abraham, Gary Gerstle, and the other Davis Center fellows and visitors working on the migration theme between 2001 and 2003. These scholars read my work, talked to me about migration, and provided useful input and suggestions as I prepared my manuscript. At Princeton, I coordinated a major conference on North American migration and a conference on the War on Poverty, both of which put me in contact with two important communities of scholars. These scholars have stayed in touch and helped each other over the years, and I am grateful to the assistance and friendship of the many people who constantly remind me that historians are a collegial bunch. Special thanks go out to Bob Bauman, Bill Clayson, Tom Kiffmeyer, Rhonda Williams, and Kimberly Phillips.

The University of Notre Dame has been an excellent place to do Latino studies work. Timothy Matovina, as director of the Cushwa Center for the Study of American Catholicism, along with the programs of the Institute for Latino Studies, has integrated the study of Latinos into the life of the leading Catholic university in the United States. In nearby Chicago, with the assistance of Gilberto Cardenas and Jim Grossman, I founded the Newberry Library Seminar in Borderlands and Latino Studies, which each year brings new scholars to Chicago to share their work. At the University of Notre Dame, I wish to thank John McGreevy, Gilberto Cardenas, Walter Nugent, Patrick Griffin, Jaime Pensado, Sandra Dedo, Sabine G. MacCormack, Tom Guglielmo, Jim Turner, Brad Gregory, Linda Przybyszewski, Theresa Delgadillo, Timothy Matovina, Jon Coleman, Gail Bederman, Robert Sullivan, Bill Miscamble, John Deak, Lauren Faulkner, Jason Ruiz, Mikolaj Kunicki, Karen Richman, Margaret Meserve, Maurizio Albahari, Pierpaolo Polzonetti, and Hector Escobar, for their guidance, friendship, and advice these past years. In many ways, this book is a response to Gil Cardenas's refrain that scholars of Latino history and life pay attention to the Midwest.

None of this would have been possible without the migration of my parents to Wisconsin in the 1960s. My mother and father were both committed educators and activists who played a role in the tumultuous civil rights activism of the 1960s. They marched in Milwaukee in support of migrant workers, open housing, and a variety of causes, and in the months before I was born, traveled to Washington as members of the Poor People's Campaign and camped in Resurrection City. My mother, Virginia Mary Flynn, a native of Massachusetts, and my father, Guadalupe Medina Rodriguez, a Tejano former farmworker, met as their lives crossed paths and spent their lives committed to social justice and educational reform. In particular, my mother's parents, Simon and Virginia Flynn, encouraged me constantly and challenged my assumptions about so many things over the many summers I spent at their retirement home in Maine. My father's mother, Maria Medina

Rodriguez, from her kitchen table in Texas told me stories of her long life as a single parent following the premature death of my grandfather from tuberculosis and remembered the difficulties faced by migrants in a way that was always attentive to the sublime in a life of struggle. My brother and sisters, David, Melissa, and Jessica, watched me go from steelworker to college professor, and while they might not understand why I chose this path, they have always been proud of me for doing so. I am happy that my two grandmothers, both over ninety years old now, saw this project become a book.

I am extremely grateful for all the people, institutions, and opportunities that have helped to support my academic career. They each contributed to making this book better than it might otherwise have been, and any errors or omissions in the final text are my own.

Abbreviations in the Text

AGIF   American GI Forum

CAP   Community Action Program

CASA   Citizens Association Serving All Americans

CSO   Community Service Organization

CU   Ciudadanos Unidos

EOA   Economic Opportunity Act

GCML   Governor's Committee on Migratory Labor

HEW   Department of Health, Education, and Welfare

LAUCR   Latin American Union for Civil Rights

LULAC   League of United Latin American Citizens

MALDEF   Mexican American Legal Defense and Educational Fund

MAPA   Mexican American Political Association

MAYO   Mexican American Youth Organization

NAACP   National Association for the Advancement of Colored People

NFWA   National Farm Workers Association

NLRB   National Labor Relations Board

OEO   Office of Economic Opportunity

OU   Obreros Unidos

PASSO   Political Association of Spanish Speaking Organizations

RUP   La Raza Unida Party

TEA   Texas Education Agency

UFW   United Farm Workers

UFWOC	United Farm Workers Organizing Committee
UMOS	United Migrant Opportunity Services
WERB	Wisconsin Employment Relations Board
WERC	Wisconsin Employment Relations Council [*now* Commission]
ZCEDC	Zavala County Economic Development Corporation

Introduction

In 1963, Crystal City, Texas, shot onto the national scene when a group of five Mexican Americans dubbed "Los Cinco" swept all seats on the common council. This "revolt" made its way onto the front pages of the *Wall Street Journal*, the *New York Times*, the *Los Angeles Times*, and *Life* magazine. The events in Crystal City forced Americans to ask questions about the other "race" problem in the United States during a period of civil rights turbulence that focused on the dramatic African American freedom struggle in the South. Led by flamboyant Teamsters Union representative Juan Cornejo, Crystal City's activism caused some to speculate that these events in Texas marked the start of an expanding political role for Mexican Americans in southwestern politics and might provide African American activists with a framework for political success in the South.

The activism of Crystal City did not emanate from a large city, but it reflected the tensions in one of the largest-population regions of Mexican American settlement in the nation and stood out as one of many national events that placed Mexican American politics on the national agenda after 1960. Yet there was more to Crystal City than its place in one of the many Mexican American–majority counties of South Texas from Del Rio to Brownsville. The city's residents, over 80 percent of Mexican ancestry and nearly all engaged in migratory farmwork, lived in a translocal world of labor that, because of Los Cinco and the emerging labor movement among farmworkers, increasingly incorporated politics into existing repertoires of social action. One key link emerged three years after the Los Cinco action, when twenty-three-year-old Crystal City native Jesus Salas, with a group of farmworkers, college students, and clergy, marched to Wisconsin's capital in solidarity with similar protests in California and Texas. This 1966 march, like the rise of Los Cinco three years earlier, expanded the activism of the community into the interstate world of migrants.

By considering the translocal dimension of Mexican American politics, this book challenges a geographically settled understanding of U.S. history and suggests new ways to consider the vast diaspora that made Mexican American life a rich tapestry of interrelated and overlapping communities. Each spring, entire families in Crystal City boarded up their homes and moved north and west to work. Unlike transmigrants, these U.S. citizens crossed no national border, yet they traversed a variety of cultural and structural boundaries. In doing so, they participated in a migration stream that was both annual and linked to a deep history of interstate migration and urbanization. Lacking any clear point of concentration, Tejano migrants created footholds in a variety of small, medium, and large cities from the Great Lakes to California. Like the African American migrants who moved in overlapping streams of migration from the South to settle permanently in the cities of the North and West, Tejano migration reacted to some of the same transformative economic pressures, yet continued its circular pattern. Thrust into migration by changes in the North American labor market and agricultural economy that often pitted them against Mexican workers, Tejanos fashioned flexible labor, economic, and social networks that functioned for much of the twentieth century. This "Tejano diaspora" allowed for a near-seamless flow of workers and ideas across the country, linking a variety of people together as "Tejanos" as they engaged the major upheavals in Mexican American politics and culture nationwide.[1]

To explore the history of activism across the Tejano diaspora with precision, this book considers how Mexican American activism after World War II emerged as a "translocal" politics emanating from South Texas to other parts of the country, notably the Midwest, and especially Wisconsin. Young Mexican Americans traversing this interstate web of seasonal labor migrations articulated a kind of "Mexican Americanism" in school and politics that embraced a politics of ethnic inclusion generated in the Texas postwar period and a politics of reform activism with roots in the Wisconsin progressive and labor tradition.[2] In this way, the migrant-labor world produced a unique political outlook and activism among young Tejanos coming of age in the United States in the 1950s and 1960s. These young activists exited classrooms to participate in the main social movements that grew in force in the 1960s and 1970s, pressing for a place in the mainstream of the nation as well as space for those things that made them different.[3]

The turbulent story spanning the worlds of Texas and Wisconsin that is at the center of this book provides a corrective to the overly settled focus of Mexican American history on events in California and Texas. The traditional approach to the study of this history has focused to a large degree on the local preservation of urban and countryside society and the process of resistance to the culture of the United States. Mainly centered on Southern California and South Texas, these studies show the ways Mexican colonials and the communities they formed became the basis for persistent settlements of Mexican Americans in Los Angeles, San Antonio, Santa Barbara, and other cities. Later studies, while expanding our understanding of gender, intercultural relations, and popular culture, have essentially followed this same model of settlement and resistance, even as they increasingly mark out the terrain of acculturation. While preservation and resistance represented important responses in most places where Mexicans settled, these places and the people in them changed as waves of immigration and migration from a variety of sources created several generational and nativity strata within Mexican-ancestry population groups and as some, rather than resisting American culture, embraced certain parts of it. Some research suggests that the inflow of transmigrants regenerates and strengthens community life, while translocal Tejano migrants challenge and undermine the process of cultural resistance. Other examinations of Mexican American life routinely explore the role of hybridism and of Americanization campaigns yet leave the resulting acculturation understudied, particularly in California, where Mexican Americans traditionally intermarried with Anglos at relatively high rates.

This study takes place within the Texas and Wisconsin segment of the national "Tejano diaspora," by which I refer to the permanent dispersion of several hundred thousand Mexican Americans from Texas across the rest of the United States. This migration grew significantly after World War II as part of the broader "southern diaspora," linking Tejanos to one another through the annual movement of nearly two hundred thousand farmworkers between South Texas and established communities of Tejanos in the urban North and West.[4] As U.S. citizens,

Tejano migrants enjoyed greater ease of movement between states than noncitizens, but their access to the political, legal, and other rights of citizens varied, a fact that facilitated the development of labor, civil, and political protest between Texas and Wisconsin.[5] Tejano activists articulated a commitment to a pragmatic Americanist politics: operating across community and state boundaries, and working at both ends of the Tejano diaspora, they pursued inclusion and acculturation, yet they often did so in opposition to Anglos and institutions that excluded or limited the life chances of Mexican Americans.[6]

The migrant stream that comprised the Tejano diaspora emerged in the early twentieth century as a labor network established by interstate agricultural industries. Mexican immigrants settled by the thousands in South Texas after 1900, joining older communities and forming new ones. This settlement accelerated during the Mexican Revolution, making Texas one of the primary entry points for migrants, including many who later moved to other southwestern states and to California in search of stability. Some entered already established Mexican-ancestry communities, whereas others settled in entirely new farm and ranching cities in South Texas where they formed distinct Mexican districts.[7] Among those who established their homes in the agricultural cities of South Texas, the majority worked as harvest hands in the vegetable and citrus industries, often joining the annual "big swing" migration of cotton workers within Texas. These settlements rapidly became collection and recruitment areas for migrant farmworkers in Texas and eventually the rest of the nation.

Migration and settlement in Texas alone did not make these people into "Tejanos," a term most commonly used to describe the Spanish and Mexican colonial settlers of Texas and their descendants. In a more expansive use of the term, migrants increasingly became "Tejano" as a result of the extension of these labor networks, which thrust Texas-based workers into the North American migrant labor market. By midcentury, agricultural industries and canneries were increasingly recruiting workers in Texas, and in response South Texas migrants had expanded the range of their labor movement to include California, the Northwest, and the Midwest. Competition with Mexican immigrants and contract workers in Texas agriculture served as an incentive for Tejano farmworkers to seek out seasonal work at higher wages in states like Wisconsin. In this search for stability, Tejano migrant workers scattered across

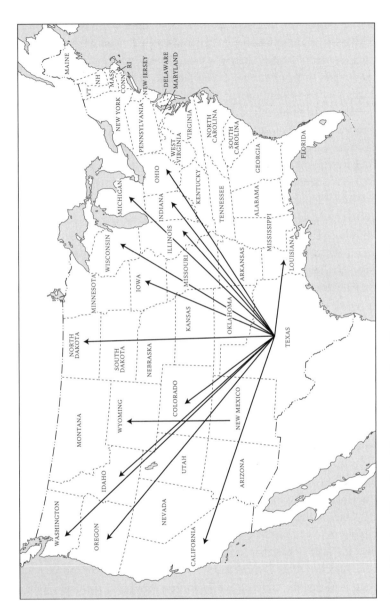

Map 1. Migration of Texas-based farmworkers northward in early spring, mid-1950s

the United States, but as they established themselves within broader Latino and Latin American neighborhoods in the North and West, they strengthened their Texas-origin identities—their sense of connection to often recently established Texas hometowns.[8] In an unstable world, migrant workers made these places in South Texas home and remade themselves as Tejanos, even if their families had left Mexico in the decades after the revolution.

More than employment drew Tejano workers to the North and West: a variety of other social, economic, and political factors influenced the decision to migrate or relocate. Western and midwestern communities in places like Wisconsin often allowed for greater flexibility in the use of social space, more economic mobility, and a potential for interracial and interethnic cooperation often lacking in Texas.[9] Crystal City novelist Tomás Rivera characterized migrant workers as "searchers" seeking stability and self-discovery beyond the segregation, poverty, and racialized worldview of South Texas. Rivera came to view the midwestern United States as a place with opportunities and outlooks uncommon in Texas.[10]

The Mexican Americanism that developed in Texas and Wisconsin reflected the influence of this emerging national politics taking shape after World War II. The call for equality, upward mobility, and the preservation of ethnic identity grounded postwar demands for a place within the United States as full citizens.[11] This politics of Mexican Americanism allowed for the maintenance of specific cultural and political traditions within the more general Americanist framework. In accepting their status as Mexican-ancestry citizens in and of the United States, young Tejanos pressed for a place within a framework defined by increasingly hardened nation-states and citizenship regimes. They also borrowed from Texas- and Wisconsin-based political traditions as well as changes in Mexican American politics during the 1960s, altering Mexican Americanism along the way.[12] As radical Mexican Americanism evolved into the Chicano movement, the rhetoric of cultural pride took over. Activists began to outwardly reject acculturation and instead sought control over the institutions that served the Mexican-ancestry community. Far from rejecting ethnic or cultural self-definition in favor of 100 percent Americanism, the Chicano movement emerged as a politics of pragmatic engagement and choice when activists and everyday people confronted the contradictions between high-minded national rhetoric of American freedom and local racial and ethnic discrimination.[13]

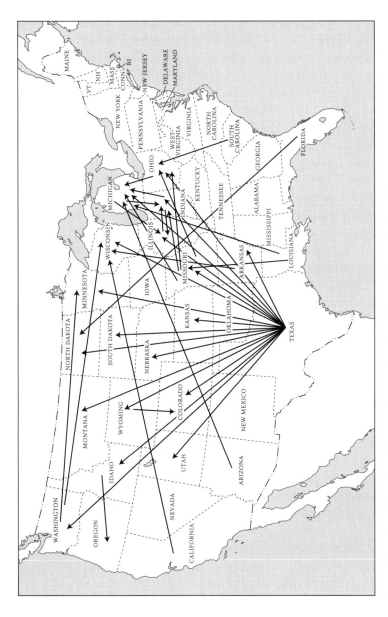

Map 2. Migration of Texas-based farmworkers northward and from spring work sites, mid-1950s

The Chicano movement emerged in the 1960s as a radical phase in the long history of Mexican American civil rights activism. With no central leadership, this social movement grew from a variety of roots and expressed the concerns of a large number of local communities across the United States. Although it was not a single movement, several key groups and leaders served as its organizational base in California, Texas, Colorado, and across the Tejano diaspora. Some Chicano ideologists called for a separatist movement or for armed resistance, yet most participants, while attentive to the legacy of discrimination and political oppression, mainly sought to reform the American political and educational systems. Movement leaders borrowed militant tactics and rhetoric from the Mexican radical tradition and the Black Power and Third World movements in creating what Ignacio Garcia has termed the "militant ethos" of the movement. In making the Chicano movement, young people voiced their concerns, utilized the rhetoric of race and resistance, and sought to build a place for Mexican Americans and other Latinos in the social fabric of the United States.[14]

The young activists and the community movements they led, which lie at the center of this book, reflect a coming-of-age story for some of those who grew up in the 1950s and early 1960s shaped by the cold war and educational reforms that increased Mexican American school attendance. The major reform of the postwar period in Texas was the passage of a law linking school funding to compulsory attendance. Once inside the doors of the schoolhouse, young Tejano men and women interacted with the Americanist political imaginary.[15] Daily contact with the ideology of Americanism in school provided young people with ready ideological tools for future use.[16] Teens and young adults underwent a "segmented" process of acculturation, accepting certain aspects of Americanism while also preserving a distinct Tejano and Mexican American worldview based on their lived experiences as American minorities.[17] Mexican American men and women, veterans, and young people in particular grew increasingly aware that as American citizens they had civil and social rights that petty local officials, institutions, and individuals had no legal or moral power to deny them, and they began to articulate the moral failures of the Anglo establishment.[18]

More than a rural story, this book also documents the migration from small cities to larger ones. The transformation of cities and urban space after World War II has garnered significant attention from scholars, yet these narratives, which make claims about national developments, overwhelmingly remain tied to a black/white paradigm. Scholars often overlook the story of continued economic vitality and Latino in-migration in the spatial history of American cities. For Mexican-ancestry people from Texas, the story of urbanization continued even as the larger processes of white migration from cities, urban decline, and African American social mobilization captured the attention of the nation. These Mexican American citizens moved from urban communities (but often considered rural) in the farming and ranching counties of South Texas to the larger barrios in the medium and large metropolitan areas of the northern and western United States. Although they formed a much smaller population group than African Americans for much of the twentieth century, their internal migration to northern and western cities developed in tandem with the increasing growth of African American and other minority populations in central cities. In places like Chicago, New York, and Los Angeles, this in-migration expanded the space occupied by Mexican- and Puerto Rican–ancestry people.[19]

The city of Milwaukee was one of many midwestern receiving cities for Tejano migrants after World War II, and it offered an abundance of factory work and a well-established labor movement. Each year, roughly fifteen thousand Texas-based migrant workers entered Wisconsin to undertake summer work after completing springtime harvest work in the Pacific Northwest, Great Plains, or other midwestern states. In Wisconsin, a social movement developed that linked Milwaukee's southside barrio, a well-established neighborhood with roots in the migration following the Mexican Revolution, to nearby agricultural regions where the mainly Tejano migrant community worked each year. In Milwaukee, Tejanos encountered an established Mexican American, Puerto Rican, and Latin American presence in the diverse Spanish-speaking milieu of the city's industrial neighborhoods, and they entered into a diverse urban politics, building coalitions with long-settled Mexican-ancestry residents, African Americans, Puerto Ricans, and other Latinos and embracing a variety of identities simultaneously.

The increasingly militant Mexican American activism expanded the definition of politics for young people in Milwaukee, as it did in several other large cities, yet they did not reject key pillars of Americanism even when they embraced a Chicano identity and felt greater cultural pride. Responding to the key development of the growth of the United

Farm Workers (UFW) movement in California after 1966, young activists in South Texas took up the UFW banner in the Rio Grande Valley, and Wisconsin migrants established an independent union named Obreros Unidos. All of these movements relied on the AFL-CIO, which coordinated and funded their organizing efforts. In the late 1960s, Crystal City native José Angel Gutiérrez became the voice of a celebratory Chicano nationalism that made cultural and political claims in resistance to American mainstream society without abandoning the whole of Americanist ideology. Activists in Milwaukee blended these two frameworks—that of labor activism and that of Chicano nationalism—within a mixed-race and mixed-ethnicity urban environment that maintained connections to cities in agricultural-producing regions of Wisconsin and South Texas.

Although Chicano nationalism often appears as a wholly oppositional movement, it was far more diverse and contradictory in practice. Certainly, many voices spoke of an irredentism that considered the Southwest the Chicano or Aztec homeland (Aztlán), yet often these same activists or organizations demanded affirmative action and bilingual education, and they made other Americanist claims on states, institutions, and the federal government. In Milwaukee, Tejanos participated in a movement that linked the broader contours of *el movimiento* (the collective civil rights movement of Mexican Americans) with the struggles of Puerto Ricans and other Latinos, often blurring the lines of ethnicity and identity within and between groups. Wisconsin was amenable to such movements as a birthplace of the Progressive movement and one of the few places where Socialists and academics often held office and had long played an active role in government reform. In this setting, Tejano and Latino activists in Milwaukee expanded and reformulated notions of Americanism, Progressivism, and ethnic citizenship through protest and real opportunities to implement change.

Mexican Americans increasingly moved beyond merely building community within the ethnic enclave, moreover: during this period of protest, they also expanded out into the larger society in a thoughtful way. Politics, by its very nature, tends to fix itself in some degree to a place, be it a high school, an electoral jurisdiction, a state labor board, or a local political party office. As such, this study seeks to understand the activist movements that emanated from Crystal City as both settled and translocal phenomena. Activists from Crystal City living and working in Texas and Wisconsin spoke as Mexican-ancestry Americans with pride in their origins when they demanded acceptance of their status as persons and citizens in both places. This orientation toward citizenship rights was the result of a long process of resistance, accommodation, and adjustment to life in the United States.

By considering the 1950s roots of the radical Mexican Americanism that grew in the 1960s, the precursors to the social movement that took root among the young emerge as the extension and expansion of local efforts by a mix of working-class and upwardly mobile Mexican Americans to push for civil rights. Following the lead of African Americans, adult activists in Crystal City pressed with moderation for school reform and a political voice. They failed at both efforts when the conservative Anglo political community waged negative campaigns and moderate Anglos abandoned the effort. But in light of the heretofore lost history of their failed moderate, inclusionist insurgency, the subsequent movements of Crystal City emerge as an expansion of and radicalization of earlier attempts to claim the rights of citizens. Histories like this one, analyzed in chapter 1, reflect the way local people implemented and altered the ongoing national efforts of organizations to press for "cultural" and other citizenship rights.[20] While the shift from a moderate to a radical Americanist politics led many middle-class leaders to abandon activism, many of the goals and demands remained the same, even as the tactics and rhetoric changed under the influence of new leadership.

Never confined merely to the world of electoral or school politics, activism also takes place within other institutions, such as the public schools themselves. If moderates and acculturated members of local communities were pressing for change, Mexican American students were also engaging in a politics of inclusion and acculturation within the context of the American high school. As chapter 2 makes clear, the high school environment enabled Mexican American teens to engage the "proto-politics" of school life as they made demands for a greater role in what became a testing ground for future public politics. Most histories of Mexican American politics in Crystal City document the rapid success and failure of Los Cinco to govern in the face of Anglo harassment and pressure from the notorious Texas Rangers. This study seeks to shift the emphasis onto the role played by the young people who took their activism out of the schools and into the public world of electoral politics. Through observation and participation, young Mexican Americans learned from Los Cinco and other past efforts as they conceptualized a distinct translocal politics in Wisconsin shaped by their experiences in Texas.[21]

Just one of the many states that Texas-based migrants traveled to each season, Wisconsin became a central arena in the development of translocal labor organization among the migrants of Crystal City. Inspired by recent California and Texas state capital marches on behalf of farmworkers, Crystal City natives, college students, and religious leaders in Wisconsin led a similar march to Madison that served as the spark for the establishment of an independent farm labor union. The progressive state regulatory and legal institutions created by reformers John R. Commons, Elizabeth Brandeis-Raushenbush, and Robert La Follette made Wisconsin a seemingly perfect place for organizing migrant workers. Yet the situation was far from ideal: the Wisconsin case foreshadowed the failure of the UFW as a national union and serves as an example of the way that legal rights supposedly meant to protect labor in fact create mechanisms for the protection of employer interests. The Wisconsin effort, detailed in chapter 3, also suggests how traditional union leaders like César Chávez and institutional unions often worked against the expansion of labor leadership and independent labor organization, despite public calls for solidarity and mutuality.

This is also a book about the urbanization of Mexican Americans from the small cities of the Southwest to the larger cities of the North and West. The development of urban life in San Antonio, Southern California, and, more recently, Chicago form the backbone of Mexican American urban history. Although some scholars detail the long history of Mexican-ancestry settlement in the Great Lakes, Midwest, and Pacific Northwest, few have focused on the move of urbanized people from small cities to larger ones or the ways their urban roots affected the processes of activism and policy formation during the turbulent era of the War on Poverty. Chapter 4 of this book explores the way a Texas-origin migrant community took shape in Milwaukee and the politics this group built with an understanding of themselves as "migrants," despite the fact that many had settled permanently in Wisconsin. Their migrant politics served as the foundation of calls for community control and led to the takeover of an important War on Poverty agency, United Migrant Opportunity Services, Inc. (UMOS), by Tejano and Crystal City migrant activists. They remade it into a migrant-centered arena for service delivery and a form of Tejano politics—and alternatively Chicano, Latino, and poor people's politics—informed by diverse interactions with other minorities and progressive reformers.

By the late 1960s, activists had completely transformed the system of labor recruitment established by employers to serve as the foundation for a translocal migrant and Tejano politics. Chapter 5 shows how this same network provided the mechanism for the circular transfer of activists and organizers when Crystal City again became a center of radical politics after 1960. As La Raza Unida ("the United Race") Party (RUP) grew in Crystal City, the migrant stream became key to the growth of a leadership core for the party in Texas. The RUP in Crystal City grew as a party of migrants linked to the activist campaigns and organizational activities of migrants in Wisconsin. Experienced organizers and managers from Wisconsin moved back to Texas to assist in the formation of the party, and activists from California and Texas who were based in Crystal City entered into this system, enabling the growth of the RUP. Although originally based on a localism born out of community life and the process of migration, the politics of migration defined the contours and personnel of the movement for civil rights in Wisconsin, Crystal City, and other places by the late 1970s.

This book seeks to show how activists adapted broader national themes and activist practices while maintaining a focus on expanding the meaning of Mexican American citizenship on what was a unique translocal stage. Influenced by the turbulence of the 1960s, activists like Jesus Salas, Francisco Rodriguez, José Angel Gutiérrez, and many others engaged the various aspects of the liberal state in Texas, Wisconsin, and again in Texas as they pushed the limits of citizenship in an effort to topple a discriminatory system that limited their lives and those of their parents and immigrant grandparents. This story is not, however, a linear tale of social movement emergence, buildup, and victory. With each organizational success, these Mexican American activists also experienced failure and internal dissention as they often built temporary defenses against the unfettered power of big business, conservative elements within government and legal institutions, and their own limitations as minority group members, as well as those of their leaders and the movements of which they were a part. To some degree, this is a story of organizational success and structural failure. The legacy of this social movement is a mixed one. Like many social movements that emerged from grassroots ethnic life in America, translocal Mexican Americanism left a legacy of accomplishment different than those teens had dreamed of in high school classrooms in the late 1950s and early 1960s.

Post–World War II Mexican Americanism in Crystal City, Texas

In early 2003, the *Zavala County Sentinel* ran a newly discovered photo of nearly a dozen uniformed service men and women posing in downtown Crystal City. The image captured the high level of World War II military participation among Mexican Americans in this small South Texas city.[1] Many of the veterans pictured spent their lives as politically active citizens in motion between Texas, the Midwest, California, and beyond. In the early postwar years, some engaged in a civil and patriotic form of activism in an effort to remake their hometown in the image of the America they had imagined and defended in uniform, seeking a place for Mexican-ancestry citizens within the broader society.[2]

For Mexican Americans throughout the Southwest, as for African Americans in the South, the post–World War II period witnessed increasing civil rights activism. Among the southwestern states, Texas served as a central location of postwar militancy on the part of Mexican Americans, in part for reasons of demography: although California would surpass Texas in total Mexican-ancestry population by 1960, Texas had the largest established Mexican American population in the United States after the war, with 1,033,768 Spanish-surnamed residents in 1950 compared to California's 760,453. Texas hosted both of the nation's largest Mexican American civil rights organizations. The League of United Latin-American Citizens (LULAC), a national organization founded in 1929, fought discrimination against Latinos, particularly through its long effort to end discrimination against Mexican-origin children in public education. The American GI Forum (AGIF), established in 1948 by Dr. Hector P. Garcia to advocate for veterans' rights, subsequently committed itself to the elimination of the poll tax and to Mexican American voter registration, and it joined with LULAC in bringing a number of antidiscrimination court cases in the 1950s.[3]

To understand the successes and failures of postwar Mexican Americanist politics and the foundation it created for subsequent activism across the migrant stream, this chapter sets the efforts of the AGIF within a local context in Crystal City, Texas. It begins with an examination of spatial separation from the early twentieth century through the 1950s to reveal the way Anglos and Mexicans structured what was a racialized community. From the founding of Crystal City, Mexican-ancestry people served primarily as an agricultural and increasingly migratory labor force—a position that compelled a large majority of this population to spend much of the year in transit, working in Texas and other locations across the United States. The postwar era brought the introduction of Mexican braceros, or contract workers, whose presence strengthened divisions between Mexicans and Anglos in ways that benefitted some ethnic entrepreneurs but also preserved the perception of all Mexican-ancestry people as foreign.

Within this social environment, AGIF members practiced a politics of civility in an attempt to carve out a role for themselves as representatives of the Mexican American majority. This approach failed repeatedly: Anglos rejected it as a threat to the hardened racial boundaries they had created to control the participation of the Mexican American majority. Indeed, the virulence of Crystal City Anglos' reaction to the efforts of the AGIF's "moderate" politics suggests the radical challenge that early Mexican Americanism represented to the social and political practices of Anglo-controlled South Texas. Its limitations and its failure led subsequent activists to fashion their own, more radical version of Mexican Americanist politics.[4]

Social Separation in the Heart of the Winter Garden District

From its establishment in 1907 from the culled-together remains of the Cross-S Ranch, a property built by combining unperfected Spanish grants in Zavala County, Crystal City grew as two cities, one Anglo and the other Mexican. Located 120 miles southwest of San Antonio and 50 miles from the Mexican border at Eagle Pass, Crystal City experienced significant growth in its first twenty years, as entrepreneurs, speculators, and labor migrants from Texas and Mexico joined the small ranching class that had settled Zavala County in the late nineteenth century along the banks of the Nueces River. Between 1920 and 1930, the population of Crystal City grew from 3,108 to 10,349 as the region experienced a farming boom, and this population remained stable and divided, with Anglo and Mexican urban communities on separate sides of the railroad tracks, following a widespread pattern across the Southwest and California.[5]

Boosters seeking to develop the region dubbed the area around Zavala County the "Winter Garden District." The district encompassed the border county of Maverick as well as Zavala and Dimmit counties and part of LaSalle County; it had close economic and other relationships with settlements in Uvalde and Frio counties, as well. By the late 1920s, Crystal City had emerged as the primary urban, commercial, and labor center for the district. In many ways, it was a typical farming city, which lacked the established Mexican landholding class of Laredo or Brownsville as well as the paternalism and patronage systems of the ranch-dominated, Anglo-run counties of the Rio Grande Valley.[6]

Like Crystal City, whose population had peaked by 1930, the Winter Garden District as a whole experienced rapid population and economic expansion between 1920 and 1930, with Zavala County surpassing nearby Dimmit and Maverick counties in population. Mexican immigrants from Coahuila, Nuevo Leon, and Tamaulipas who may have already worked as transmigrant laborers in Texas journeyed to Crystal City, built simple homes, and established businesses. Even as they settled permanently, however, they remained a migrant laboring people. Workers planted the two dominant crops, onions and spinach, in September, and in October they harvested fall crops. In the late fall, they began the labor-intensive period of transplant and harvest work in onions and spinach that provided employment through late spring. Summer brought work in cotton and, for an ever-larger number of workers, migration to find harvest work in the Great Lakes and Great Plains states.[7]

Even as the population of Mexican-ancestry workers boomed, Anglos used their temporary majority status in the early decades of the century to shape and establish control of the district's city and county governments. This control extended to the selection of candidates for county and city office. In Dimmit County, to offer the most glaring example, the White Man's Primary Association worked to exclude the Mexican-ancestry majority from the candidate selection process.[8] Elsewhere in the district, Anglo political control was less blatant but equally real.

After World War II, Crystal City continued as a small, now mainly Mexican-ancestry city with just under ten thousand residents. Over 85 percent of the population in 1960 was of Mexican origin, with 32 percent being foreign born. Sixty-three percent of families had annual incomes of less than three thousand dollars, and over 80 percent of the Mexican-origin population engaged in annual migratory agricultural work. Several prominent Anglo families owned most of the county's land, while the majority of the city's Anglos worked as teachers, professionals, civil servants, ranch workers, and shop owners whose incomes, homes, and lifestyles stood in stark contrast to those of their Mexican-ancestry neighbors.[9]

Residential separation defined the boundaries of community life and infrastructure in Crystal City, as it did across much of South Texas. The Anglo neighborhood expanded eastward from City Hall on East Zavala Street along paved roads lined with modern ranch- and Victorian-style homes served by major utilities. Other, smaller Anglo neighborhoods lined the west side, yet this area was also home to what locals referred to as "Mexico Grande," the largest concentration of Mexican-ancestry residents and businesses in the city. The city had smaller Mexican settlements at Campo Santo, near the Catholic cemetery, and Mexico Chico, on the south side of the city. In general, Mexico Grande, Mexico Chico, and Campo Santo had limited or no street paving, as well as uneven utility service, with some homes lacking running water well into the 1960s.[10]

The commercial center boasted a well-developed shopping district that ran along East and West Zavala Street on both sides of the railroad tracks, which served the centrally located cotton gin and vegetable packinghouse. This main street, lined with tall palms and mature citrus trees, served as a regional shopping destination for families of the Winter Garden District.[11] As the heart of the Winter Garden, the city's center was home to regional governmental and professional offices and national retailers, including the Department of Agriculture, the Zavala County Bank, a Chevy dealership, and a Dodge dealership, as well as the Guild Theater, which showed recent Hollywood releases.[12]

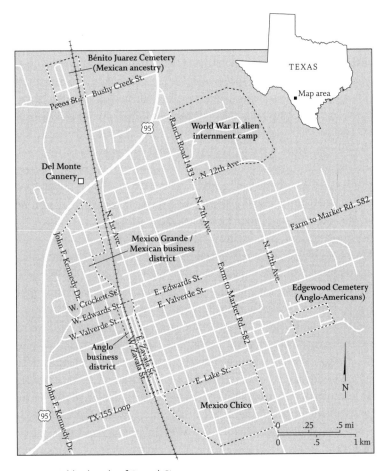

Map 3. Neighborhoods of Crystal City

For Crystal City—and much of South Texas and the Southwest—where street pavement and sidewalks ended, the "Mexican section" began. The downtown shopping district faded as West Zavala Street became Avenue A in the center of Mexico Grande. Well-developed when compared to barrios or *colonias* in other nearby towns but shabby when compared to Zavala Street, Mexico Grande provided a full array of Mexican-style shops, such as bakeries, barbershops, taverns, restaurants, fruit stands, two Spanish-language theaters, and a medical office.[13] Longtime resident Gloria Cuellar remembered that the downtown "was so pretty, with citrus trees, and . . . full of nice places, fruit stands, and many taverns."[14]

Although there were signs of Mexican American prosperity in Crystal City's Mexican section, the poverty of the Mexican American majority was palpable as one walked the streets of Crystal City.[15] Throughout the 1950s, tuberculosis threatened the lives and prosperity of both the Anglo and Mexican American communities, and the Tuberculosis Association, vigilant in pressing its X-ray exam program, became one of few points of cooperation in the city: it appears that middle-class Mexican American women worked with the county's Anglo medical establishment to assist residents in taking the test. Poverty also had other costs. The low income of many Mexican American fathers contributed to cases of child abandonment and desertion. Some workers traveled north, never to return alive; dying in accidents across the diaspora, their bodies would be returned home for burial at the Catholic Bénito Juarez Cemetery. As migrants continued to labor and suffer the sting of intergenerational poverty, some advanced to moderate prosperity by supplementing earnings made in the Midwest and California with work in Crystal City and temporary work in large urban areas outside of Texas.[16]

The contrast between Anglo prosperity and Mexican American poverty nonetheless remained stark even when, in the postwar period, the Anglo management of local businesses and national retailers began hiring more Mexican American employees and courting the Mexican American trade. Gloria Cuellar remembered, "The shops began to hire mostly Mexican American clerks, and I clerked at all those stores when I was in high school."[17] Large chains, most prominently J. C. Penney, entered Crystal City in the 1950s and employed young Mexican Americans like Cuellar on the showroom floor. As Sears and Montgomery Ward opened stores in Crystal City later in the decade, they likewise hired Mexican American sales staff.[18] Local merchants also hired young Mexican Americans as clerks and ran bilingual advertisements. The Leonard Furniture Company, for example, ran two advertisements, one in English and one in Spanish, featuring photographs of Neno Certantes, an employee, and "El Patron," presumably Mr. Leonard.[19] Opening commercial space to people of Mexican ancestry made sense, as Mexican Americans were the majority population in the city, county, and region. In order to survive, Anglo businesses needed to attract Mexican American shoppers.

The postwar period also witnessed limited commercial integration on Zavala Street when a small number of Mexican American businesses expanded by opening stores downtown, seeking customers from both communities. Longoria's Department Store, for example, was located downtown on West Zavala Street and ran large English-language advertisements in the *Zavala County Sentinel*.[20] Other such businesses ran advertisements in English, such as Canela's Bakery, which featured "French Pastries and Bread Cakes for all Occasions" as well as traditional Mexican *pan dulce*, and the Salas Call Taxi Service operated by Manuel Salas Sr., which offered "service day and night."[21] In the main sections of the paper, Mexican American–owned grocery stores ran advertisements in Spanish and English featuring a mixture of traditional Mexican foods and American brands. The large Rodriguez Grocery, Guarneros Food Stores, and Gomez Meat and Groceries advertised free delivery, sales, and weekend specials.[22]

Even though the shopping district opened to Mexican-ancestry consumers and some businesses, traditional fears about crossing the lines of separation kept many Mexican Americans from shopping in the Anglo section on more than special occasions. Perhaps because of past discrimination, some felt uneasy entering the Anglo district. Life-long resident Amalia Aguillar remembered that some older residents feared that Anglos "would fight with them or shoot at them."[23] Although death while shopping along Zavala Street was not a serious threat in the 1950s, resident Arturo Gonzales recollected that he felt there "were several places that you weren't allowed to go."[24] As Oscar Cervera put it, even friendly Anglos "would never allow their kids to play with . . .

the Mexican kids."[25] In Crystal City of the 1950s, Anglos and Mexican Americans lived parallel and often interdependent lives, but they seldom did so as equals.[26]

As its small steps toward business integration suggest, Crystal City made some progress in race relations after the war. The local newspaper incorporated coverage of Mexican-ancestry social and religious life into its pages each week. Early in the 1950s, the *Zavala County Sentinel* began a Spanish-language society and news page titled "El Noticiero" written by Olga Lopez, who reported on community life, and it also began publishing Mexican American and AGIF news in the main sections of the paper, running important stories in both English and Spanish. During the Korean War, Mexican American service members routinely appeared in front-page veterans' profiles. In the late 1950s, the paper increasingly covered Mexican American weddings, funerals, birthday celebrations, *quinceañeras*, and visits from former residents living in the Midwest alongside Anglo community news.

Even as the pages of the *Sentinel* increasingly integrated, however, the social lives of Anglos and Mexican Americans revolved in separate and unequal orbits.[27] Most common social and membership organizations had no Spanish-surnamed members, segregated churches prevailed, and few Mexican Americans held office or employment at the city or county level unless appointed by Anglos.[28] The Lions Club and Chamber of Commerce, for instance, had no Spanish-surnamed members well into the postwar period.[29] Women's social groups, including the Twenty Four Club and Athena Study Club, continued into the postwar period with an exclusively Anglo membership that included the daughters and wives of Crystal City's ranch and business elite.[30]

Mexican Americans founded social organizations of their own as they became more active in public life after World War II. Indeed, the exclusion of Mexican Americans from civil and polite society necessitated the creation of their own groups, and these largely replaced rather than invigorated older Mexican nationalist organizations. Only the Miguel Hidalgo Association continued with any vibrancy after World War II, operating a death benefit and managing the Bénito Juarez Cemetery. But veterans and business owners established a local American GI Forum chapter, as well as a Mexican Chamber of Commerce, both of which played increasingly important public roles.

Mexican-ancestry women also found homes in separate social organizations. In June of 1954, the AGIF established a Ladies Auxiliary. As was the case nationally, this group supported cultural and social events for Mexican American girls and women analogous to those organized by Anglo community groups. Although the positions of Crystal City high school homecoming queen and the annual Spinach Festival queen were theoretically open to all, for example, these honors went exclusively to Anglo girls. In response, yet without challenging the Anglo honor system's functioning, the AGIF sponsored its own "GI Forum Queen" competition for Mexican American girls. Likewise, a local radio station that featured rock and roll and Mexican American disc jockeys began awarding a "Miss KBEN" crown in the early 1960s. Even little girls found space for enjoyment in this racially separate environment in the Ladybug Club, which hosted social events and parties for the elementary school set. Too often ignored by scholars because they conformed to traditional gender roles and religious practice, these spaces for Mexican American women and their daughters were an important aspect of social progress and ethnic pride.

The Catholic Church functioned as another segregated center of social and organizational life. Mexican American women founded organizations of their own at Sacred Heart Catholic Church, which included the Women's Club, Women's Study Group, and La Sociedad de la Vela Perpetua (Society of the Perpetual Flame), all similar to the church and social groups organized by Anglo Catholic and Protestant women, whose "Mary and I Guild" hosted tea parties. The church also permitted separation between Anglos and Mexican-ancestry parishioners in social events held at the parish hall. It appears that this segregation of church-club life existed in the Presbyterian, Methodist, Baptist, and Nazarene churches as well.[31]

The social segregation of Crystal City conformed to a pattern common to agricultural communities from Texas to California. In all aspects of local residential, commercial, and associational life, the separation was uniform and enforced by coercion as well as social practice within both groups. Even as interactions increased within the commercial sphere and the imagined community spaces of newsprint opened to the Mexican American community, daily lives shaped by neighborhood, associational, and religious interaction remained separate and defined by race and class. The addition of Mexican contract workers, or braceros, in the postwar period only added to these preexisting divisions.

Bracero Workers and Local Society

The introduction of braceros added significantly to the local economy in the 1950s by providing an important economic foundation for ethnic business while affirming the "alien" or "foreign" status of Mexican-ancestry people in Texas. Established in 1942 as a wartime expediency, the Bracero Program brought 4.6 million Mexican workers to the United States in the twenty-two years of its operation. Mexico banned Texas from participation for nearly a decade, citing the long and persistent history of discriminatory treatment of Mexican-ancestry people in Texas. With passage of Public Law 78 in 1951, however, the United States and Mexico agreed to continue the Bracero Program and allow Texas to recruit workers.

After the removal of the ban, Zavala County growers readily contracted braceros, even though domestic farmworkers were available. They worked mainly as harvest hands for the Del Monte Corporation, known locally as "Cal-Pack," which produced over one million cans of spinach per year in a union facility organized by the International Brotherhood of Teamsters. Del Monte housed the braceros in barracks located behind the cannery and on the company's three-thousand-acre spinach farm. Braceros and some local workers harvested the spinach, and local Anglos and Mexican American citizens worked in the unionized plant.[32] The mix of foreign and native workers was nothing new, as Crystal City had long contained a mixture of citizens, legal residents, and undocumented workers, but the bracero community formed a legally present yet foreign and socially isolated group of men with paychecks to spend and few transportation options.[33]

Braceros traveled frequently to Mexico Grande's commercial center to shop, drink, and relax. This new market demand led to the expansion of taverns in Mexico Grande, creating jobs for adult bartenders and cooks. For some, the bracero trade made up for the loss of winter harvest work, and several neighborhood migrant entrepreneurs prospered.[34] Rosa Martinez, who grew up in Mexico Grande, remembered that local children played marbles and spun tops afternoons outside the Salas tavern. Then, at nightfall, some of the same young boys worked as shoeshine boys or bar hands in the many taverns of Mexico Grande.[35] Several single mothers and families made their living operating these establishments. Other residents took advantage of the added demand to sell liquor and beer without a license or operate after-hours clubs during the height of the Bracero Program.[36] Occasionally, Mexican workers, presumably braceros, were involved in barroom fights that led to criminal convictions and deportation.[37] Yet despite such common rowdiness, the bracero taverns became a central hub in the social and economic activity of the barrio, perhaps also revitalizing its "Mexican" roots.

The presence of braceros also created a variety of ancillary opportunities for Mexican American entrepreneurs. Since the braceros did not own cars yet wanted to get to town to socialize and shop, several migrants used their vehicles to serve this market as taxi drivers, offering fifty-cent rides between Mexico Grande and the Del Monte camp.[38] Other entrepreneurs supplied services directly to braceros at the labor camps. The Galvan family, for example, owned a corner grocery, provided bail bond money, engaged in ranching, and operated the workers' cafeteria at the Del Monte camp, feeding hundreds of braceros daily. The Bracero Program allowed the Galvans to prosper throughout the 1950s and in so doing provided employment to Mexican American teens and adults. On a more modest level, other residents prepared food, which they sold outside the camps in cars and trucks as a way to supplement winter earnings.[39]

As it functioned in Crystal City, the Bracero Program was both a blessing and a curse for Mexican contract workers and the local Mexican American working class alike. While the program brought benefits to the community, it also reduced the number and quality of available winter employment options for returning migrant workers. Filling jobs at many of the counties' largest harvest operations, the braceros made it difficult for local farmworkers to find winter work.[40] As the 1950s wore on, Mexican American migrants increasingly spent winters in Crystal City unemployed, underemployed, or on relief, a fact that may have prompted some to settle permanently in the larger cities of the Midwest, Texas, and the West. Although labor unions and the AGIF strongly opposed the Bracero Program as abusive to Mexican and Mexican American workers alike, it survived for over a decade in places like Crystal City.[41]

Grassroots Mexican Americanism

Veterans returning from World War II and the Korean War to places like Crystal City established organizations that relied on the contributions of an often-small group of activists and members who sought to improve their own communities and open public life to Mexican Americans. As one historian has remarked, "Mexican-flavored patriotism became All-American patriotism" when veterans returned and demanded civil and citizenship rights.[42] There was more to Mexican Americanism as it developed after the war than the singular embrace of Anglo-American culture: activists continued to speak Spanish and did not hide a pride in their Mexican heritage as they pledged themselves to the perfection of the social and political system in Texas and the United States. Their hybrid organizational politics contained elements of what some have termed "cultural citizenship," embracing Tejano or Mexican folkways as well as a desire to acculturate following established practice among ethnic and immigrant group organizations.[43] In Crystal City, the activism of the 1950s shows many of the ways AGIF members attempted to embrace ethnic and racial politics, counter fears among Anglos that the organization was "subversive," and refute charges that Mexican Americans were not prepared for the responsibilities of citizenship.[44] Similar to returning African American veterans, Mexican Americans collided with the exclusionary system of local racism yet struggled to find meaning in and preserve the social and religious worlds that gave purpose to their lives. The mixed results of this history show the ways minority activism that is often considered moderate posed a direct challenge to Anglo rule.[45]

Those involved in the activism of the 1950s and early 1960s were "elites" within the Mexican-origin population to be sure, yet their class status in mainstream society was tenuous at best. A blue-collar or union job that is working-class within the dominant society may very well be a high-prestige occupation within a minority community. The often working-class veterans who joined the AGIF sought upward mobility via the regular pay and hours provided by employment with national retailers or the veteran-friendly post office, a step up from migratory labor or work as part of the relatively unstable sales or professional class serving a Mexican-ancestry clientele. Although the AGIF counted several entrepreneurs and professionals among its members, even these white-collar workers were dependent on a clientele of largely migratory workers, and they did not have access to the social networks of Anglo middle-class professionals. Thus, it may be better to describe these leaders as middle-class aspirants, even if they were elites within the ethnic community.

E. C. Munoz, president of the AGIF's Crystal City branch and State Board of Directors representative for the Winter Garden District, epitomized the AGIF's upwardly mobile orientation. Crystal City residents remembered Munoz as a heavyset and boisterous man who was a familiar face on the dusty streets and doorsteps of the city after World War II. He stood out in this primarily working-class migrant community because, unlike most workers, he wore a tie in public when he traveled the streets and byways of his hometown, clinging to his giant insurance book while collecting premiums for the American National Insurance Company. In this dog-eared record book, Munoz recorded the policies and names of the many Mexican Americans in Crystal City who paid weekly installments for small life insurance policies. As someone who often visited families in their homes, outside the view of Anglos, Munoz was well positioned to assume a leadership role, and organizing apparently became part of his regular work duties.[46]

As the local head of a reform organization that tried to maintain a moderate position vis-à-vis Anglo politicians, Munoz addressed claims to Mexican American citizenship to the world outside of Crystal City. In one letter to a congressional representative, he proclaimed himself one of the "veterans who fought in the last War" as he called for a ban on child labor in "agricultural work during the school session and school hours." He made this argument based on the belief that "educating our children is more important than picking the farmer's cotton." In this letter to Dixiecrat Graham Barden of North Carolina, chair of the House Education and Labor Committee, he mentioned that "prior to World War II and during World War II, Texas had a system of education . . . [that] segregated our children throughout the state merely because of their origin." Munoz wrote on behalf of "Americans of Mexican Origin" to express a clear hope that "children . . . be educated and not . . . used as cotton pickers all their life."[47] For Munoz, Mexican Americans and their children had earned the rights of citizens.

The local movement Munoz represented built on long-standing civil rights claims made by a string of Mexican American organizations in

Texas. Before and after the establishment of LULAC, Mexican Americans fought against discrimination and for access to jobs, education, and human dignity in Texas and across the Southwest. The long effort to desegregate Texas schools and expand the meaning of the Fourteenth Amendment continued after the war with the founding of the AGIF, which together with LULAC worked in Texas, the Southwest, and California to support civil rights legal cases. These efforts, often the result of local grassroots organizing and community mobilization, became tied to the cold war rhetoric of Americanism. The AGIF and similar organizations, such as LULAC and California's Community Service Organization (CSO), tied their quest to expand Mexican American citizenship beyond the "third space" of the insular barrio to patriotism, anticommunism, and a call for democracy.[48] Their "aspirational politics" sought access to the ideal of American citizenship and called on the Anglo community to reject racist policies in favor of American ideals.[49]

The message of American freedom was everywhere available to Mexican Americans and Anglos in the 1950s. Anticommunist rhetoric mixed with an homage to American freedom was available nearly every week in the *Zavala County Sentinel*, which featured Lyndon Johnson's "Your Senator Reports." In one 1954 letter, Johnson argued that the nation faced one "basic question," which was "whether free, representative government—the kind of government we have in the United States—can survive." Johnson tied this anticommunist message to the sacrifices of those who went to war in the defense of "freedom in government, freedom of enterprise, and individual freedom."[50] The local and national AGIF, borrowing heavily from this same cold war rhetoric, made a similar argument to local Anglo elites and machine politicians when they demanded that Mexican Americans had earned a place at democracy's table as full and equal citizens. To continue the policy of segregation and marginalization so common in South Texas was not just morally wrong, they argued, it was also unpatriotic and un-American.

Texas was also a "southern" state, and in the mid-1950s it increasingly confronted the system of segregation and discrimination for both African Americans and Mexican Americans. Anglo Democrats of a conservative stripe sought to resist the implementation of the *Brown v. Board of Education* decision by creating state laws to nullify the verdict. Henry B. Gonzalez, a liberal Democrat and Mexican American state senator from San Antonio's westside barrio, blocked the anti-*Brown* legislation by filibuster, a move that won him a "Man of the Year" award from the National Association for the Advancement of Colored People (NAACP). These were heady times. Expressing the virtue of his commitment to racial justice, Gonzalez also worked to get San Antonio to pass antidiscrimination laws as Martin Luther King marched in the Deep South for similar reforms. In 1958, Gonzalez ran for governor as a liberal candidate committed to racial and civil rights for all Texans. With strong ties to LULAC and the AGIF, Gonzales represented the Mexican Americanist impulse at the state level and the possible future of Mexican American politics in Texas. But San Antonio was a large metropolitan area with a well-developed Mexican American middle class. In the highly segregated farm communities south and west of San Antonio, more limited, yet no less important, struggles for participation also took place.[51]

Grassroots organizations such as AGIF chapters were often unstable groups that met irregularly and were driven by the strong personalities of a few primary members. Much as in local NAACP chapters, a local leader could be a strong force for change, yet these organizations often had extremely small budgets, if any at all. Unlike the NAACP, the AGIF, despite the strong leadership of its founder, Dr. Hector Garcia, had no Washington office, lacked a powerful group of outside supporters, and functioned without a full-time litigation team. Although it aspired to national status, it remained a mostly regional organization, with its national headquarters in Texas rather than Washington. In the Winter Garden District, the AGIF had few resources, and as the organization spread to Carrizo Springs, Cotulla, Eagle Pass, Uvalde, and other cities, it did so as an outgrowth of the efforts of one or two veterans operating on a shoestring budget of their own.[52]

The Winter Garden District was a central hub in the wheel of migrant labor, and often AGIF members migrated and settled permanently outside of Texas, further weakening the organization. Eduardo Idar Jr., executive secretary and Texas chairman, worried as early as August 1953 that "our GI Forums at Crystal City and Carrizo Springs have died out."[53] Later that month, Idar wrote E. C. Munoz that the organization understood that "it is a difficult job to keep our groups at Asherton, Crystal, and Carrizo organized because so many of the people have to migrate or have left the area permanently." In this letter, Idar asked Munoz to take over direction of District 4, covering most of the counties of the Winter

Garden region.[54] The loss of members and residents from South Texas due to labor migration provides one explanation for the AGIF's stand against the Bracero Program. One statewide 1956 petition claimed that braceros had "driven us out of our homes seeking better jobs and pay in other parts of the state and other states."[55] The national AGIF was relatively weak and had a difficult time coordinating investigations into local acts of discrimination, a fact that worried Idar, who felt that the failure to come to the aid of local members' requests placed the reputation of the AGIF in jeopardy in the already unstable organizational territory of the Winter Garden District.[56]

Even with these problems, the Crystal City AGIF expanded its role in community life by sponsoring various programs and assisting the Mexican American community with basic services. In June 1951, the AGIF sponsored the expansion of the water line to the Catholic cemetery, with AGIF head E. C. Munoz and fellow veterans Guadalupe Ledesma Sr. and Mauro Torres organizing the program. The AGIF also supported the building of a new plaza for Mexican American social and community events, commonly known as la placita, in Mexico Chico.[57]

Joining the AGIF in sponsoring such positive efforts on behalf of Crystal City's Mexican American community was the Mexican Chamber of Commerce, established in 1953 as a social and business organization by some of the city's Mexican American businesspeople. Most prominent after 1955, the Mexican Chamber appears to have been an outgrowth of the entrepreneurial prosperity that had developed after the institution of the Bracero Program. The chamber provided for social welfare needs, offered student scholarships, and sponsored social events, such as a free circus and concerts.[58] Although ostensibly nonpolitical, the chamber, like the AGIF chapter, encouraged electoral participation and offered critiques of Anglo governance.[59] Evidence gathered by sociologist Douglas Foley, among others, demonstrates that the chamber, working together with the AGIF, advocated civil rights and limited direct action in ending the mistreatment of Mexican Americans in public and private facilities. It led a boycott of the Guild Theater, for example, after an employee slapped a Mexican American girl. Along with the AGIF, the chamber also sought the desegregation of the Crystal City swimming pool, which African Americans and Mexican Americans were only permitted to use in the last days before the water was drained and replaced.[60]

In 1951, Mexican Americans in Crystal City took the first steps on the road to political participation by forming a loose coalition with whites who were not beholden to or supported by the entrenched city and county machine. The coalition supported an interracial ticket of opposition candidates for the Crystal City school board and other offices, seeking to elect a single Mexican American as part of the slate. The candidate, Abbie Guevara, a mild-mannered store clerk who was the son of a prominent Mexican American Protestant minister, ran for an open school board seat against several white opposition candidates.

Hector Garcia of the AGIF wrote to E. C. Munoz in the weeks prior to the campaign, providing him with information on Texas election law. In his letter to Munoz, Garcia informed him that attorney Hector De Pena of Corpus Christi would be in contact to assist him and encouraged Munoz to "keep working on this," promising to send additional materials and wishing him "good luck."[61] Neither Munoz nor the AGIF publicly endorsed the Guevara campaign, but they offered their support behind the scenes. If they wished for this support to be kept secret, that wish is understandable in light of what soon followed.

As the campaign began, the *Zavala County Sentinel* reported in a conspiratorial tone that someone had distributed a "mimeographed letter printed in the Spanish language and . . . circulated among the Latin-American people of Crystal City . . . presumably sponsored by someone, or a group, in opposition to the city administration."[62] As reported in the newspaper, the flyer accused the city of using public monies to beautify Anglo sections of town while neglecting the Mexican American neighborhoods, and it reminded the city administration that the Latin American community would remember these deeds on election day. The pamphlet also accused now-deceased members of the city administration of funding the construction of private homes, the American Legion Hall, and church gardens using Works Progress Administration funds.[63] Described as a "deliberate attempt at race prejudice," the protest letter was, according to the editor, "vigorously condemned by the great majority of Anglo Americans as well as Latin Americans"; the *Sentinel* called on opposition candidates to "protest an attempt at race discrimination."[64] By the bizarre logic of this account, defeating racism presumably meant voting against Guevara and supporting the status quo.

If the flyer in question was in fact written by the AGIF and Anglo coalition, then even moderate criticisms of past cronyism and corruption, if tied to the "Latin-American" vote, were enough to prompt local Anglos to speak out against what twenty-first-century politicians might label "reverse discrimination." Rather than make explicitly racist arguments against Guevara, his opponents deployed this language of antidiscrimination in true colorblind fashion to speak against Guevara without naming him. Following this strange series of events, the inter-racial attempt to oust the local machine faltered as the Anglos on the opposition slate abandoned the campaign. In the wake of the flyer's distribution, Anglo voter registration exploded: the city machine mobilized nearly eight hundred voters for Anglo incumbents, contributing to the highest voter turnout in school board election history. Guevara lost the election.

For Mexican Americans, this election demonstrated that the airing of complaints about problems such as corruption, cronyism, unpaved roads, and a lack of water, sewer, and electric service in their neighborhoods resulted in massive resistance. In the weeks before the election and during the flyer scandal, Mexican American service members were front-page news nearly every week as they left for the war in Korea or were killed and wounded in combat. Ironically, following the defeat of Guevara, the paper ran a series of letters from the sons of Frank De La Rosa. One of his sons wrote, "Yes dad, this is one army under the United Nations . . . fighting for what we hold dear to our hearts." Each week, Mexican Americans from this community of fewer than ten thousand residents made blood sacrifices for their country, yet the local machine fought to keep a sole Mexican American off the school board.[65] Though Anglos did not support a single Mexican American candidate for office, Anglo politicians spent the 1950s appealing to the majority population of Mexican Americans for their votes.[66]

Four years later, a statewide land scandal broke that brought national attention to the corruption and racial discrimination prevalent in South Texas and Crystal City. In the mid-1950s, a number of state and county officials manipulated loopholes in the recently created Texas Veterans' Land Act (1946) to enrich themselves by defrauding Mexican American and African American veterans through the exploitation of a program designed to help veterans purchase land. State, county, and city officials used hundreds of minority veterans as pawns in a shell game that involved some of the state's most powerful Democratic politicians in a crass manipulation of the law. In 1954, the scheme was uncovered in

Cuero, Texas, ninety miles southeast of San Antonio, by reporter Ken Towery, who won a 1955 Pulitzer Prize for his investigative reporting.

The perpetrators of the scheme set out to enlist African American and Mexican American veterans to file for land, purchase it, and then lease it to white politicians or the original owners for a fraction of its true market value. Prominent lawyers and politicians led minority veterans to believe that they were receiving cash bonuses in return for their service in the U.S. military. Some veterans apparently had no idea that the "bonus" forms they had signed were actually purchase contracts and rental agreements. When the state attorney general was done with his investigation, the commissioner of the General Land Office, Bascom Giles, a man some thought a potential gubernatorial candidate, was sentenced to jail time for his corruption of the Veterans' Land Program he helped create.[67]

In Zavala County, those accused of participating in the abuse of the Veterans' Land Program included the mayor, the county judge, and several prominent lawyers. The scheme functioned at the local level as a veteran benefit operating directly out of City Hall and the county judge's office. In Crystal City, Mexican American veterans like Jose Guadalupe Ledesma, an AGIF member, thought they were applying for veterans' benefits when they signed the papers put before them by an accountant and the county judge. One Mexican American veteran said, "[I] thought [I] was getting my veterans' bonus"; he received no information "about any land." Given some papers to sign, veterans were paid one hundred dollars. Later, they returned to the county judge's office, signed more paperwork, and received the remainder of the "bonus," an additional two hundred dollars. In fact, these veterans first applied for and purchased land under the program; then, at the second visit to the judge's office, they executed an agreement to lease the land back to its original owners, who profited from the sale to the state of Texas.[68]

Ledesma only found out that he had in fact purchased land when he started receiving rent checks. The local official who was managing the fraudulent scheme told Ledesma to sign the checks back over to him, but he refused to do so, since the checks were in his name. Ledesma then agreed to testify against local officials, assisting the state as a witness. The attorney general sued several local landowners, the county judge, and the mayor in suits to recover money paid for land in Zavala County. All of the veterans manipulated in the Zavala County scheme were Mexican Americans.[69] The graft cost the state tens of thousands of dollars and demonstrated how the Anglo city and county machine viewed even the most patriotic Mexican Americans as mere pawns.

Very few politicians resigned from office or served jail time for violations of the law. In Crystal City, the city regime remained in power for nearly another decade. Ledesma, on the other hand, paid a personal toll for providing testimony to the state and doing his duty as a citizen. When he returned to his job as a milkman after giving testimony, Ledesma found that longtime customers were unwilling to accept his deliveries, and he was forced to give up his business. He traveled the migrant stream with his young family, settling first in California and then moving on to Milwaukee, Wisconsin.[70]

The outcome of Ledesma's participation in this prosecution suggests the extent to which the early activism of Crystal City veterans ended in severe disappointment. Nonetheless, nearly a decade after Abbie Guevara failed to win office, E. C. Munoz of the AGIF ran for a seat on the school board in 1960 with the same limited goal of informing the Mexican American community of educational events and issues. If Guevara had been considered unqualified by the white majority, Munoz, a member of the Mexican American middle class who lived in an integrated section of town, represented a qualified candidate. As the local head of the AGIF and a key participant in its many programs, Munoz worked to bring news of the local and national AGIF to Crystal City. He apparently sought to participate within the system as it functioned rather than to topple it. His candidacy, like other Mexican-ancestry leaders' postwar moves toward participation in Crystal City, was tentative and mediated by the lived experience of past oppression and a genuine desire to alter rather than dismantle the core values of Americanism.

Since the record 1951 turnout, school board elections had brought few to the polls, and Munoz, with support from the Mexican Chamber of Commerce and representing a talented and prosperous segment of the Mexican American community, might have won a seat on a school board representing a district that now overwhelmingly served Mexican American students.[71] He ran a low-key campaign in an election commonly won with fewer than two hundred votes cast. In reaction to the Munoz candidacy, however, the Anglo incumbents apparently monitored Mexican American registrations and waged the same sort of get-out-the-vote campaign that brought Guevera's defeat. They did not stoop to attack Munoz himself; indeed, the local paper offered little if any reporting on campaign activity. Nonetheless, the election campaign resulted in "the largest number of votes cast since the creation of the Crystal City Independent School district"—at 1,034, it surpassed even the Guevara total. Munoz, who polled 311, lost to the incumbents, who each polled more than 700 votes. Twice within a ten-year span, AGIF members had run for the school board, and twice the Anglo community had mobilized to keep a Mexican American veteran from serving as an elected official.[72] According to one social scientist, this defeat "corroborated Mexicano judgments that Anglos were unwilling to allow even an established Mexicano businessmen to participate in schooling decisions affecting the majority of Mexicanos in the community."[73] In 1961, with no comment in the newspapers, perhaps as a response to the AGIF efforts of the past decade, two prominent Mexican Americans with close ties of dependency and family relationships with the Anglo establishment were elected with the majority of the Anglo vote to serve on the school board.

Within the year, the AGIF once again pushed its educational agenda at the local level, this time in an effort to dismantle the early tracking of Mexican American students. In 1960, Rev. Arnold Lopez, an evangelical minister new to Crystal City, attempted to enroll his child in school, but an English language proficiency test given to Mexican-ancestry students placed the student in one of the "Mexican" schools. In response, parents and students held mass rallies in July 1960 with the support of local AGIF member Geraldo Saldana—perhaps the city's first grassroots mobilization. The AGIF sent prominent Tejano Democrat Cristóbal P. Aldrete, the Val Verde county attorney. Aldrete, an ally and friend of Hector Garcia and Texas senator Lyndon Johnson, had a long history as an advocate for Mexican American schoolchildren dating back to his own family's participation in the landmark case *Del Rio Independent School District v. Salvatierra* (1930), the first to address the segregation of Mexican-ancestry pupils in Texas.[74]

Aldrete and a group of "something close to 100 Latins" marched to a meeting of the Crystal City Independent School District and forced its relocation to the high school auditorium. There, the group protested the school board's maintenance of segregated elementary schools on a separate campus for children of Mexican descent who had limited English proficiency, the continued segregation of children in these schools through the second and third grades, and the operation of tracks composed entirely of children of Mexican descent in the elementary grades. Aldrete complained that that these practices violated the 1948 *Delgado v. Bastrop Independent School District* decision, which disallowed the segregation of Mexican and Mexican-ancestry children from white pupils, as well as both the letter and the spirit of Texas Education Agency policies. He asked the school board when it would inform him as to when and how it would remedy this situation, as he and his fellow demonstrators wanted relief "when school opened in September."[75]

Even a room of over a hundred Mexican American residents did not force the Anglo school administrators to budge. Dr. Peters, president of the school board, reminded the crowd that "this was a very poor district" and that "he did not know how soon the board could give [Aldrete] an answer" but promised that the board "would give [the problem] every consideration." The district decided to avoid possible litigation by following the letter of the law: it placed all nonmigrant first- and second-grade students at the Airport School, with nonmigrant third through fifth graders attending the traditionally Anglo elementary school.[76] The former "Mexican" schools remained open, in accord with the *Salvatierra* and *Bastrop* decisions, as "migrant" schools. At its August 8 meeting, the board voted to write Aldrete to inform him that "the school would be carried out in a lawful way . . . to utilize its resources in the best and most economical way possible."[77] This result brought integration for some yet continued to segregate the Mexican American majority in so-called "migrant" schools. The organizing efforts of the AGIF failed to alter the structure of ethnic and class segregation in the face of Anglo resistance. However, everyday people learned how to organize as a result of these early AGIF campaigns, as they grew increasingly wary of courteous protest in the face of hardened formal and informal Anglo opposition to even limited Mexican American participation in the social life of the city.

Conclusion

This chapter has sought to reconsider the organization, mobilization, and politics of Mexican Americanist conflict. Over the course of the 1950s, Mexican Americans in this migratory working-class community witnessed vigorous resistance to Mexican American entry into the mainstream of social and political life—resistance that suggests the extent to which their activism came across as far from moderate, far from unthreatening. The events of 1960 brought an end to the era of AGIF-led Mexican Americanist activism in Crystal City. Despite the associational and organizational growth within their own community, Mexican Americans still had neither the respect nor the acceptance of Anglo residents as equal citizens. Yet the era of moderate Mexican Americanist politics in Crystal City may have softened the ground for the militant activism rooted in labor unionism and working-class consciousness to come—for what became an important and sustained translocal movement for Mexican American civil rights based out of Crystal City.

2

Inclusion and Mexican Americanism

HIGH SCHOOL ACCULTURATION AND ETHNIC POLITICS
IN CRYSTAL CITY

In the late 1950s and early 1960s, mainstream public school systems of the Southwest became increasingly open to Mexican American students. A variety of changes, including statewide public school reform and a shift in attitudes among some parents, brought large numbers of Mexican American teens into high school for the first time, where they began an epistemological encounter with the meaning and practice of American citizenship.[1] Some Mexican American students in Crystal City embraced idealized forms of Americanism and their identity as Mexican-ancestry people while rejecting the racial hierarchies of South Texas. Much as Mexican American and African American veterans did in the decades after World War II, teens and young people born in the United States sought inclusion and acceptance within a framework of Americanism in contrast to what they increasingly considered the local misinterpretation of the nation's values.

These changes took place as state reform efforts brought about a restructuring of Texas schools after the war. By 1955, one in six students attending Texas schools had a Spanish surname, and thirty-one counties, including Zavala County, enrolled a Mexican American majority. Though dropout rates remained high among students from families engaged in migrant work, the 1950s witnessed an overall growth in the number of Spanish-surnamed students completing high school across Texas, the Southwest, and California. Indeed, the number of Spanish-surnamed students attending Texas high schools increased 63 percent between 1950 and 1960.[2] In Crystal City, Mexican American students became a majority population in the high school for the first time.

As historians of education have pointed out, public schools in the United States often provide a forum for the expression and maintenance of the dominant social hierarchies outside the schools. The politics of the schoolyard, while often considered "game play," tend to reproduce dominant class relations and affirm the social biases of the dominant group. In most cases, these "games" are of limited political consequence. In the case of newly integrated school systems, however, wherein racial and ethnic change alters the social life of the school, they take on an oppositional character as minority students seek inclusion within preexisting institutions. Reflecting broader changes taking place outside the schools, they can also have serious "real-world" consequences.[3] Across the Winter Garden District of South Texas, Mexican American students sought inclusion in the full range of student activities. In the process, some of them became politicized for life.

To understand the origin point for later Mexican American migrant activism among *Cristaleños* (Crystal City residents) in Texas and Wisconsin, this chapter explores how the contested space of the high school facilitated the creation of a student activist vanguard. After graduation, several of these school-based organizers, now attending junior college, joined to aid a coalition of local Mexican Americans, the International Brotherhood of Teamsters, and the Political Association of Spanish Speaking Organizations (PASSO) in 1963 to elect an "all-Latin" slate to the city council. Teens and young adults, many too young to vote, joined this campaign and learned the basics of electoral organizing from the professionals sent to their city. These young volunteers familiarized themselves with grassroots organizing, as well as the factors that work against social movements. These lessons served them well as they matured politically and followed the migrant stream to Wisconsin, taking their activism with them.

The Transformation of South Texas Schooling

The post–World War II era witnessed rapid structural changes in Texas education. At the federal level, the United States implemented the Good Neighbor Policy under the direction of the Office of Inter-American Affairs to encourage cross-cultural understanding between the United States and Latin American countries, and through this policy it funded educational and other outreach efforts in Texas. After Mexico banned the importation of its guest workers to the state in 1943, Texas sought to reform its image as a border state with a history of racial and ethnic discrimination against Mexican-ancestry people. This same year, Texas established the Good Neighbor Commission to improve the lives of "Latin Americans," avoid embarrassing cases of discrimination, and encourage Mexico to allow the contracting of braceros. Made permanent in 1945, the commission promoted education reforms, sponsored a Pan-American teacher exchange, funded a number of international scholastic projects, and brought a degree of hemispheric Americanism and tolerance to Texas schools. In complicated ways, the demands of Texas farmers for braceros affected the social standing of Mexican American students and the way schools were to treat and teach them.[4]

Reform efforts under way during World War II brought about postwar legal changes as Texas modernized its educational statutes. Governor Beauford Jester, a segregationist who fought the integration of the University of Texas as regent, strongly supported the improvement, if not the desegregation, of Texas public schools through the reform of state administrative laws. In 1947, the Texas state legislature, with the support of Jester, established a joint legislative committee chaired by Representative Claud Gilmer and Senator A. M. Aikin Jr. to research and plan the overhaul of Texas education law. The following year, the Gilmer-Aikin Committee issued *To Have What We Must*, a report that proposed the overhaul of a school system with little uniformity, few standards, no statewide curriculum, and limited opportunities for African Americans and Mexican Americans.[5] The resulting Gilmer-Aikin laws of 1949 linked state funding to average daily attendance, a move that brought more minority children into schools even as racial and pedagogical segregation continued. In an effort to prevent districts from providing shorter school sessions to minority and rural students, the state required them to offer a uniform twelve years of schooling over a nine-month term. These legal reforms also professionalized the teaching occupation through the establishment of a State Board of Education, which became the Texas Education Agency.[6]

At the local level, the Texas Good Neighbor Commission and the statutory reforms transformed the Crystal City schools. The main lobby of the Crystal City High School displays graduating class photos for most years after 1900 and reveals an overwhelmingly Anglo student population prior to the mid-1950s. Some scholars have compared Crystal City High School to a private club where Anglo students practiced hazing until the county banned it in 1948.[7] But in the wake of the school reforms, the Crystal City district reclassified Mexican-origin students as "Latin Americans" and introduced Spanish-language instruction at the high school. With an "increased importance . . . placed upon schooling for patriotic citizenship and college preparation," Mexican American students entered South Texas high schools dedicated to the rhetoric and practice of a cold war Americanism.[8] Greater enforcement of attendance laws in Crystal City led to significant changes in the social status of Anglo students as they lost dominance in a variety of school-based groups; teachers put up limited resistance while seeking to protect Anglo positions in some student groups and honors. The passivity of the response perhaps reflected a limited acceptance of the Mexican American students as fellow citizens within the school.

Throughout the 1950s and into the early 1960s, the mainly Anglo administrators at the state level continued to include Mexican American students in Texas in pedagogical and curricular policy discussions and support the teaching of a more balanced history of the Southwest. Continuing statewide efforts begun in the 1940s, *Texas Outlook*, the official publication of the Texas State Teachers Association, focused its readers' attention on the well-being of Mexican American children. In one 1955 issue, the publication called for bilingual education and the teaching of Spanish to Spanish-speaking pupils. In 1957, the call again went out for teachers to learn Spanish if they taught Spanish-speaking pupils. In an article titled "Texas History Seldom Told," teachers were given a brief primer on the Spanish and Mexican heritage of Texas. As the official mouthpiece of the teacher's association—one that perhaps reflected a more liberal politics than that of most of its audience—*Texas Outlook* encouraged educators to integrate Mexican American children and their culture into curriculum and practice.[9]

More than structural reform changed the school environment in Crystal City: parental attitudes toward education also evolved in the 1950s, as migratory and settled parents alike made greater efforts to keep their children in school as long as possible. Some within the Mexican American communities of South Texas had long sought educational opportunities for their children, even as agricultural industries in Texas and the Midwest demanded these children's labor. Yet following World War II, more farmworkers chose to alter migration schedules, returning earlier from the Midwest and West so that their children could attend Anglo-majority schools rather than pedagogically segregated "migrant" schools.[10] Others found ways to stop migrating and remain in Crystal City to improve educational opportunities for their children, while still others settled permanently in the Midwest and West. Future student activist Severita Lara, whose father owned a gas station and lived permanently in Crystal City, attended school year-round in the 1960s with her siblings. Members of Lara's extended family traveled to labor as harvest workers in California, Wisconsin, and Minnesota; these relatives placed their children in school in these states or made efforts to return to Crystal City for the regular school year. In Lara's family, some also settled year-round in California, Minnesota, or Crystal City to make sure their children attended school for the full academic year.[11]

Parents across South Texas also supported the establishment of prekindergarten schools for their children. These barrio preschools gave students basic instruction and bettered their chances of initial success in public schools.[12] The preschools in Crystal City prepared students to pass the English proficiency tests. In classes often held in grocery stores or other businesses, for instance, two local teachers, Hermania Sifuentes and Suzie Salazar, taught English and Spanish and covered a basic curriculum of reading, writing, and math for children as young as three years old at a cost of fifty cents per week.[13] Future organizer and migrant worker Francisco Rodriguez remembered, "We learned the basic skills spoken in English and in Spanish," and the "result of that was the ability of the kids to . . . participate in the public schools with minimal difficulty."[14] Such schools, attended by an important minority of future activists, highlighted elements of ethnic pride and patriotism by staging annual pageants honoring the history of Mexico and Texas. Although they by no means offered a system of mass schooling for the mainly migratory Mexican American community, they did give a small group of children an introduction to a transnational form of civic nationalism and key skills needed for initial success in the public schools.[15]

Preparatory schools like the one in Crystal City may have served as the model for the LULAC "Little Schools of 400" established in 1957 and funded by LULAC president Felix Tijerina. Like the barrio preschools, the LULAC schools taught Mexican American children four hundred words in English to prepare them for the English proficiency exams. These schools used local Mexican American teachers and some Anglo volunteers to cover a focused language training curriculum, teaching classes in private homes and barrio business. Tijerina pressed for and won state funding for a broader project in 1959, which became a model for the federal Head Start Program. In increasingly creative ways after World War II, then, Mexican Americans struggled to provide a quality education for their children.[16]

The school district, meanwhile, struggled to cope with much larger enrollments at all grade levels. The district had constructed a high school meant to accommodate the small, mainly Anglo student population that continued beyond the elementary grades, but the facility proved inadequate for the rush of new students in the 1950s. The high school campus, established on the site of a World War II alien internment camp, held some classes in sheet metal buildings from the camp.[17] In another response to the growing number of Mexican American students, districts like Crystal City implemented a skills tracking program. Although there is little evidence in school records of this system, oral histories and research conducted by social scientists reveal its existence.[18] The district placed the majority of Mexican American students in lower-skill tracks and most Anglo children in the higher-skill tracks. Parents were also given the authority to move children from classrooms or schools through an open transfer system.[19] According to a 1962 graduate of Crystal City High School who became Crystal City school superintendent, "Anglos were not placed in the fourth, fifth, or sixth track" with Mexican American "slow learners."[20]

The Mexican American students who stayed in school entered a social and educational environment that reflected the distinct local culture of the Anglo community. From the early twentieth century, high schools in the United States shaped the development of youth culture and the formation of adult identity, an "extraordinarily durable" role that took on a new form and resiliency in the 1950s.[21] Across the country, high school students fell into specific categories according to race, ethnicity, income, and social status, often carrying these identities for the rest of their lives. In Crystal City, Anglo educators and administrators were often the product of the same school system and were thus committed to the maintenance of the local social order. But the Mexican American students who entered Crystal City's high school in the late 1950s were in a unique position to both encounter and interrogate the identities expected of them.

The separation between "Anglos" and "Mexicans" outside of the schools provided Mexican American teens in Crystal City with real-life experiences to challenge undemocratic hierarchies inside the schools as they sought inclusion. Adopting the rhetoric of Americanism, these students made claims to social prestige in school and organized electoral campaigns to win class offices and yearbook honors for members of their own ethnic group. Boys tried out for teams and the status of "jocks," and girls sought positions as cheerleader and pom-pom squad members.[22] Signaling this desire to join in all aspects of high school life, Jesus Salas, who left Crystal City High to attend school in Wisconsin, remembered that young Mexican Americans had "a real desire to be elected Most Popular."[23] As Mexican American high school students blended and refined a politics of ethnicity, inclusion, and Americanism, they sought the high-prestige elective and athletic positions long reserved for Anglos that functioned as uncontested status markers within the schools.[24]

Changes within school society, politics, and sports were mapped in the high school yearbooks, which encapsulated each year's various activities and the ethnic makeup of student life. From the mid-1950s onward, nearly every page is a testament to the growth of Mexican American teen participation in athletics, clubs, and student government and to their success at winning those honors that came with full-page photos.[25] After 1955, Mexican Americans won most elective school offices and honors in Crystal City. A small group of Mexican American students also played leading roles in high-prestige nonathletic clubs overwhelmingly populated by middle-class Anglo students, such as band, debate, Future Farmers of America, and the academic honor societies. In this way, the school—even as it continued to be a segregated space for many Mexican American students—provided a greater degree of integration for those who participated in politics and club life, and it was increasingly socialized across the color line.[26] It was often this group of students—perhaps the most acculturated in the Mexican American community—whose members ran for political office in school and who became leaders of outside activist efforts after graduation.[27]

In reaction to this changed environment, school officials supported the creation of faculty-selected honors and the tailoring of extracurricular activities to appeal to Anglo students and alumni. Teachers selected several important honors, including "most beautiful" and "most representative," and in effect reserved them for an Anglo woman and Anglo man, respectively. By placing certain honors under school control, teachers preserved the school's important place in local Anglo society while also accepting the rise of Mexican American majority politics in other areas of student life.[28]

Perhaps the greatest integration and highest level of acceptance came in the arena of boy's sports. Beginning in the 1950s, local sports fans celebrated team victories led by Mexican American boys on the basketball court, baseball diamond, and increasingly on the football field. Nearly every week, the local newspaper highlighted and celebrated the achievements of baseball and basketball players with Spanish surnames.[29] In 1957, the district hired Juan Rivera, a Mexican American graduate of Crystal City High School and former varsity "football star," as an assistant varsity football coach and head coach of the mainly Mexican American B-team.[30] Francisco Rodriquez remembered: "We were very competitive. . . . lot of folks went into the sports. . . . so I think that that began to motivate other Mexicanos."[31]

For girls, a de facto quota continued to restrict participation in high-status athletic activities, most prominently cheerleading squad, which remained Anglo-dominated well into the 1960s, when these squads and their quota system became the focus of teenage female grassroots activism.[32] Mexican American girls, restricted to a quota of one on most cheerleading squads, did, however, participate in a variety of other high-prestige activities at the high school. The homemaking clubs, for instance, witnessed integration. In a rural city surrounded by remote ranches and farms, making clothes and sewing were important aspects of family economic life for Mexican-ancestry and Anglo families alike. Early in the 1950s, young girls had an annual garment review and fashion show that increasingly became an affair of importance. In 1954, students modeled the clothing they made for a variety of settings, including "travel" and "garden party" attire. The competition required skill, style, and frugality. The local newspaper highlighted several of the designs and featured photos from the fashion show in both its English- and Spanish-language sections. Faculty supervisors presented awards for design and improvement in skill.[33]

Mexican American students' participation in high school activities was not necessarily oppositional in nature. In 1959, for example, Hector Nevarez, high school student council president, attended school board meetings to discuss and support the school's clothing regulations, everyday student concerns, and the constant controversy over "displays of affection at school."[34] Yet as the school became more integrated across the full spectrum of activities, Mexican American boys and girls joined a process that aligned their interests according to ethnicity and race. As the proportion of Mexican American students grew, students noticed the ways administrators sought to preserve some aspects of Anglo privilege while allowing others to be challenged.[35] Restrictions led to "silent anger" among many students, and this anger led to organization: elected offices, particularly the lower class presidencies and administrative positions, were increasingly held by Mexican Americans and those Anglos willing to win the votes of all students. (Anglos still held major offices in the senior class well into the late 1950s.)[36] Mexican American teens acculturated in the mid-to-late 1950s within the local Anglo-managed society of high school life in ways that their parents had been unable to do. Crystal City did not have to wait long to see the impact of increasing education levels and Americanist ideology in practice.

The Los Cinco Campaign

One year after his graduation from Crystal City High School, José Angel Gutiérrez, a champion debater, a member of the National Honor Society, and the 1962 Senior High School class president, gave a speech to his community at *la placita* in the Mexico Chico barrio in the midst of a political campaign. Gutiérrez, then attending junior college, remarked: "They say there is no discrimination, but we have only to look around us to know the truth. We look at the schools . . . the houses we live in . . . the few opportunities . . . the dirt in the streets . . . and we know."[37] Gutiérrez spoke these words on April 1, 1963, to a crowd of between fifteen hundred and three thousand Mexican Americans assembled in Crystal City to support the candidacy of "Los Cinco," an "all-Latin" slate for city council. Surrounded by a contingent of armed Texas Rangers in patrol cars, this group of interstate farmworkers and their children held signs that read "Vote for All 5." Under the glow of a single light bulb, this "shirt-sleeved crowd" of migrant workers and their children came together in support of Mexican American political participation.[38]

The crowd reflected the unity of the working-class and migrant community mobilization, as well as the emergence of an educated youth leadership in Crystal City, a city whose Mexican-ancestry adults were still plagued by low educational attainment. The leader of the Los Cinco slate embodied the differences between the young high school graduates and their parents' generation. Juan Cornejo, the charismatic business agent of the Teamsters Local 657 at the Del Monte spinach canning plant, had only an elementary school education plus some additional schooling in the armed forces. The other candidates included a photographer, a car salesperson, a truck driver, and a store clerk with similar educational backgrounds.

The most warmly received speaker that evening was not one of the candidates but the eighteen-year-old Gutiérrez. While too young to vote, Gutiérrez gave voice to the growing rejection of discrimination on the part of Mexican American youth and their parents, using the language of Americanism to call for better roads, schools, and more opportunity—and sounding a lot like a reform politician. The majority of early comers to the rally were Mexican American school-aged children and teens, with Gutiérrez merely one of many young Crystal City High School graduates, some of whom, like him, now attended Southwest Texas Junior College in nearby Uvalde. Francisco Rodríguez, vice president of the Crystal City High class of 1962, and other high school graduates managed the stage crew, orchestrating the arrival of speakers from San Antonio and the entry of Juan Cornejo from among the crowd.[39] The rally was the culminating preelection event' in what had been a busy winter and spring for young and old in Crystal City's Mexican American community.

The all-Latin slate in 1963 extended and amplified the Mexican Americanism expressed by the AGIF rather than rejecting it outright. The Los Cinco campaign and youth activists linked Americanist politics to an explicit rejection of the racially restricted system local Anglos had made. Young people carried a more aggressive Americanist politics out of the schoolyard and onto the streets, where they blended it with a working-class politics of confrontation, ethnic pride, and citizenship rights. The Teamsters and the Political Association of Spanish Speaking Organizations provided important material and psychological support during the 1962 voter registration drive and 1963 city council election, yet the participation of young adults and teens played a foundational role in this campaign. These young activists, already trained in the politics of democratic participation in the high school, gained practical political experience moving door-to-door in their own neighborhoods and through interactions with organizers—experiences that had a lasting impact long after the demise of Los Cinco and PASSO.[40]

The political campaign to elect Mexican Americans to public office in Crystal City developed as a social movement at two levels in 1962 and 1963. The first involved the creation of an organizational system and a formal politics using the resources of the Teamsters and PASSO, which brought local adults, regional politicians, and union leaders together in the name of democracy for Mexican American citizens. Scholars have documented this movement and its rise and fall well. The second, less well-known mobilization witnessed the expansion of internal community resources to serve the sometimes informal needs of a grassroots politics, which relied upon the persuasive power of the young adults and women who wholeheartedly embraced the electoral campaign. This movement used everyday neighborhood, church, and migrant social networks as political tools.[41]

By 1963, the AGIF had failed several times in attempts to elect a Mexican American to the Crystal City School Board. In this unpromising context, an unrelated series of events in 1962 led Mexican Americans to mobilize another electoral campaign, this time without AGIF leadership. Andrew Dickens, a transplanted Anglo oil worker who settled in Crystal City to open a doughnut shop, came into conflict with the local city machine over a right-of-way decision that would harm his new business. Angered by what he considered an unresponsive and self-serving administration, Dickens grew determined to destroy Crystal City's "machine." He sought out local Teamster business agent Juan Cornejo, a former migrant and veteran—but non-AGIF member—who had helped organize the Del Monte cannery.[42] In October 1962, Dickens and Cornejo visited San Antonio to meet Ray Shafer, president of Teamsters Local no. 657, who agreed to lend Teamster support to a poll-tax drive.[43]

As home to a large, unionized agricultural processing facility, Crystal City stood out in antiunion Texas. In 1946, Del Monte Corporation, the largest canner of fruits and vegetables in the United States after World War II, had established a facility in Crystal City. The cannery employed many local Mexican Americans, including women, migrants, and former migrants, for winter work, even as the company hired braceros to do harvesting. Del Monte earned millions of dollars from a three-thousand-acre farm that annually produced over a million cans of spinach. The Teamsters organized this facility in the 1950s, hiring local workers as union representatives who reported to regional offices in San Antonio. The Teamsters Union played a part in hundreds of seasonal hires, kept in contact with these mainly Mexican American migrant workers, and helped some receive unemployment compensation in the off months. This labor recruitment mechanism, together with similar migrant labor and teenage social networks, gave the Los Cinco movement a solid organizational backbone.[44]

The Teamsters were joined by PASSO in supporting the effort in Crystal City. With organizational roots in the Viva Kennedy and Viva Johnson clubs of the early 1960s, the PASSO leadership was struggling in 1963 to maintain its relevance as a political force in Texas and the southwestern states. Headed by Bexar County commissioner and AGIF member Albert Peña, the organization grew to include the Mexican American Political Associations of California and Texas, the CSO of California, and LULAC. PASSO sought to unite the largest and most influential Mexican American political groups and expand the political power of Spanish-speaking people both regionally and nationally by supporting Mexican American and other political candidates. The effort in Crystal City gave San Antonio's PASSO leaders a chance to prove themselves an effective political action group. The *Dallas Morning News* referred to Crystal City as a "pilot project" for PASSO.[45]

The San Antonio representatives sent by PASSO and the Teamsters contributed to the political learning of teen activists. Teamster and PASSO campaign workers gave young leaders like Gutiérrez and others daily lessons in the tactics and practice of electioneering. They provided the teens with role models and demonstrated the importance of knowing the rules of election law, as well as having well-organized speeches and rallies in attracting and reinforcing voter support.[46]

The campaign began with a poll-tax drive to boost Mexican American voter registration. Crystal City voters were obligated to go to the city or county building in person to register and pay the poll tax. Not only did the expense of the tax impose an economic burden, but the experience of in-person registration must have made first-time voters nervous. In 1963, however, Crystal City's organizers freed Mexican Americans from the poll-tax burden: the Teamsters and PASSO compelled the city to appoint Mexican Americans as registrars, as allowed under Texas election law. Young people acted as preregistration activists, canvassing neighborhoods and doing much of the work for the registrars. Thus, rather than face an Anglo registrar at City Hall, new voters greeted neighborhood kids and a registrar at their own door, making registration an easy affair.[47] The activists also made the cost of the poll tax less burdensome by giving prospective voters something in exchange for payment. Mothers sponsored tamale sales, for example, which involved the whole community. Much as they did for church events, mothers and children requested donations of supplies from Mexican-owned grocers, monitored which stores made donations, and boycotted those that refused. With the donated foodstuffs, the women made tamales, which the young men and women sold door to door in exchange for a completed poll tax form and payment of the $1.75 poll tax. The activists also used the Catholic parish hall for dances and cakewalks; admission required payment of the poll tax.[48]

If the Teamsters Union and PASSO provided one form of structure to the campaign, Mexican American young people and their social networks provided another. Young people were central, as Albert Peña Jr., state director of PASSO at the time, remembered: there were "a lot of young people," and "Albert [Fuentes] organized the young people, and they brought in the senior citizens."[49] In the poll-tax drive, high school organizing experiences blended with and provided a foundation for formal political participation. Teen activists assembled an organized core of leaders who encouraged everyone—young and old, men and women, residents and migrants alike—to pay the poll tax.[50] José Angel Gutiérrez remembered that "in the schools you had a kind of symbolic exercise of what it is to be a good citizen and practice citizenship," which created in him "this thing of being a Chicano leader."[51] This training in the rhetoric of liberty, democracy, and personal freedom resonated with the Mexican American youth who joined in the challenge to remedy the local misapplication of Americanist principals by Anglos in Crystal City.[52] According to Francisco Rodriguez, "Even in the . . . civics course, for example, we would always ask the question, 'If we are the majority, why aren't we in key governmental positions . . . why don't we have a mayor, and why are all the cops non-Mexicanos, and why is the city Council non-Mexicanos if we are the majority?' Then the response was, 'Well, you are not educated.' . . . We were involved because we were active within our class. For example, Angel was the president, and I was the VP . . . in '62."[53] Gutiérrez remembered, "This was the most exciting thing happening in Cristal [sic], and we were eager to be a part of it."[54]

The campaign also revealed the degree to which Mexican American deference toward Anglos was on the wane as young people pressed for a role in civil society. Ezequiel Guzman, a self-described "propaganda" worker on the 1963 campaign, said, "A lot of the older people had a lot of reverence for the Anglos. We kind of lost that, [thinking,] 'Well shit, we're about the same.' A lot more confident about our culture . . . and ourselves, and I think that the education . . . provided that confidence in a sense. Being able to think like Anglos do, see them, read about them—they're no different than we are."[55] Serving as the "workhorses" of the movement, as one future Wisconsin migrant activist put it, Crystal City high school students took to the streets in support of Los Cinco by leafleting, organizing and attending rallies, and getting others to participate.[56] Another future Wisconsin activist explained this grassroots youth energy as the actions of a "little group . . . getting people . . . involved" even though they were "only" teenagers.[57]

The combined efforts of local grassroots organizing and national support and political expertise resulted in a successful poll-tax drive. The Teamsters and PASSO kept the city police, the county sheriff, and the Texas Rangers at bay, allowing the Mexican American migrant community to out-register Anglos: a total of 1,139 Mexican Americans registered, versus only 542 Anglos.[58] The Teamsters and PASSO assigned organizers to Crystal City to ensure that that the incumbent Anglos ran the election in compliance with state election law. The Teamsters dispatched organizer Carlos Moore, whom future Los Cinco candidate Juan Cornejo considered "the guy that helped the most," to keep eligible voters unified behind the effort.[59]

Middle-class Mexican Americans of the sort who had run in AGIF-supported candidacies tended not to support the Los Cinco campaign. Local Anglos branded what would become the campaign as a movement of outside agitators, of communists, and they weakened middle-class Mexican American support by appointing some middle-class Mexican Americans to government posts.[60] In an apparent shift from its position in the AGIF efforts of the 1950s, Mexican Chamber of Commerce chair José Mata, speaking on behalf of the group, stated that the "organization is not a political one. . . . we do not take part in political campaigns . . . nor support candidates."[61] The AGIF also played no role in the campaign. As Cornejo explained, "We begged them to run . . . . the educated Latins did not want to join with us. . . . [So] we poor Latin-Americans with fifth-grade educations had to run."[62] The five candidates later chosen to run reflected the majority of the adult Mexican American population, in that they all had limited education, had been migrant workers, and had played no role in the earlier AGIF electoral efforts.[63]

As news of the candidate selection spread through the community, the Anglo and middle-class Mexican American reaction was confused and contradictory. The *Zavala County Sentinel* reported, "Attempts have been made . . . to create strong racial feelings and charges of discrimination have been tossed around freely."[64] One local Anglo citizen ran a full-page advertisement that read in bold letters "Think Before You Vote," reminding voters, "A split ticket is a vote for outside control." In an interesting sign of segregation and class unity, the Mexican Chamber of Commerce and the Crystal City Chamber of Commerce sponsored an advertisement that read, "We believe in continuing the excellent racial relationships we have attained over the years and are against tactics designed to create racial issues." The incumbents, in Spanish and English, requested that voters reelect them to "continue progress and a growing economy." By stark contrast, the newspaper published no Los Cinco campaign advertisements.

The incumbents included two Mexican-ancestry members elected in 1961—E. W. Ritchie Jr., the son of a prominent local family, whose mother was of Mexican ancestry, and Salvador G. Galvan, perhaps the leading Mexican-ancestry businessperson in the community, who ran several businesses, owned a ranch, and had personal relationships that spanned both the Mexican American and Anglo communities—yet the press and advertisements made no mention of the ethnic diversity of the present council. The long-serving city administration had apparently selected Ritchie and Galvan to run, perhaps in response to the efforts of the AGIF and Mexican Chamber of Commerce, yet there is no record of these men advocating Mexican American causes, and neither made ethnicity-based appeals to the electorate.[65]

In the weeks before the election, the Texas Rangers harassed individuals affiliated with the campaign. Ranger Company D captain Alfred Y. Allee, a fourth-generation Texas Ranger and former Zavala County sheriff stationed in nearby Carrizo Springs, militarized the city on orders from Governor John Connally.[66] Governor Connally dispatched Allee to Crystal City to keep the peace, but according to several accounts, Allee did far more than this, actually interrogating youth activists and community members, and even accosting several of the Teamster and PASSO activists. Allee harassed Albert Peña Jr., who visited Crystal City as head of PASSO. Peña remembered his confrontation in these words:

> And he walks up to me and he says, "are you Albert Peña?"
> I said, "yes sir, I am Albert Peña." "Are you causing all this problems, all our problems over here?" And I said, "the people of Crystal City, it is their problem, not mine. I am just here to help them, talk to them." And he had that big cigar in his mouth and he was hitting the ground and me in the chest. I think he had two, I know he had at least one gun, maybe two guns, I think. But after that it was getting kind of hot and a crowd got around and they were all Mexicanos, so he backed off. All of a sudden, he called me a communist. He said that I was a communist. . . .
> I said, "I am an American citizen."[67]

According to José Angel Gutiérrez, Allee harassed him, and on one occasion Gutiérrez's mother drew a shotgun on Allee to protect her son from injury.[68]

The Los Cinco coalition worked in tandem with PASSO and the Teamsters to protect registered voters from intimidation at the hands of the Texas Rangers and within the Del Monte plant. Del Monte plant managers sought to restrict participation by firing six workers for wearing campaign buttons and by going into overtime production on election day. On both occasions, Teamster president James R. Hoffa contacted the Del Monte headquarters in San Francisco to force the local plant manager to reinstate workers and give them time off to vote.[69]

On April 2, 1963, Mexican Americans voted overwhelmingly for Los Cinco. The five candidates led by Maldonado and Cornejo received over 795 votes each, defeating all five incumbents. Cornejo sought and received the largely honorific post of mayor.[70]

Responses to the Los Cinco Victory

Anglo responses ran the gamut from racist anger to feelings of personal betrayal, as all claimed never to have practiced discrimination in Crystal City. One local Anglo complained, "During the Depression I went in hock . . . feeding and clothing these people" and claimed, "How this discrimination business got started I'll never know."[71] This was a common reaction. As they had done in the past when Mexican Americans ran for office, Anglos claimed that the opposition manufactured racial discrimination where none had existed before. Future county judge and Mobil Oil representative Irl Taylor, unhappy with the result, wrote Governor Connally that Los Cinco won by "effective political speech making appealing to their loyalty to their Mexican Ancestory [sic]" and "throwing in reverse racial discrimination, and keeping the flame going."[72] Tom Allee, a relative of Ranger Allee, criticized the media coverage of dilapidated schools for Mexican American children by WOAI Television in San Antonio. Making a common paternalistic argument, Allee countered that Anglos paid "95% of the taxes" for a school enrollment that was "85% . . . Latin" and that the media ignored the fact that the school board had planned to demolish the dilapidated schools but kept them open to serve the immediate needs of the migrant "Latin people coming to Crystal City for the winter."[73]

Some Anglos, backed by the Texas Rangers, at first refused to accept the victory. The Rangers did not leave after the election, and according to reports, Captain Allee refused to turn over the keys to City Hall to the newly elected mayor until ordered to do so by Governor Connally. In an effort to calm fears and perhaps force the exit of the Rangers, Los Cinco informed the people of Crystal City, "We will tolerate no unlawful acts regardless of who may be responsible for them."[74] Cornejo accused Allee of physically assaulting him, and he sent telegrams to the governor and others complaining of Allee's behavior. Cornejo's protests led Texas senator Ralph Yarborough to complain of Ranger-led "Pistol Rule" in Crystal City and to call on the Federal Bureau of Investigation to intervene.[75]

The election of Los Cinco had the unintended consequence of bringing some segments of the Mexican American and Anglo middle classes together in alliance against the upstart movement of workers, migrants, women, and young people. Several prominent Anglos, the Crystal City

Chamber of Commerce, and Frank Guajardo of the Mexican Chamber of Commerce wrote to Governor Connally expressing support for the continued presence of the Texas Rangers in Crystal City. Locally well-known ranchers and members of the Mexican Chamber met with Homer Garrison, director of the Texas Department of Public Safety, to pledge their support for the Rangers' presence.[76] Jerry Greene of Crystal City claimed that "we were robbed in the recent election" and that the Rangers were required, since "we will need protection . . . from PASSO and Teamster sponsored characters." Others informed the governor that the Mexicans supporting Los Cinco wanted "something for nothing" and accused the Teamsters and PASSO of being "reds" and using "Communistic methods."[77] As tensions mounted, all but one of the many long-serving Anglo city employees resigned their positions rather than assist with the transition, adding to the chaos and hostility in the city.[78]

Regardless of such opposition, Crystal City's "revolt" brought an emerging Mexican Americanist radical politics to national attention, drawing responses across the political spectrum.[79] Mexican Americans from across Texas expressed their concerns about the situation in Crystal City quite differently. Dr. Hector Garcia, founder of the AGIF, telegrammed the governor asking for Allee's "immediate dismissal and charges brought against police brutality" and instructing the governor to request federal marshals as peacekeepers and replacements for the Rangers.[80] University of Texas professor George I. Sanchez reminded Connally that the Rangers are "better known as '*rinches*' among my people . . . [as] sorry representatives of law-and-order" and pointed out that "the *Mexicanos* and the Negroes wield compelling political power in Texas" and "if you look the other way . . . this is not a matter to be forgiven or overlooked."[81] Tomas M. Rodriguez of Laredo reminded the governor that a "substantial group of our citizens of Latin extract are surprised and deeply concerned about your clearing the attitude of ranger [Allee] in the Crystal City situation." Rodriguez, embracing the Americanist rhetoric of democratic participation and acculturation, pointed out to Connally that "all they wish and need is to be democratically governed; thereby they endeavor to be so considered and accepted."[82] Governor Connally replied rather glibly that his "only position and sole desire is that the elected officials of Crystal City govern the city in peace."[83]

In San Antonio, home to the PASSO and Teamsters organizers, the election in Crystal City exposed similar divisions. In a series of editorials titled "In the Shadow of San Fernando," the official San Antonio Catholic archdiocesan newspaper, which often sympathetically detailed the plight of Mexican American farmworkers, the exploitation of the Bracero Program, and other areas of social concern for the strongly Catholic Mexican American community, lambasted the Los Cinco effort as an outside effort that exploited "minor forms of discrimination" and compared the activists' embrace of ethnic politics to the "Hitlerarian concept of Aryanism."[84] From the point of view of the editorials, which ran for several weeks, racial reform was already taking place in Texas, albeit quietly and slowly, and a "revolt" like the one in Crystal City put this progress at risk. Further, the editorials complained that "foreign" groups like PASSO and the Teamsters created false division in Crystal City, and the paper defended the Anglos who had long maintained segregation in most areas of adult life. As the weeks went on and Mexican Americans wrote in support of the expansion of civil rights in Crystal City, the tone of the editorials softened and called on Anglos to "labor alongside these men for the benefit of the community," but they continued to chastise PASSO for embracing "racism in reverse" and warned of a possible "tyranny of the majority" across South Texas.[85]

The political shockwave of Crystal City's radical Mexican Americanist politics spread across Texas, exposing rifts within the Mexican American political leadership. Some leaders questioned the efficacy of an explicitly racial politics for Mexican Americans, and the controversy over tactics and rhetoric weakened PASSO, whose very purpose was to act as a unified force in Mexican American politics. The PASSO wing, led by Albert Peña Jr., faced direct and open opposition from other prominent Mexican American political leaders. Peña himself faced reprisals in San Antonio as the Bexar County commissioners voted 4–1 to censure him for setting "citizens against citizens in Crystal City." Congressman Henry B. Gonzalez of San Antonio strongly protested the Peña-backed PASSO effort in Crystal City for alienating moderate Anglo voters across Texas. The arrival of a more radical and confrontational Mexican Americanism revealed the fissure between those who saw Mexican Americanism as primarily Americanist and those who saw it as defined by a radical commitment to both citizenship rights and a Mexican American or Tejano race consciousness.[86]

The Los Cinco Legacy

As tensions raged within Mexican American leadership circles across Texas, Los Cinco faced the hard task of governing. Almost from the start, it became clear that Juan Cornejo sought more control than his post as mayor provided. By becoming mayor even after coming in second in terms of votes cast, Cornejo rejected the customary practice of awarding the honorific post to the candidate with the most votes. Despite his charismatic personality and proven organizing strengths, Cornejo had little understanding of the way a city manager form of government functioned. Los Cinco, after consultation with the Teamsters and PASSO, appointed George Ozuna to the post of city manager. Ozuna thus became the first Mexican American city manager in Texas history. The hiring of Ozuna was also an effort to show that despite a clear lack of education and experience, Los Cinco could appoint educated professionals to govern.[87]

The election of Los Cinco made Cornejo a celebrity, and he traveled widely as a representative of the Mexican American civil rights movement. He appeared with the likes of Martin Luther King Jr., visited Mexico as a guest of state, and campaigned for PASSO candidates in Austin.[88] Cornejo also visited Los Angeles on several occasions to make speeches, engage in organizing, and speak on television.[89] When not traveling on behalf of Mexican American political involvement, Cornejo openly fought for control of city government, despite the fact that daily city operations rested with the city manager. He did not accept the independence of Ozuna and the weak mayor system of Crystal City's charter. Over two years of controversy and misunderstanding, Cornejo became an embarrassment to the Teamsters, who fired him, and to PASSO, which abandoned his administration after several well-publicized and foolish blunders on his part.

Cornejo was not the only problem: Los Cinco fell apart in its first year thanks to economic pressure on individual council members. Some of the five candidates lost their jobs, resigned from the council, or shifted allegiances.[90] By 1965, Anglos, together with some middle-class Mexican Americans, had formed a new interracial political organization, the Citizens Association Serving All Americans (CASA), which ran an Anglo and Mexican slate and brought Los Cinco's reign to an end. The Los Cinco victory was a hollow one for the Teamsters, who seemingly abandoned Mexican American activist causes; for PASSO, which disintegrated following the Crystal City affair; and for the candidates themselves. At the local level, however, it paved the way for further political and labor movement activity by placing Mexican American civil rights and politics on the agenda.[91]

Yet for the young men and women who participated in the election and witnessed the aftermath, Los Cinco represented more than the story of the rise and fall of five Mexican American men who lacked the education or stability to govern: the election represented a success as a catalyzing and educational event. According to youth participant Miguel Delgado, who later moved to Milwaukee, Wisconsin, "We did realize one thing—that if we were going to succeed against the Gringo, we had to educate ourselves in the Gringo world—to know how to use this new power that we could gain."[92] Jesus Salas, a Crystal City native then living and working between Crystal City and Wisconsin, argued that neither "the organizing of farmworkers" nor "the development of [the] farmworker's union" would have been possible "if Los Cinco hadn't come to the fore in the political arena when they did." He noted, "In effect, when I speak about organizational activities in the mid-1960s, it is with people that have experienced that situation who become unafraid of the challenge, who start confronting not only the political bosses, but the economic ones in Central Wisconsin."[93]

For young participants like Ezequiel Guzman, who also resettled in Wisconsin, the "importance [of Los Cinco] lay in the future," when people like Delgado, Guzman, and Francisco Rodriguez carried this political movement across the migrant stream to Wisconsin, and when José Angel Gutiérrez carried this spirit to San Antonio, where he helped found the Mexican American Youth Organization (MAYO) while attending Saint Mary's University.[94] Commenting on the broader influence of Los Cinco, Jesus Salas stated that the movement "really empowered us to improve ourselves not only politically, but economically and educationally."[95]

Often considered a precursor to the well-known 1969 Crystal City revolt that led to the rise of La Raza Unida Party, the Los Cinco movement—both its successes and its failures—changed the way Mexican American youth and migrants viewed their place within American political life. One of many important points of departure between the Mexican Americanism of the 1950s and the more radical Mexican

Americanism of the early 1960s, as well as the rising "Chicano" politics of the late 1960s, Los Cinco revealed the latent racial understanding of working-class Mexican Americans and many Anglos. It also brought about the collapse of PASSO and splintered the established Mexican American leadership in Texas and California.[96] As Juan Cornejo and Los Cinco retreated from history, young people across the migrant stream in Wisconsin and at home in Texas fanned the fires of radical Mexican Americanism.

3

Activism across the Diaspora

THE TEJANO FARMWORKER MOVEMENT IN WISCONSIN

On August 15, 1966, twenty-two-year-old Jesus Salas, a college student and the son of a migrant contractor and restaurant owner from Crystal City, Texas, organized a "March on Madison" to bring attention to the problems of Wisconsin's migrant farmworkers. This was the third farmworker march of the year. In March, the fledgling National Farm Workers Association (NFWA) had led a march from Delano, California, to Sacramento, and put the plight of the farmworker on the national agenda. In June, Father Antonio Gonzalez, a Catholic priest whose family annually traveled to the cucumber harvest area of Wautoma, Wisconsin, had led a march of La Casita Farms workers from Starr County, Texas, to the capitol at Austin. The NFWA sponsored these two earlier events with funding from the AFL-CIO in an effort to build a national farmworkers union. While the young Wisconsin activists linked the plight of Wisconsin's migrants to the national farmworker movement, the Wisconsin event remained formally independent.[1] The protest had specific local goals, as Salas hoped that the march would publicly "dramatize the plight of migrant workers" and arouse "the social conscience of progressive Wisconsin."[2] All three marches gained national attention and in so doing demonstrated that the migrant stream was truly a diasporic system that linked Tejano and other Mexican American migrant workers to one another in South Texas, California, Wisconsin, and other states.[3]

This transregional community linked the Crystal City activism of 1963 to the developing farmworker movement: Mexican American activism spread and became connected to the larger movement via the Tejano diaspora. Following the rise and fall of Los Cinco in Crystal City, young people and migrants continued to move north each spring, and they carried an activist spirit with them. The transregional migration of young workers from Crystal City became the backbone of a grass-roots movement that informed community action and brought together several related groups in a web of pan-Tejano cooperation and mutual dependence in Wisconsin.

This chapter details the development of transregional migrant unionism in Wisconsin between 1966 and 1970 as one window into the importance of the Tejano diaspora in Mexican American history. Focused on the growth of Obreros Unidos (OU), a transregionally grounded and independent labor union of mainly Tejano workers in Wisconsin, it shows how social networks function and expand within both interstate and local settings to accommodate community activism. The emergence of OU as an outgrowth of both Texas- and Wisconsin-based activism and reform movements expands our understanding of grassroots mobilization among Mexican Americans during a period of state-level legal reform, interstate union competition, interregional ethnic conflict, and multiethnic and multiracial civil rights activism in Wisconsin. Its growth shows some of the ways an ethnic movement re-lied upon both preexisting social networks among Tejano migrants and state-based networks linking a variety of Wisconsin progressives, New Left student activists, and Old Left labor activists in building a broad-based labor and reform organization.

This chapter also considers how institutional forces, particularly the legal system and bureaucratic unionism, can overcome the spirit and frustrate the goals of grassroots labor activism. With the support of the AFL-CIO legal staff, OU won victories in court and before labor boards, yet these decisions came after striking workers had returned to Texas or moved on to other work. Even with state-level protections for labor in place, the structural tendencies of labor law and procedure in one of the few states to protect agricultural workers mitigated against grassroots activism and the spirited commitment of the organizers. In addition, the national AFL-CIO and the farmworkers' union, represented by César Chávez, tried for many years to bring OU union under national control and, eventually, to dissolve the union altogether. Thus, both legal protections and the national union movement itself proved unstable sup-ports for a grassroots movement led by young people on behalf of some of the nation's neediest workers.

Roots of the Wisconsin Movement

Wisconsin was central to the annual circular migration of nearly ten thousand farmworkers, a position strengthened in the decade after World War II. Other states, including Michigan and California, received more migrants and had larger settled populations of former migrants, yet Wisconsin served as a midseason hub for workers from several labor-sending regions in South Texas, as tens of thousands of Tejano migrants traveled to Wisconsin each summer to work in the cucumber harvest after working in a number of other states. In trucks driven by crew leaders or cars driven by family members, Tejano migrants from Crystal City traveled to harvest sugar beets in Minnesota, Montana, North Dakota, or other western states. After several weeks in sugar beet work, a large number of workers traveled to Wisconsin to harvest cherries and cucumbers in late July and early August. Another stream from Crystal City carried migrants to California, where they worked before moving on to Washington and Oregon to harvest orchard crops. Each fall, these workers returned to Crystal City, just one of the many South Texas sending cities for labor migrants, with news of labor opportunities, social conditions, and gossip from across the national diaspora of Tejano workers that harvested and canned much of the nation's fruits and vegetables. In 1966, demonstrating the centrality of the Tejano diaspora to workers' movements, observers noted that many of the grape workers who went on strike for the NFWA in California were from Texas.[4]

The interstate system of migration made the Tejano diaspora a truly national network of job sites, workers, and mobile communities. In 1966, for example, the majority of migratory farmworkers in Wisconsin were Tejanos, and many had worked in other states before entering in search of work. Each year, ten to fifteen thousand workers entered Wisconsin, the vast majority coming from Texas as family groups. The peak season was mid-August, when thousands came to harvest cucumbers, cherries, canning crops, and other vegetables. After the Wisconsin harvest, large groups of workers went on to work in Indiana, Illinois, Ohio, and other states, including California. Of all these places in the diaspora, it was only in California, Texas, and Wisconsin that Mexican American civil rights activists created and sustained a national labor rights movement among migrant workers.[5]

While the Tejano diaspora functioned as a macro-level system of migration and labor, this was a system built upon social networks maintained by individuals and families of workers. In Wisconsin, the family of Jesus Salas acted as an important node in the migrant networks that linked workers and communities in Texas to labor sites across the nation. In 1959, Manuel Salas Sr., Jesus's father, a labor contractor for cucumber farms and the successful owner of a restaurant and tavern in Crystal City, established a similar bar and restaurant operation in the migrant agricultural town of Wautoma, Wisconsin, and continued to recruit workers from Texas. Like many residents of Crystal City, Texas—or "Cristal," as residents referred to it—the Salas family traveled as migrants for over a generation, and in fact Jesus and his siblings had been engaged in fieldwork before they entered public school. Farmwork was a communal process in which families traveled together and worked in farm fields as small, interdependent units. Speaking in 1969 on the foundational aspects of this social network, Jesus Salas commented that his family traveled "as a community with family, neighbors, relatives . . . all together and we reinforce ourselves continually"—a process that strengthened personal ties over the decades.[6]

Diasporic labor systems also transform the meaning of space and place: community changes and evolves as workers move and travel far away from their home region. Migrants outside of Texas like the Salas family came to identify themselves as Cristaleños within a broader community of traveling Tejanos as they lived and labored across the diaspora, an appellation that would have had little meaning if they had stayed within the boundaries of their family and kin networks in Crystal City. Because of Manuel Salas Sr.'s role as a labor contractor, the Salas family helped to sustain this annual circular migration between their former home in Texas and their new hometown in Wisconsin. The migrant networks also incorporated others into the community. Salvador Sanchez of McAllen, Texas, became an important part of the Crystal City–based migrant stream after his recruitment by Manuel Salas Sr. to bring workers from other South Texas communities. Sanchez remembered the contours of this social and labor network as comprising "a lot of pickers from Crystal City . . . [and] thousands of workers [from Texas]."[7] In this way, Manuel Salas and those he recruited, along with subcontractors like Sanchez, tied thousands of workers from Crystal City and other South Texas migrant communities to one another in overlapping networks of kinship and interdependence.[8]

Such interstate social networks allowed members to flow between both their adopted and former homes with relative ease. The Salas family had deep roots in Crystal City, where Teophillo Salas, Jesus's grandfather, had settled prior to 1910.[9] Several branches of the extended family remained in Crystal City after Manuel Salas settled in Wisconsin, a resource that facilitated continued trips to Texas in search of workers and eventually labor union organizing trips led by Jesus and Manuel Salas Jr. Even after moving to Wisconsin, the Salases, much like other migrants, maintained property in Crystal City and returned to visit friends and relatives.[10] Through the maintenance of these ties, they became aware of the 1963 political struggle in Crystal City; indeed, they returned between 1962 and 1963 to witness and become involved in the poll tax and get-out-the-vote efforts for Los Cinco. Jesus Salas participated in the Los Cinco effort with former Crystal City school classmates, including José Angel Gutiérrez, Francisco Rodriguez, Ezequiel Guzman, and others, who knew him as "Chuy."[11]

The reform-minded social, labor, and political networks based in Wisconsin also influenced Jesus Salas, who completed high school in Wautoma and attended college in Wisconsin. As a college student, Salas developed close relationships with local student activists and reform-minded academics, seeding new social nodes for the development of transregional politics. At Wisconsin State University–Oshkosh, for example, Jesus and Manuel Salas Jr. befriended David Giffey, a student journalist and campus free-speech activist. Giffey and the Salas brothers became close friends who parted ways when Giffey was drafted to serve in Vietnam. In Vietnam, Giffey, a student journalist, worked for *Stars and Stripes* and gained practical skills he would later bring to the farmworker movement.[12] Jesus Salas then attended Wisconsin State University–Stevens Point, where he met longtime progressives on the faculty who helped him begin work in early childhood programs serving migrant children and introduced him to reformers in Madison.[13]

In 1964, Salas helped establish and distribute the bilingual paper *La Voz Mexicana* to inform seasonal migrant workers of available summer services in Wautoma, Wisconsin. This newspaper, established as a seasonal publication for migrants and funded by the advertising of local merchants, brought him to the attention of state officials. As he and his brother Manuel increasingly wrote for the paper, it became more involved in migrant advocacy and increasingly lost merchant sponsorship.

Through the newspaper, Salas came to know and respect University of Wisconsin professor Elizabeth Brandeis Raushenbush, a labor economist and daughter of Supreme Court justice Louis D. Brandeis.[14] "This extraordinary woman," as he described her, served as Salas's "mentor" and had him appointed to the Governor's Committee on Migratory Labor (GCML) in 1964.[15]

Raushenbush played a central role in progressive reform in Wisconsin and dedicated most of her energies after World War II to the improvement of migrant conditions in the state. Earlier in the century, she, along with economist John R. Commons, helped establish labor and worker protections in Wisconsin, many of which became models for other states and the nation as part of the New Deal. Raushenbush was a participant in the creation of the "Wisconsin school" of labor economics and authored portions of Commons's *History of Labor in the United States*.[16] She served on the Governor's Commission on Human Rights, where she brought attention to migrant labor issues, and in 1960 she was appointed chairperson of the GCML.[17] Perhaps more than any other academic or bureaucrat, Raushenbush worked for the improvement of health, living, and labor conditions for Wisconsin's migrant workers. In fact, she considered the "migrant problem" the "unfinished business" of national labor legislation and corresponded with reformers in Washington, D.C., New York, and California to this end.[18]

The University of Wisconsin was well positioned in the early 1960s to assist in reform-minded research as a result of prior tradition and new avenues of federal funding. Raushenbush, as the head of the GCML and a University of Wisconsin faculty member, already had well-developed networks in Madison and Washington, D.C., and through these she was able to fund and assemble a research team to study migrant poverty in Wisconsin. Professor Robert Lampman, who later founded the Institute for Research on Poverty at Wisconsin as the national center for the research of poverty under the Office of Economic Opportunity (OEO), also helped find federal funding for Raushenbush's project, which sent economics graduate students to Waushara County, Wisconsin, to complete a quantitative study of wages and working conditions among cucumber harvesters.[19] From Wautoma in Waushara County, *La Voz Mexicana* published reports detailing the entry of these "young" economics graduate students and their "*Gran Proyecto.*"[20] In the previous decade, University of Wisconsin economists had completed research and pointed the way to migrant labor reform, yet Raushenbush sought new, unmediated data on the migrants in Wisconsin to provide a baseline for discussing their wages and their working and living conditions and also to refute the contrary and unsubstantiated claims of farmer and grower representatives as reformers sought to amend Wisconsin's regulations pertaining to migrant labor, housing, and welfare.[21]

This research effort significantly linked young academics and migrant leaders in the cucumber-growing region of Wisconsin. One of the graduate students sent to Wautoma, Mark Erenburg, a Jewish doctor's son from suburban Chicago, developed a close relationship with Salas and other migrants. In 1964, Salas introduced Erenburg to Salvador Sanchez, who would assist him. These three men became fast friends and, with the support of Professor Raushenbush, sought some concrete ways to aid migrants.[22] The friendships and allegiances that developed surfaced on the pages of *La Voz Mexicana*, which several of the graduate students joined as staff writers.[23] In an editorial titled "The Times Are Changing," Manuel Salas lambasted the "atrocious wages" paid to farmworkers and thanked those who lobbied to end the Bracero Program for putting Mexican American workers in "an advantageous position to ask for better wages and working conditions."[24] By 1965, the newspaper, led by a group of Tejano and graduate student writers, was providing information to workers and calling for reform in an increasingly vocal way.

In 1965, after the creation of the Office of Economic Opportunity and the extension of federal funding to the Institute for Research on Poverty, the Raushenbush-led research team was transformed into a small service program for migrants. The program sponsored various baseball tournaments and other outreach activities to attract attention to its offerings. These tournaments, often held at labor camps that housed workers from Salvador Sanchez's labor crew, brought college students, migrant workers, and migrant leaders like the Salas brothers and Sanchez together to play ball, socialize, and become friends.[25]

In the summer of 1966, the organizers held formal meetings to discuss the role migrants and reformers might play in bringing attention to the problems faced by agricultural workers in Wisconsin. These meetings, held at Saint Joseph Catholic Church in Wautoma, mainly focused on gathering information, airing complaints, and considering possible future action. Crew leaders, workers, and activists discussed matters raised at the meetings and considered a variety of approaches to reform. Just months after fellow migrant workers marched on the state capitols at Sacramento, California, and Austin, Texas, in the name of labor unionization, Wisconsin's Tejano migrants considered a similar protest action, although they were not part of an established labor union.[26] After several meetings at the church, the group decided that a march was the best way to shed light on the farm labor struggle in Wisconsin. The organizers, Salas recalled in 1967, meant to emulate "César Chávez . . . in California, and the . . . Negro . . . in the Civil Rights Movement."[27] The youthful activists inspired by the actions of the Agricultural Workers Organizing Committee (AWOC) and National Farm Workers Association (NFWA) grape strike led by Larry Itliong, César Chávez, and Dolores Huerta in Delano, California, sought to make a difference in Wisconsin.[28]

The spark of labor activism begun in California sought to resolve long-standing issues for harvest workers and created a movement that quickly spread across the nation. Various organizations had unsuccessfully attempted to unionize farm workers in California in the twentieth century. Many had succeeded at the task of organizing but failed in the effort to establish a viable trade union for agricultural workers on the vast industrial farms of California. Antiunion efforts overpowered the attempts of a number of unionization drives prior to World War II. In 1959, in response to increasing attention on the plight of farmworkers, the AFL-CIO chartered the AWOC and provided it with a significant budget. Leading several strikes, which failed to win collective bargaining agreements, the organization nonetheless proved organizing agricultural workers was a feasible project. As America focused attention on poverty and civil rights, and as the federal government ended the Bracero Program, the AWOC continued its organizing drive in California. Most important, AWOC grape harvesters went on strike in September 1965 led by Filipino workers, later joined by the NFWA—a move that quickly made farm organizing a national issue and garnered praise from African American civil rights leaders such as Dr. Martin Luther King Jr.[29]

A multiethnic effort from the start, the grape strike in California gained immediate attention and placed the issue of justice for farmworkers on the national agenda. Certainly, the airing of Edward R. Murrow's

Harvest of Shame television documentary had placed the plight of agricultural laborers in the American conscience, but the actions of AWOC and the NFWA's leader, César Chávez, served to inspire young Mexican Americans and progressives across the nation. Chávez, former state director of the CSO, had significant experience as a community organizer in Northern California and before the strike had created within the NFWA a social unionism based on the CSO model in Delano. As the AWOC and the NFWA increasingly worked together, the union movement that grew from this collaboration became a clearinghouse for a variety of migrant services. By moving beyond the basic goals of trade unionism, this community-based union model, very much a product of the CSO, responded to the diverse needs of the migrant farmworker community.[30]

César Chávez, as the charismatic head of the union, quickly became a national figure. Following the strike, religious and civil rights activists, as well as others, including Walter Reuther of the United Auto Workers (UAW) and Senator Robert F. Kennedy, visited Delano to meet with Chávez and his union, which quickly made this devoutly Catholic activist an iconic embodiment of the Mexican American community's struggle for civil rights. Religious groups, many already assisting migrant workers, also responded to Chávez's pilgrimage-based activism, and a variety of denominations increasingly provided financial and personal support to the union. Student volunteers and members of African American civil rights organizations also lent a hand to the California farmworkers' cause. Throughout his career, Chávez was a leader among many within an organization that included Dolores Huerta and many other competent organizers, yet it was Chávez who became the identifiable leader of the movement for most Americans.[31]

Inspired by the marches and labor organizing drives in California and Texas, former migrants from Texas and a small group of college students organized a march to focus attention on the needs of farmworkers in Wisconsin. In the absence of direct union leadership, the demonstration was a protest and informational march. In an effort to keep sympathetic workers who wanted to join the march employed and avoid the impression that this was a labor strike, the crew leaders and migrants agreed on a "representative" march of activists joined by a small number of farmworkers. The protesters selected one member of each crew to participate, a move that allowed a small group of marchers to stand in for the agricultural workers while guaranteeing that the majority continued to earn their wages. To protect families, single men and those without children volunteered to make up the bulk of participants. The organizers did their best to calm fears on all fronts while protesting the mistreatment of migrant workers.[32] The announcement that workers would march on the state capital brought a rapid call for negotiation on the part of the state government. Salas, now the de facto leader of the Wisconsin movement, agreed to meet with state officials but resolved that the protest would continue because the problems of the migrant workers could not "be solved immediately."[33]

On Sunday, August 14, Salas and others gave speeches outside the Waushara County Courthouse and rallied several hundred supporters. After an early-morning mass at Saint Joseph's Catholic Church, the marchers, joined by Saint Joseph's Father Michael Garrigan and Rev. Barry Shaw, head of the Wisconsin Council of Churches, left Wautoma holding signs that read, "*Juntarnos para ser reconocidos, hablar para ser oidos, La Raza tiene causa*" (Join us to be recognized, speak to be heard, The People have a cause), as others carried images of the Virgin of Guadalupe, the U.S. flag, and the black thunderbird of the California-based NFWA.[34] The following day, Salas met with state officials before rejoining the march on its way to Madison.[35] At the meeting, state agency representatives and Joseph C. Fagan, chair of the Wisconsin Industrial Commission (WIC), the primary state-level regulatory agency for labor and employment laws, discussed a variety of issues facing agricultural workers and pledged to help. Following this meeting, Chairman Fagan announced, "I think your demands are reasonable, your cause is just and you should be encouraged."[36]

Plagued by rainfall, the migrants were assisted by groups of Madison activists, Catholic Church members, and unionists as they traveled the eighty-eight miles to Madison. As the march neared the capitol, workers from Racine and Kenosha, Wisconsin, joined it.[37] On August 19, Salas, with fourteen of the original twenty-six marchers, entered Madison, along with several migrants and their families who had been discharged for participation. Madison residents and labor leaders came out to join the marchers at the capitol, swelling the ranks of supporters. Bill Smith, an African American graduate student in history at the University of Wisconsin who had met Salas while working on a summer construction crew, organized the Madison reception and rally

Jesus Salas (front left) and Salvador Sanchez (front right) lead a march leaving Wautoma for Madison, Wisconsin, August 15, 1966. Photo courtesy of David Giffey.

at the state capitol building. At the reception, attended by Governor Warren P. Knowles and several key state labor leaders, WIC chair Fagan thanked the marchers for giving the people of Wisconsin "the chance to look at something much better than we have had for some while . . . [and] care about someone who is trying very hard to care about his own people."[38]

From the capitol steps, the speeches of politicians and the migrant activists avoided the topic of unionization, yet the AFL-CIO and the NFWA were clear supporters of the movement. Salas embraced the language of Americanism as he reminded the crowd that the march was not an attempt to exert "economic pressure" over the agricultural industry, nor was it a "walk-out," but rather an assertion of the migrant's "constitutional right . . . to be heard."[39] This statement was contradicted by other reports, however: in Wautoma, *La Voz Mexicana* reported that the march was an NFWA event, and César Chávez informed Governor Knowles on August 13 that the protest was "led by the National Farm Workers Association, AFL-CIO."[40]

Although no migrant workers' union technically existed in Wisconsin, the march had the support of organized labor and the close attention of the AFL-CIO and affiliated unions. Charles Heymanns, longtime labor organizer from Kohler, Wisconsin, and director of Region 12 of the AFL-CIO, gave the keynote speech at the rally. Heymanns reported directly to Bill Kircher, a former journalist and UAW leader and the AFL-CIO's national director of organization. Kircher served as the highest-ranking union official responsible for coordinating and providing financial support for the farmworker union drives in California and Texas and reported directly to AFL-CIO president George Meany. More than any other nonfarm labor activist, Kircher funded and monitored the national drive to unionize agricultural farm labor. From the start of the march, the national AFL-CIO followed developments via the state union leadership and gave support to what soon became the Wisconsin front in the battle to organize farmworkers.[41]

The response to the protest in and around Wautoma in central Wisconsin was markedly negative. Journalistic reports and letters sent by readers characterized the movement as an outside, unrepresentative, and even subversive affront to the foundation of the local economy, to Christianity, and to core American values. The *Appleton Post-Crescent* reported that "ninety five percent" of migrant workers in central Wisconsin were happy. One resident went so far as to compare Jesus Salas to Adolph Hitler. Religious leaders attacked Salas in the newspapers, and the local John Birch Society asked for an investigation of the leadership.[42] Many in central Wisconsin's agricultural regions clearly saw the march as a first step in the establishment of an "instant" union by those who they felt failed to represent the views of "responsible" migrant workers.[43]

Sensing that the divide between growers and farmworker supporters might become a political issue, the state called for meetings between these groups. Joseph Fagan organized a meeting to include growers, activists, workers, and government officials so that all parties could sit and "talk turkey."[44] Growers maintained that workers made more than the minimum wage, that the migrants were free laborers who moved about as they wished, and that further regulation would harm the industry and the individual's ability to maintain wage rates.[45] In an ominous sign of things to come, a local company tested a pickle-harvesting machine in Waushara County the same week as the march.[46] One industry representative, in perhaps a veiled threat to the state and the activists, pointed out that "even a minor change affecting . . . [grower] return . . . would very likely eliminate the crop."[47] Nothing came of the meeting between the two sides in what was now a clear divide between growers and workers in the cucumber industry.

Despite the failure of the growers and migrants to find joint solutions, the march led to significant results at the state level. The governor appointed more former migrant workers to the Governor's Committee on Migratory Labor headed by Raushenbush. The Board of Health hired more housing inspectors and moved to improve enforcement. The Chamber of Commerce of Wautoma agreed to pursue plans to build more public toilet facilities, answering a long-standing migrant complaint. The WIC began a program to inform migrant workers of their rights under the Wisconsin Workmen's Compensation Law, raised the state minimum wage for women and children from $1.10 to $1.25, considered its extension to men, and barred employers from deducting rental fees from migrant wages.[48]

Salas's position within the migrant community, his charismatic presence, and his sense of duty grounded in migrant life quickly made him the obvious leader of this emerging farm labor movement. Inspired by a Mexican Americanism with roots in activist Crystal City and heightened through his learning experience as a young man interacting with progressive Wisconsin, Salas had useful contacts and skills for such leadership. Likewise, crew leader Salvador Sanchez of McAllen, Texas, had learned from similar experiences and embraced the union effort. The two graduate students, Mark Erenburg and Bill Smith, joined the movement intent on doing their part and stayed on longer than either anticipated. In September of 1966, these four "summer revolutionaries" had put Wisconsin on the map as part of the national farmworkers' movement, and they headed back to school and work unsure as to what lay ahead.[49]

The cucumber workers of Wautoma were key to the success of the march, as they would be key to any potential migrant labor organizing effort in Wisconsin. Salas's and Sanchez's leadership grew from the relationships the two men had within this community and the respected position of Salas's father, Manuel Salas, who still actively worked for the cucumber harvesting and processing operations of central Wisconsin. Cucumber harvesters were employed across state lines before and after the harvest and often moved on to potato work after the cucumber season ended. This move to nearby work in potatoes proved an unexpected opportunity to test the ability of the young activists—an opportunity that caught them completely off guard while also teaching them meaningful lessons about union organizing, including the importance of having state-level support.

Independent Farmworker Unionism in Wisconsin

In September 1966, a group of cucumber harvesters who participated in the march brought the idea of unionizing the potato processing warehouses of Wisconsin to Salas and the other organizers. Soon after these discussions, an executive at James Burns and Sons, a potato processing facility, humiliated an employee, and his coworkers began preparations for a walkout in response.[50] At this point, the workers again contacted Salas, who quickly sought volunteers among those who had marched with him to Madison and the assistance of the Wisconsin AFL-CIO.

There was a direct link between the August march and the union now forming in the potato facilities just fifteen miles away from Wautoma. Between four and five hundred migrants worked both harvests, and they were active in the meetings with Salas and in the march. These workers, like Salas and Sanchez, were mainly from South Texas, with many hailing from the Winter Garden District and from Crystal City in particular.

By the early fall of 1966, the march leaders had become labor organizers, though none had prior experience with union organizing.[51] Salas remembered the challenges: "[It is] very . . . painful for me to talk about it because we knew so little about the strike. . . . We didn't know that we had to establish membership. We didn't know that we had to petition the WERB [Wisconsin Employment Relations Board] to get an election. We simply walked out. We said, 'We have a majority of the workers, we want you to recognize us.'"[52] Bill Smith remembered that the group was "just completely baffled because first of all, we had no idea how to form a union, we knew nothing about a union, and we didn't know what to do." Smith also thought that "since we were the big mouths . . . then we obviously owed those workers up there something . . . [and] we decided that what we should do, is what all revolutionaries did . . . we would formulate a list of demands."[53] Researchers for the United Packinghouse, Food and Allied Workers, AFL-CIO, were concerned with the leaders' lack of organizing experience and recommended that the AFL-CIO provide the union with "an experienced organizer and a labor lawyer familiar with Wisconsin and Federal labor laws."[54]

Organizing in the potato processing industry was no easy task. The potato industry had an exceptional level of processor control and a labor force divided between local Anglo workers and Tejano migrants. Potato processors were family-owned businesses that managed the harvesting, packing, warehousing, and shipping functions. Within this system, local Anglo workers operated the harvesting machinery, and Tejano migrants did the sorting, grading, washing, and bagging at lower wage rates. Tejana women tended to do most of the sorting, earning about $1.25 an hour for removing dirt, rocks, and other debris from the potatoes. Men tended to do the bagging and loading, with older men doing the sewing of the ends of the sacks. Men earned from $1.35 to $1.50 an hour for this work. Unlike in harvest work, children did not participate, and the work took place in industrial facilities.[55]

With support from the state AFL-CIO, the activists established OU as an independent labor union. At the Burns plant, the organizers, led by Salas and Carolina Reyes, also a native of Crystal City, quickly won the support of the majority of the processing workers, who signed membership cards designating OU as their exclusive bargaining agent.[56] Since other work crews from the cucumber harvest worked in nearby potato plants, the union also organized employees at Central Sands, Paramount Packing, and Frontier Packing Company. At Burns, Bill Smith and a group of workers formulated the list of demands, which included time and a half for overtime hours, optional overtime, a twenty-five-cent raise, paid breaks and lunch hour, and cheaper rent in company housing, among others.[57] On October 5, OU informed Burns and Central Sands Produce that it represented a majority of workers and called for union recognition and the start of collective bargaining. Monsignor Finucan of the nearby Stevens Point Catholic Archdiocese served as the mediator and go-between for negotiations between Burns and OU.[58]

James Burns ignored the union's request and reacted to the organization of a union by forcing workers to declare in writing whether or not they were affiliated with the union and firing the twenty-seven union workers, as well as one other who refused to sign an affidavit. On October 7, 1966, in response to these actions, sixty-five of the ninety packing-shed workers at Burns went on strike, and OU began picketing the Burns plant at Almond, Wisconsin.[59] The success of the organizing drive and the pickets brought newspaper coverage and cast light on Burns's failure to negotiate and the interrogation of the workers. Local press coverage by the *Waushara Argus* was expectedly harsh on the workers: the paper ran a front-page editorial attacking the drive and labeling Jesus Salas and Mark Erenburg "self appointed" union leaders, even though the workers had formed the union and then called on Salas and Erenburg for help.[60] Central Wisconsin provided little support for these young activists; instead, they drew on the assistance of Milwaukee-based AFL-CIO attorneys, Madison-based academics and students, and the Tejano workers' families.

The union soon had an opportunity to prove itself to the workers by defending their rights and the needs of their families. After the first day of picketing, Burns had a deputy sheriff of Portage County block them from entering their rented homes. The union's attorney informed the deputy that since the workers had paid their rent in advance, such a no-notice eviction was illegal in Wisconsin. The deputy, now under media scrutiny, informed the sheriff of the demand for entry, and the sheriff ordered the opening of the camp to the workers.[61] The workers and their families entered their homes and went about their daily lives with support from the union and its allies.

The potato harvest is a time-restricted operation, since potatoes have to be harvested in the late fall before the first winter frost. The union reasonably hoped that since it was negotiating in October, the weather might help in bringing the processors to the bargaining table. The Burns family came to the table with an offer to bargain and called for a new election to determine representation. Rather than deal with the processing workers alone, of whom there were fewer than one hundred, however, the Burns family wanted all two hundred employees to cast votes, including the harvesters, truck drivers, office staff, and supervisors. The union rejected this offer and planned for protracted negotiations.

Although the union was technically independent, the fact that the strike action could continue indefinitely required that it strengthen its financial position. OU sought additional support from the Wisconsin AFL-CIO, which was then holding its annual convention in Madison. To show solidarity and draw attention to the OU unionization drive, the state AFL-CIO invited Jesus Salas to speak to the convention. During the convention, Wisconsin's unions elected John Schmitt, head of the United Brewery Workers Union in Milwaukee, as their first president with roots in the CIO.[62] At his election ceremony, Schmitt called on Wisconsin workers and trade union organizations to support the needs of migrants and other minorities.[63] From the unions at the convention, Salas raised over $2,500 to support the efforts of OU.[64] Charles Heymanns and Henry Santiestevan, the national AFL-CIO organizer sent to assist OU, and others returned with Salas to attend a rally on October 12 in Wautoma.[65]

Even with national and state-level AFL-CIO support, the union fell apart. The weather remained mild, giving the processors time to wait out the strike. Burns hired strikebreakers from outside of Portage County and completed the potato harvest. Adding to the workers' woes, local businesses placed pressure on them by curtailing credit at grocery stores, and some called in notes on used cars purchased in town. Facing these difficult realities, the union agreed to accept the failure of the Burns strike even as the AFL-CIO continued the legal battle on behalf of the workers. Nearly a third of the workers returned to Texas, and the rest found work in Milwaukee.[66]

As the striking Burns workers settled into winter in Milwaukee or returned to South Texas, the state AFL-CIO pursued the case even as it appeared that the potato workers' union was a lost cause. Represented by AFL-CIO attorneys, OU sought to defend workers' rights before the WERB, a state-level equivalent to the National Labor Relations Board (NLRB). Unlike most state and national labor laws, Wisconsin's laws protected agricultural workers. Much as it might have done before the NLRB, the union argued before the WERB that Burns had engaged in unfair labor practices by forcing workers to sign union membership affidavits and that the resulting firings were wrongful discharges.[67] The AFL-CIO pursued the case for several reasons. It sought to establish under state law that Burns's actions were illegal in order to protect Wisconsin workers from these types of unfair labor practices. It also aimed to preserve the right of agricultural workers to form unions.[68] Handing the union and its workers a victory in December 1966, the WERB decided that the interrogation of workers as to union affiliation amounted to an unfair labor practice under state law.[69]

The struggle to unionize the workers at the Burns plant taught the new organizers useful lessons. Though deeply concerned with the plight of migrant workers in Wisconsin, the activists were forced to realize that inspiration and organization were not enough to create a sustainable labor movement. They learned that labor organizing and collective bargaining were two different things. The first required organizing skills and charisma, which the young activists had in abundance, but the second required expertise and experience, things they relied on others for. As William Forbath has pointed out, the administrative regimes of labor law both structure and limit the arena for the struggle between workers and employers, a fact that militates against new unions, which often lack the resources to survive the procedural pitfalls of formal legal process. The WERB and NLRB exercised the power of life and death over start-up unions like OU, and employers took advantage of the labor board to delay the resolution of many strikes, thereby claiming victory against the best-organized workers.[70]

Independent Unionism and the Organizing Drive of 1967

The activists entered the holiday season of 1966 set on establishing a labor union in cucumber harvesting the following summer. To avoid the pitfalls of the failed potato organizing drive, any future effort had to incorporate legal procedure as well as the seasonal nature of agricultural work. The union needed more organizing support from the AFL-CIO and a commitment from the WERB that it would hear its cases as rapidly as possible. César Chávez, now heading the United Farm Workers Organizing Committee (UFWOC), which combined predecessor farmworkers' unions, wrote to Charles Heymanns of the Wisconsin AFL-CIO that he supported efforts to "work together in extending the rights of collective bargaining to farm workers in the agricultural areas of Wisconsin" after meeting with labor leaders and Jesus Salas when visiting Milwaukee to raise funds for his union.[71] As they entered the New Year, OU and the AFL-CIO decided to target the multinational agricultural canning and processing giant Libby, McNeill, Libby, which controlled the bulk of cucumber processing in Wisconsin.

In an effort to strengthen its position, the union incorporated the migrant recruiting system as a tool for organizing workers across the Tejano diaspora. Texas sent more workers into the migrant stream than any other state, and organizing at both ends of the stream made sense. Much as workers were contracted by Libby in Texas before the season started, the leaders of OU decided that they could build the union in Texas by using the company's crew leaders to identify workers who might be susceptible to unionization before they arrived in Wisconsin. With inside knowledge of the cucumber recruiting system, OU knew which cities to visit to sign up Libby workers.[72] "As we began to talk about a union in a real sense," Bill Smith remembered, "we came to the conclusion that unlike California, where workers work in the fields year round, in the Midwest our assumption was that if we were going to be successful we had to organize at least a core group of people at the home base" to avoid "scrambling to do things" in the summer months.[73] Interstate preseason organizing across the Tejano diaspora enabled the union to avoid the misuse of key Wisconsin harvest time and strengthen the union's position vis-à-vis the employer. This strategy allowed the union to focus its Wisconsin energies on maintaining solidarity and to counter the AFL-CIO's fears that the "rather seasonal periods" migrant laborers spent in the state posed a real problem to organizing.[74]

In the early months of 1967, Jesus Salas traveled to his hometown of Crystal City with Mark Erenburg, his brother Manuel Salas, Salvador Sanchez, and Bill Smith to seek out workers across South Texas coming to Wisconsin to work for Libby. According to Erenburg, "We knew it would be Libby from the get go" because there were "too many connections for it not to be."[75] Both the Salas brothers' father and Salvador Sanchez worked as Libby recruiters, and it was Salvador Sanchez's and Manuel Salas Sr.'s crews who had made up the core of participants in the 1966 march on Madison and the Burns strike. Jesus Salas deemed organizing workers in Texas "very important," since the workers were in Wisconsin for "such a short period."[76] By traveling to Texas, ou sought to establish an "inside" committee to place "[a] number of credible and supporting Libby workers in place before the season" began.[77] In Crystal City and other Texas cities where Libby contracted workers, ou held organizing meetings with crew leaders and other influential workers. Among the organizers, according to Erenburg, "the notion was that this movement could succeed because [the union now had] resources not available [at the Burns strike]."[78]

Transregional networks played a role in providing the workers with an added layer of trust when it came to the Salas family. Manuel Salas Sr. had successfully settled his family in Wisconsin's cucumber harvesting region after many years of circular migration as a recruiter and patriarch of a large migrant family rooted in both Texas and Wisconsin. The fact that the Salas family had lived at both ends of the migrant stream provided another resource. The Salas Café in Wautoma, Wisconsin, "was a Mecca for communication and the like" and was familiar to the migrants who spent time at the original Salas Café in Crystal City. The social position of the family and the fact that Salas led the union "gave the movement, [and] gave Jesus, a good deal of credibility."[79]

In Texas, Jesus Salas and the organizers relied on local workers as they hitchhiked from Crystal City to other nearby towns, moving in reverse along the migrant stream to organize from the Texas Winter Garden to the Rio Grande Valley. Once the organizers were in the barrios and colonias of South Texas, workers provided them with lodging and meals and entrance into their communities.[80] The trip to South Texas was a wake-up call for Mark Erenburg in particular, who was shocked and saddened by the poor housing stock, lack of indoor plumbing, and other problems faced by the Tejanos in Crystal City's barrios. Impressed by the seemingly limitless generosity of the migrants who fed and provided shelter to the organizers, Erenburg, a suburbanite from Chicago's

North Shore then in graduate school, felt the respect that he already had for migrant workers deepen.[81]

In the spring of 1967, OU established its union headquarters in downtown Wautoma, Wisconsin, hanging two large red UFWOC thunderbird flags in the front windows. While the union remained officially independent from its California counterpart, it received financing from the state and national AFL-CIO.[82] In another preparatory move, Jesus Salas approached his college friend David Giffey and asked the veteran and former *Stars and Stripes* writer and photographer to give up his job at a local newspaper and convert *La Voz Mexicana* into a union publication.[83] By early spring, OU felt confident that it had won the support of enough workers in Texas to organize cucumber harvest operations in Wisconsin. The union had an office, AFL-CIO support, a newspaper, and a core group of organizers and members ready to take on one of the nation's largest fruit and vegetable producers.

At this time, OU maintained a position in the middle ground between the Teamsters and the UFWOC, which both sought to incorporate it. Since Wisconsin was the third front in the farm labor movement centered on California and Texas to a lesser degree, there was much discussion among UFWOC and AFL-CIO officials about abandoning the Wisconsin effort as a practical matter. As long as it remained independent and did not seek to organize workers in areas of fruit and vegetable canning already controlled by either the Teamsters or AFL-CIO unions like the Amalgamated Meat Cutters and Butcher Workmen (AMC), the OU was able to preserve itself and its AFL-CIO support as a union focused on harvesting operations. Because the AFL-CIO unions and the Teamsters were in a battle for control of agricultural canning and harvesting nationwide, the OU protected itself by continuing its discussions with the Teamsters during a period in which the UFWOC and the Teamsters were in direct competition for harvest workers in California. Chávez increasingly pressed the AFL-CIO for direct control over the Wisconsin effort, while Salas sought to maintain local control by keeping his union independent. In April, Chávez visited the Spanish Center in Milwaukee and met with Salas. Despite the tensions at the organizational level, Salas viewed Chávez as a mentor. Throughout his career as an activist, he looked to Chávez for inspiration and guidance, often sending Chávez handwritten letters about his concerns, fears, and hopes for the young Wisconsin union.[84]

Jesus Salas (partially visible at left) and César Chávez, UFWOC (right), during Chávez's first visit to Wisconsin for four hours. (Unidentified photographer at center). Chávez met with Salas and other labor leaders and activists at El Centro Hispano-Americano on National Avenue, Milwaukee, Wisconsin, April 25, 1967. Photo courtesy of David Giffey.

The Wisconsin AFL-CIO provided the bulk of OU's funding. Wisconsin AFL-CIO president John Schmitt of the CIO brewery union based in Milwaukee worked closely with OU and helped its leaders gain an understanding of the organizational structure of the state's labor hierarchy. With this help, OU efficiently directed its solidarity and fund-raising campaigns to utilize Wisconsin's labor councils, affiliated unions, and local prolabor organizations and publications. This support and sponsorship gave the young activists entry into union halls with the blessing of the state president—invitations that might not have been forthcoming otherwise—and helped keep the newly established union afloat.[85]

As the migrants returned to the cucumber fields after working other crops in the Dakotas, Minnesota, and elsewhere, many of them sought out the union office—a sign of the success of the winter organization drive. David Giffey remembered the spring of 1967: "It was wonderful then when the season began . . . because people would come up to Wautoma, and then the union office started to . . . flourish as a place of activity, as more of a [community] center. Because the workers knew about it and they would look us up, even just to socialize, but it got to become a place that was available to workers."[86] By June, the union began preparing for battle with Libby. The state AFL-CIO assisted with staff needs and fund-raising, and it paid the rent in Wautoma.[87] AFL-CIO organizing officials had their legal staff confirm with the national union leadership that Wisconsin labor law protected the collective bargaining rights of agricultural workers.[88] Staff at the University of Wisconsin School for Workers in Madison helped Salas "set up the bylaws in the organization, the real standard things you do in forming a labor union."[89]

To encourage solidarity among workers, the organizers planned a variety of events, including baseball games, camp workshops, and dances for the workers. The union did its best to create a community atmosphere and make organizing enjoyable for workers and union representatives alike. As Erenburg and Sanchez had done when working on the OEO demonstration program in 1965, they established a union baseball team to play against the men from the various Libby camps.[90] According to Salvador Sanchez, "We would play for a half-barrel" of beer, and "while we were playing . . . we were talking to the people" about joining the union.[91] The games offered a ready and safe venue for the solicitation of membership as players relaxed and socialized during and afterward at beer parties.[92]

There were seventy-five worker camps in Waushara, Marquette, and Portage counties, making individual camp meetings impractical. To protect the workers from possible employer harassment at more remote camps and streamline the organizing process, the union held meetings at friendly camps and invited workers to attend. These brainstorming sessions compelled the union to take on a broader advocacy role on behalf of agricultural workers and their families, as workers often brought complaints about housing and sanitary issues to the attention of the union at these meetings and expected the organizers to follow up. Salas brought worker concerns to state officials and spoke before the state assembly during the 1967 union drive to press for reform of the state housing code and the expansion of the minimum wage law.[93] By working as both a labor organizer and an advocate for state reform, Salas reaffirmed his position within his community and won the respect and trust of workers.

The union also used the newspaper as an investigative and informational tool in the drive. In 1967, *La Voz Mexicana* published special sections that provided workers with basic information on the rights of workers under Wisconsin law and printed investigative stories pertaining to migrant health, housing, and sanitary issues.[94] The newspaper ran a housing exposé that revealed that the Wautoma city dump sold discarded mattresses to local migrant camp operators, who used them to furnish farmworkers' homes.[95] Similar housing issues played a significant role in bringing workers, and especially their families, into the movement. Salas remarked, "Most of the housing was overcrowded . . . [so] all I had to do was . . . refer to [the] physical condition of the housing [and say,] 'Look at what you're living [in],' [and ask,] 'How many people are sleeping in one bed?'" before workers who had not made up their minds started to seriously consider joining the union.[96] Through its newspaper, the union also brought news from across the Tejano diaspora to the workers in Wisconsin, detailing events in the drive to organize farmworkers in South Texas and California, as well as describing the growth of Mexican Americanist politics across the nation.[97]

The union was calling for not only workplace citizenship but also social citizenship for the mainly Tejano workers it sought to represent. This commitment to social citizenship led OU to establish a variety of service programs. It created a Lawyers Defense Committee to provide free legal assistance in Wautoma for migrants. Future Milwaukee district attorney E. Michael McCann and state assemblyman Frederick P. Kessler founded the committee and recruited attorneys from Milwaukee to donate their services.[98] According to Kessler, "We formed the Lawyers Committee because [after] speaking with Jesus we knew that people weren't getting adequate legal representation."[99] The legal committee put powerful Wisconsinites behind the workers, giving them "an opportunity to know that they have support if they stick their necks out."[100] This group of "idealistic young lawyers" spent weekends helping migrants with a variety of legal and other problems. According to David Loeffler, attorney for the union, the Lawyers Committee was "staffed by a group of college students and recent college graduates, who could be accurately described as more or less New Left or 'Movement' people in their general political or social stance."[101] In Milwaukee, the committee raised enough money to cover the costs of most lawsuits brought by migrants and successfully blocked the deportation of twenty undocumented Mexican workers jailed by the Immigration and Naturalization Service on the grounds that it failed to give the Mexican nationals a hearing and the opportunity to be represented by counsel.[102] The union's offices were a "clearinghouse" for basic legal information, whether it was for "small claims" cases or referrals in the case of serious legal issues. Expressing the commitment of the committee to the workers in 1967, McCann remarked that for the migrants, the "sense of protection cannot come from local government or the legislative process" but rather had to come "from the courts."[103]

The Old Left, embodied by its new CIO-based union president, John Schmitt, made its presence felt in rural Wisconsin as the state's leading labor leaders highlighted the farmworkers' organizing drive. To support and strengthen OU, the state AFL-CIO held its 1967 Executive Council meeting in Wautoma, a move that brought statewide attention to the union just weeks before the workers' election was to take place and demonstrated organized labor's firm support for the farmworkers. OU used this meeting to the union's benefit, including a prominent story on the topic in the union newspaper, along with stories highlighting worker concerns at Libby.[104] The WIC responded to the increased emphasis on migrant issues by hiring Spanish-speaking outreach personnel. By showing solidarity with the AFL-CIO, OU, still an independent union, hoped to show growers and workers alike that it had the ability to organize and the outside resources to defend the rights of cucumber workers.[105]

Just as they had piggybacked on a system of labor recruitment and migration, the union likewise used the daily institutions of the cucumber harvest to organize workers and maintain solidarity. As the season began, the union paid attention to the daily harvest schedule in arranging to meet workers and discuss issues with them at times that were appropriate. Knowing when workers took breaks and when they could relax and talk allowed the fledgling union to respect the wage-earning needs of workers as it also sought members. After the daily harvest of cucumbers, the vegetables were brought to a number of grading stations, where the cucumbers were separated according to size (with the smallest being the most valuable) and weighed. As the cucumbers were divided, household heads, mainly fathers and single men, waited around and talked. Salas and the other organizers joined workers at the four grading stations operated by Libby because "one member from each family showed up" to be paid for the cucumbers picked each day. Since most of the Tejanos who ran the grading stations knew Salas and his family quite well, these workers kept him informed; in this way, Salas was able to contact and speak to most household heads as they put the final touches on the organizing campaign.[106]

The interstate organizing, together with the Wisconsin-based organizing and solidarity work, paid off, at least initially. On August 18, OU successfully organized the majority of the Libby harvest workforce and called for recognition. The company refused to accept the union as the employees' representative while also claiming that the harvest workers were not Libby employees: rather, they worked directly for the crew leaders or the growers. Rejecting Libby's interpretation of the employer-employee relationship, on August 23 over 80 percent of the Libby field harvesting force walked out of the fields to display the union's strength. The next day, the union demanded recognition again and called on the Wisconsin Employment Relations Council (which replaced the WERB in 1967) to request an emergency representation election among all Libby harvest employees, arguing that the perishable nature of the crop meant that the hearing could not, in fairness, be made subject to the WERC's normal scheduling procedures.[107] At the hearing, the union presented evidence that showed that on February 21 Libby had placed a clearance order for agricultural workers and harvest hands with Wisconsin

State Employment Services. This order designated Libby as the "employer" and requested "700 workers, 16 years and older (family groups preferred) to weed, thin and harvest cucumbers." This request, alongside the admission that Libby sent management and recruiters to Texas each year to hire workers and paid the workers with Libby checks, was enough to convince the WERC that Libby, not the crew leaders or growers, employed the harvest workers. The WERC further ruled that due to the perishable nature of the crop, an election should be held quickly.[108] The election, which took place on August 31, demonstrated the overwhelming support of Libby workers for OU. Harvest workers voted 405 to 8 in favor of the union as their bargaining representative.[109] The WERC certified OU as the exclusive representative for migrant harvest workers employed by Libby.[110] Confident after these victories before the WERC, the union reached out to Libby to begin bargaining for the next season's harvest.

Libby, like Burns before it, refused to bargain in good faith, but rather used the legal system to avoid unionization altogether. On September 26, Libby informed the union that it was examining the profitability of the Wisconsin cucumber operation.[111] On November 16, it delivered a letter to OU stating, "A decision has now been made to continue our cucumber program, but . . . all harvesting aspects will be handled mechanically starting with the 1968 season."[112] The letter further explained that because of this change in business operations, Libby needed "no migrant agricultural workers in cucumbers" for the coming season, and "continued labor negotiations would appear to be superfluous."[113] Much as Burns had done, the company ignored the union for the most part, and through its own policies fought it while its attorneys used the WERC and the courts to defend these actions and delay and postpone any resolution. This process of antiunion action and legal engagement made hollow these workers' rights to unionization and collective bargaining. Much as they had done the preceding year, the workers returned to Texas or sought work in Milwaukee, having failed to enter into collective bargaining with the employer.

The legal team appointed by the AFL-CIO fought through the winter to preserve the rights of OU's workers and to maintain the position of organized labor in the state of Wisconsin. OU attorney David Loeffler spent the winter of 1967 filing claims of unfair labor practices before the WERC. In July, the commission held that Libby had failed to bargain over the decision to mechanize and had committed an unfair labor practice in doing so, handing another precedential victory to the union and the AFL-CIO and providing nearly nothing to the workers. This was not a victory for the union, since the WERC also held that because Libby had made a "business decision" to mechanize harvesting operations and move processing to another region in the state, the commission lacked the power to restore workers to jobs that no longer existed. In an effort to find a middle ground, the WERC ordered the creation of a preferential hiring list for the operation of mechanical harvesters that was to contain the names of union workers displaced by mechanization who were qualified to do the job.[114] Just two years after its birth in Wautoma, the union had twice succeeded in organizing migrant laborers, yet farmworkers in Wisconsin continued to lack union representation at the beginning of 1968.

An Awkward Middle Ground: The Rise and Fall of Social Unionism in Wisconsin

With the season before it and no organizing goal in sight, OU shifted focus from organizing to providing social unionism services to workers and supporting a UFWOC national grape boycott. OU sought to maintain its independent status, to continue to play a role in the lives of Central Wisconsin's farmworkers, and to demonstrate solidarity with the fledgling California union. This shift in focus resulted from the ongoing legal battle with Libby, still pending as the 1968 season began. The union had to monitor harvest developments in the coming season to see whether Libby had in fact made the "business decision" it claimed before the WERC. Adding to the confusion, the UFWOC increasingly insisted that OU send all funds to California and abandon the social unionism project. The UFWOC won from the AFL-CIO concessions that gave it control over the farmworkers' budget in Wisconsin and thus over OU. Although OU was still an independent union, the AFL-CIO placed it under the tutelage of UFWOC and the boycott office in Chicago. At the behest of the national AFL-CIO, in recognition of his skills as an organizer, Jesus Salas was asked to join the UFWOC as a special assignment organizer working between Texas and Wisconsin and as a grape boycott organizer in Milwaukee reporting directly to César Chávez.

The UFWOC leadership focused on the coordination of the national grape boycott in an effort to preserve itself in the difficult period after its initial success in 1966. The Delano operation continued to pressure the Wisconsin activists to stop organizing workers and focus on support for the California grape boycott. The grape boycott became the single focus of the UFWOC as it apparently abandoned the goal of unionizing farmworkers across the United States. The grape boycott had the power to make or break the UFWOC as a viable union. This period was one of organizing success and triumph for the UFWOC in California, which found support for its grape boycott in many of the labor-friendly states, cities of the Northeast and Midwest, and on college campuses across the nation. The union also won the support of consumers nationwide who chose not to purchase grapes or grape products from California. This effort pressured many of the largest grape producers to sign labor contracts in 1970 and made the UFWOC the first union to win a bargaining agreement for agricultural harvest workers in California. Between 1967 and the demise of OU, the desire on the part of UFWOC to focus all of its efforts on survival and the grape boycott rather than attempt national organizing became the primary point of tension between the UFWOC, always focused on California, and affiliated organizations in Texas, Wisconsin, and to a lesser degree Arizona and Florida.[115]

Even with the union and Salas now reporting to the UFWOC, the California leadership continued to pressure the AFL-CIO to exercise greater control over the Wisconsin union and its organizers. Chávez, in letters to the AFL-CIO, pressed national organizing officials to make it clear to Salas that he was now directly under the control of the UFWOC.[116] In Wisconsin, many supporters of the California grape boycott also wanted to continue to support the effort to unionize local migrant workers, and this caused tension between the UFWOC and local activists over fund-raising and other commitments. In fact, in the fall of 1968, several Wisconsin organizers became concerned that relations between Wisconsin and California were on the decline, and they considered possible affiliations with the Teamsters or the AMC union. Chávez and his colleagues saw this as a "period of terrible confusion," with Jesus Salas working between Texas, Milwaukee, and California and OU considering "good offers" from the Teamsters that the UFWOC was apparently unaware of. In Wisconsin, the Teamsters pledged to give OU enough money to support "social unionism" and ongoing organizing

Jesus Salas (front right), Francisco Rodriguez (behind Salas), and
Ernesto Chacon (center, with sunglasses) prepare a fruit-boycott
picket line in the Wautoma office of Obreros Unidos, August 1968.
Photo courtesy of David Giffey.

among farmworkers if the organizers would abandon the UFWOC's grape boycott.[117] Considering a broader community role, moreover, OU began discussions with the many small farmers who contracted with the large processors in an effort to build solidarity against the processors between the often struggling and low-income farmers and the migrants who harvested their crops.[118]

Now employed by UFWOC, Jesus Salas spent 1968 traveling between Texas and Wisconsin, an interstate work schedule that enabled his greater involvement in the political activities in his hometown. On one of his first visits to Texas after joining UFWOC, he reported to Chávez that there were "two Mexican factions," a "gringo incumbent" who left "the barrio vote . . . split" and the incumbent in office. It also appeared that the relationship with the Teamsters Union in Crystal City's cannery was weakening. Salas met with some of the workers who wanted to remove the Teamsters at the same time that OU, now under the direction of his brother Manuel, was considering an affiliation with the Teamsters. Perhaps knowing the tensions UFWOC had with the Teamsters in California, he reported to Chávez that he had listened to the workers but had not advised them. Within two years, these workers would establish an independent union and borrow the name "Obreros Unidos" for it.[119] Throughout the summer and fall of 1968, Salas migrated between Wisconsin and Texas in an effort to keep all of his competing commitments active while doing his best not to alienate himself from César Chávez and the AFL-CIO.

This pattern of circular migration continued for much of the year. Salas spent time in April informing workers in Crystal City and through the Rio Grande Valley of the status of the OU court case while also checking in with UFWOC staff in Starr County, Texas.[120] In Wisconsin, he routinely traveled between Milwaukee, Wautoma, and Madison and continued to work with OU to organize workers. In particular, Salas fought to protect workers' rights to free association and sought to block efforts by politicians from Central Wisconsin to amend the state trespass law in order to forbid organizers from visiting migrant workers in rented homes on land owned by growers and processors. When AFL-CIO and UFWOC staff members criticized his interstate travels, Salas argued that to keep OU's workers organized he had to visit and keep an eye on developments in Crystal City and to support the boycott in Wisconsin by making the case for Chávez in South Texas. Salas and the young activists he worked with considered "La Causa" to involve more than the mere establishment of a grape workers' union in California— something Chávez never fully understood. In a series of heartfelt letters to Chávez, Salas explained the importance of his travels and expressed his hope for the future of the farmworkers based in Wisconsin, Texas, and California as part of the broader struggle for civil rights for Mexican Americans.[121]

Evolving in 1968 even as the UFWOC sought to weaken it, OU embraced and expanded many of the social union principles pioneered by the California union as the grape boycott increasingly overshadowed its organizing efforts. New services included arranging for a social worker sponsored by the National Association of Social Workers to field questions related to government benefits and opening a health clinic headed by a Wautoma physician. The Wisconsin Council of Churches, Migrant Ministry division, long a supporter of the union, established a center for migrants, and, as in years past, the Lawyers Committee expanded its commitment by adding more lawyers to help "workers obtain their rights under the minimum wage" and defeated new piece rate regulations in Wisconsin.[122] In July, OU established a cooperative gas station and repair shop managed by Jesus Salas's "old friend and political organizer" Francisco Rodriguez. Rodriguez, a fellow Cristaleño then living in Madison, worked for United Migrant Opportunity Services, Inc. (UMOS), an OEO-funded program. Rodolfo Palomo, also of Crystal City, joined the union as a field organizer. The cooperative provided union members gasoline at 10 percent off and parts at cost for a membership fee of $2.50, with the "major contribution" being "contact with workers."[123]

OU also pressed other unions to support solidarity walkouts in unionized Libby canneries to show support for the displaced field harvesters. Despite its many efforts to continue on, however, OU appeared in 1968 to be a union without workers, reduced to picketing mechanical harvest operations to compel Teamsters Union operators to honor the OU strike. The threat of unionization had apparently convinced the processing companies to raise the rate paid to pickers by 35 percent over the previous year. Libby ensured that it hired no migrant workers directly, and a thousand fewer than the average of about forty-five hundred workers entered the pickle fields as harvest hands. This smaller group of workers, joined by a small army of Teamsters-driven machine harvesters, brought in one of the largest crops in recent history. These conditions made organizing the remaining fieldworkers difficult at the same time that the AFL-CIO shifted funding to the California union to placate Chávez. In an interview with a *Chicago Tribune* reporter, Manuel Salas expressed his frustration, saying, "Maybe we should be organizing the bees"—a reference to the bees kept by farmers to pollinate the cucumbers.[124] Throughout the summer, young activists from Crystal City and college student volunteers flowed between Madison, Wautoma, and Milwaukee as they supported both the grape boycott and the continued operation of OU as a service organization and labor union.[125]

Despite OU's divided attention, the Wisconsin-based grape boycott led by OU activists drew significant support to the California farmworkers. In Milwaukee, the boycott brought African American civil rights leaders, Tejano migrants, Catholic priests and parishes, and members of the long-established Mexican American urban community together in support of the UFWOC and increased cross-community cooperation. In Madison, due to the combined efforts of students and others, the university and several large wholesalers agreed to honor the UFWOC boycott, as did several of the state's largest grocery chains. At the University of Wisconsin–Milwaukee, student activists led by Avelardo Valdez pressed for the same policy and led pickets at area grocery stores. In smaller towns, local people tended to associate the grape boycott with OU and to express hostility toward both, yet the pickets continued across the state in support of the California-based union. Under Salas's leadership, Wisconsin gained widespread political support for the UFWOC effort and reached one of the highest levels of participation in the national boycott.[126] OU achieved this success at a cost: by the end of 1968, the union had sacrificed most of its organizers to support the California union's boycott.

In 1969, Manuel Salas, now heading OU with several of the original organizers, set the union on its final and most militant course of action. While continuing to support the California grape boycott, OU launched an effort—against the wishes of both the AFL-CIO and the Teamsters— to organize cannery and processing workers in Wisconsin.[127] With OU now supposedly under the control of UFWOC, fund-raising became a major issue, since the Wisconsin union was already struggling to raise sufficient funds to keep its social service operations alive. César Chávez pledged support to Manuel Salas at both his Wisconsin and Texas addresses, promising him "what you need to keep you going," yet he also continued to complain that the Wisconsin activists were not sending money to California.[128] Indeed, as OU fought to stay alive, the UFWOC and the AFL-CIO began to demand that the Wisconsin union send all funds from Wisconsin to California, abandon the Obreros Unidos name, and change its letterhead to UFWOC. Jesus Salas defended the local union's policy of keeping the funds it raised to Chávez: "The little we get has gone to pay our expenses (rent & phone in Wautoma . . . [and] the co-op)."[129] It also appears that the UFWOC was not paying Salas or the other organizers on time, if at all. As a result, OU had started letting payments for utilities and automobiles go past due. In a direct letter to Chávez, Salas complained that he had had very little feedback on the status of the Wisconsin union from Eliseo Medina (the UFWOC representative based in Chicago), and he worried that "the boycott has pre-empted any . . . close look at our situation here."[130]

After a winter visit to Delano, California, Chávez informed Salas that the UFWOC planned to abandon the Wisconsin effort and called on Salas to curtail his OU-related trips to Texas. Describing the Wisconsin effort as "loose ends," he reminded Salas that OU was the only "affiliated group . . . for whom we have made some exceptions and we are trying to bring that into line." First, Chávez demanded that Salas clear all of his organizational activities with California and stated that there was "no clear cut assignment in the minds of many of us as to what you are doing in Wisconsin." Significantly weakening the union, Chávez wrote, "You will be assigned to the boycott in Milwaukee under the supervision of Eliseo Medina." Even though most monies raised by OU in Wisconsin were in support of the local union established by local leaders, Chávez again demanded that OU send all funds raised to Delano before ending his letter with "Viva La Causa!"[131]

By moving into the canneries in 1969 and 1970 against the wishes of the AFL-CIO's AMC, the Teamsters, and César Chávez, OU energized migrant workers in a sector where they had become the dominant seasonal workforce and where unionization was already the norm for migrant workers. In most canneries, there existed a clear divide between the small group of year-round employees, who tended to manage the affairs of the union, and the much larger group of seasonal workers, who were not adequately represented by collective bargaining agreements negotiated in their absence. Since OU maintained its status as an independent union, it was able to proceed despite its affiliation with the UFWOC and for a time at least sought to bargain with both the AMC and the Teamsters on behalf of the workers.[132] It is unclear if OU did this in an effort to maintain its relationship with the UFWOC or to preserve its local independence in the face of pressure from California by courting the Teamsters, who were clearly a competitive thorn in the side of the California union.[133]

Even as OU challenged the authority of the AFL-CIO, the Teamsters, and the control of the UFWOC over its affairs, the union worked diligently on the grape boycott in support of California's farmworkers. Chávez visited the boycott offices and met with AFL-CIO leaders in Milwaukee in November 1969, escorted by OU veteran organizers. The union played a significant role in staffing the boycott effort across the state while participating in most major Milwaukee events.[134] For OU activists, this effort was part of a broad-based attempt to create labor unions for agricultural workers in Wisconsin, California, and Texas and to enact a reform agenda for Mexican Americans nationwide. As the union entered its last year of existence, many veteran organizers hoped to organize the mainly Tejano migrant workers in Wisconsin while also assisting the struggling California union.

By 1970, Manuel Salas and Bill Smith were the sole veteran organizers attempting to keep OU afloat with the assistance of an influx of young activists from Crystal City. As they came into conflict with the AMC over the organization of cannery workers in Wisconsin, the union called on César Chávez for support in negotiating a settlement. Concerned over what appeared to be a lack of support coming from Chávez and the UFWOC, Manuel Salas wrote Chávez asking why the California union would "keep us from perhaps the best union drive in Wisconsin in the last decade?" Salas informed Chávez that Texas-based migrant workers were poorly represented by the contracts negotiated by the AMC year-round employees; OU had discussed the matter with the representative union but found it unwilling to "do what was necessary" to improve the seasonal workers' contracts. Salas made it clear that OU did not seek to join the Teamsters, who had indicated willingness to organize Wisconsin's canneries. But he wondered how OU could support the AMC, given the contract that union had negotiated "without migrant representation."[135]

In an effort to resolve the issue of affiliation and jurisdiction brought on by entry into cannery organizing, Bill Smith and Jesus Salas arranged for a meeting with Chávez in Chicago. Smith and Salas called for a meeting with the OU, Teamsters Local 695, and the AMC Local 248, according to an AFL-CIO representative, to "discuss the problems of organizing the migrants and who can do the best job in working with them." Salas and Smith, in a highly unconventional and perhaps naive move, proposed that representatives of the rival unions responsible for migrant cannery organizing meet and settle the issue of representation. The UFW had no role in cannery operations under AFL-CIO agreements. With jurisdiction over Wisconsin's cannery operations, the AMC union demanded that if the OU cannery did not come under its control, the AFL-CIO should suspend support for the grape boycott led by OU for fear AFL-CIO donations might be "used against them in the organizing efforts of the independent."[136] This request made sense since the AFL-CIO funded the OU and it was now organizing against an AFL-CIO union in Wisconsin's canneries. After the meeting in Chicago, Chávez, apparently following AFL-CIO policy, severed all ties with OU and requested that Larry Itliong, national boycott coordinator of the UFWOC, "hire Will Smith . . . but *move* him."[137] Soon after this, Jesus Salas, now working for an OEO-funded organization, wrote to lament that Chávez had abandoned the "concerted effort" he had promised the Wisconsin activists when OU became an affiliate.[138] By failing to intervene with the AFL-CIO to improve the two-tier contracts negotiated by the small, year-round AMC union membership, Chávez finally killed off the Wisconsin migrant labor union. This move sacrificed the Tejano migrant workers employed in Wisconsin canneries to the archrival Teamsters, who strengthened their position in Wisconsin's canneries following OU's collapse. Sadly, this jurisdictional competition had a solution in prior agreements made by the AMC in New Jersey, where it had used its position in canneries, where the National Labor Relations Act (NLRA) applied, to bargain on behalf of the three classes of workers: year-round, migrant, and harvest workers.

Why none of the parties in Wisconsin or at AFL-CIO headquarters thought to find a solution through mediation is a surprise considering prior AMC success in bargaining for unified field and cannery agreements. In a sad postscript, OU no longer existed when the Wisconsin Supreme Court decided the Libby case in its favor, holding that the law made it mandatory for Libby to bargain with OU regarding the effects of the decision to mechanize. The AFL-CIO's attorneys preserved a right for workers even as the union on whose behalf they argued had been broken on the rock of interunion squabbling and jurisdictional disputes.[139]

Conclusion

The failure of OU as a labor union is evident. This view, however, obscures the fact that the movement that produced and sustained OU was not simply an effort to establish a trade union but also a part of the broader civil rights movement among Mexican Americans. From the start, Jesus Salas and the New Left organizers who spent two to five years working on building the union saw it as part of a broader push for social justice that took root and expanded in the late 1960s.[140] Viewing grassroots, working-class, or low-income activist efforts as failures because they did not radically alter the status quo is counterproductive and obfuscates the myriad successes of these social movements. Viewed in this light, OU succeeded by helping to raise the consciousness of migrant farmworkers, training an increasing number of activists who continued to work in other movements, and sending ordinary people into new areas of the economy and society with greater awareness of their civil rights and more than willing to fashion a place for themselves as citizens.

The unionization effort shocked many growers and those in the Wisconsin agricultural industry and altered the debate on workers' rights for years to come. Future Supreme Court justice Jon Wilcox remarked after being brought before the WERC on charges of unfair labor practices for firing a worker wearing a "Viva la Causa" button that this use of state power was proof that the union "was out to get" him.[141] Others in Wisconsin's government learned different lessons from these workers and activists and later sought their input and support. Wisconsin attorney general Bronson La Follette, Wisconsin Progressive Robert La Follette's son, for example, visited Jon Wilcox's family labor camp and opined that the migrant workers there were "as badly in the need of help as are the ghetto poor" and had to be recognized. The efforts of OU in Wisconsin taught many white politicians and reformers that race and poverty in America existed beyond the black/white binary.[142]

The efforts of OU and of migrant workers in general also led Wisconsin's African American leaders to notice the similarities between the Mexican Americans' struggle and their own civil rights activities. By the late 1960s, African Americans and Mexican Americans, although often at odds, were working together on many issues.[143] By bringing together supporters from the ranks of Progressives, the New Left, the Old Left, African Americans, and migrants, OU had changed the nature of state and local discourse about working-class life and the rights of farmworkers of Wisconsin. The consciousness-raising that resulted from the OU endeavor and the transfer of talent between Texas and Wisconsin, and between the union and other Mexican American and Latino organizations in Milwaukee, stand as the lasting victories of the movement. Far more than a short-lived and failed trade union movement, then, OU fed into and trained activists for the broader Mexican American civil rights movement. The OU movement also revealed the tensions within and between a "national" farmworker movement based in Delano, California, and the movements of farmworkers in Texas, Wisconsin, and Ohio, where the Farm Labor Organizing Committee (FLOC) was inspired by the Wisconsin effort, and perhaps aware of the pitfalls of working with the UFWOC, maintained strict independence from the California union.[144]

4

Making a Migrant Village in the City

TEJANOS AND THE WAR ON POVERTY IN MILWAUKEE

On November 25, 1968, a large group of "concerned south-side citizens" packed the Milwaukee offices of United Migrant Opportunity Services, Inc. (UMOS), a social service agency established under the auspices of the Office of Economic Opportunity (OEO), to protest the mismanagement of this poverty program. The demonstrators sought a meeting with UMOS management to call on the agency, created under the War on Poverty, to better serve the needs of migrants by hiring more former migrant farmworkers and promoting those already working for the organization to management positions. Many of the protesters filling the room at UMOS headquarters that night were former farmworkers from South Texas, the primary sending region for Wisconsin's migrant farmworker population. Others included leaders of Wisconsin's Obreros Unidos (OU) farmworkers' union and participants in the then-developing pan-Latino activism of Milwaukee's urban barrios. The call for community control at UMOS in Milwaukee mirrored efforts in dozens of locations across the country where the War on Poverty faced low-income communities mobilized for change.[1]

This autumn meeting was no sudden uprising: it resulted from several meetings that brought Tejano and Latino employees, farmworkers, and community activists together to demand that the all-white UMOS management consider "problems relevant to the UMOS program." At the meeting, Dolores Aguirre, a young former migrant and graduate of the UMOS adult basic education program, held the floor. Speaking to the crowd as a UMOS board member and a farmworker, she outlined the ways "those upstairs" were failing to manage the Community Action Program (CAP) in a way that facilitated the efforts of the employees who worked directly "with the people." Although not publicly request-ing the ouster of the white administrators based on race, these charges implied that it was time for farmworkers and Tejanos to control the largest migrant-serving agency in the state.[2]

A clearly identifiable group of the protesters had roots in Crystal City, Texas, and the cities of the Winter Garden District of South Texas more broadly. Crystal City migrants participated in the founding of UMOS and made up an internal community within the agency. More-over, within the agency and the community, a pan-Tejano movement played a unifying role among former migrants now settled in Wiscon-sin. Among the leaders of this protest were Jesus Salas of Crystal City, then working for UFWOC, and Ernesto Chacon of Pearsall, Texas, one of the founders of the Latin American Union for Civil Rights (LAUCR), a pan-Latino organization also heavily representing former residents of South Texas and Crystal City.[3] Linkages between both Wisconsin's farmworker movement and Crystal City's activism expanded and were refined within UMOS, an organization that represented an urban out-post fourteen hundred miles to the north of Texas. This transregional community evolved outside of Texas as the localism of home-city identi-fication broke down in the urban milieu and gave way to a broader spirit of cooperation among Tejanos now living in Milwaukee.

The protest and its call for community control shocked and dis-mayed the all-white management staff of UMOS. William Kruse, execu-tive director of the agency, responded that he "was confused" by the requests, noting that there had been "no great outcry" for change before this meeting. Kruse's comments indicated the rejection of community control and a lack of attention to the changing nature of migrant poli-tics and to the variety of minority-group civil rights movements then spreading across Milwaukee, Wisconsin, and the nation. By 1968, Mil-waukee's farmworker community, inspired by the growth of local farm labor unionism, the California grape boycott's Wisconsin effort, and an increasing degree of pan-Latino cooperation, had mobilized an urban social movement in Milwaukee that sought control of UMOS.

This event revealed two competing frameworks for understanding the War on Poverty, which I explore in this chapter. First, the poor—in this case Tejano migrants and Crystal City–based activists—had their own understandings of their place as workers and American citizens (though they did not always express them clearly) and of their place within the institutions of the local War on Poverty. Tejanos, in rejecting nonmigrant management of an organization they claimed for migrants, were defining themselves in terms of the War on Poverty, taking actions that led to large-scale protests and perhaps nearly as often to negotiation and cooperation. Second, well-meaning progressive reformers in Wisconsin brought an opposing set of definitions to the table when they established an organization meant to assist a group they considered visitors and potential settlers. Although migrants were encouraged to join the community, many whites considered them outside the "local" community when it came to management. These opposing viewpoints had important consequences for both parties, as both sought to define the local community in ways that shaped this War on Poverty agency to their own advantage. Within the resident white community, several people, including academics and clergy members working for UMOS or serving on the board, assisted the Tejanos in their effort to win control of the institution, and a majority of board members ultimately embraced the ethic of migrant community participation and control.

The War on Poverty and Tejano Migrants in the City

Few historians of the social movements of the 1960s consider the Community Action Program and the Office of Economic Opportunity as more than well-intentioned failures, and not one considers the efforts of the migrant labor provisions of the law. William Chafe, among others, demonstrates how, despite the inspired efforts of the CAP, the program helped bring about the end of the New Deal consensus rather than an end to poverty.[4] Attentive to the failure of particular undertakings, other scholars have detailed controversial cases of contention in some of the nation's most polarized cities without exploring CAP successes nationwide. Several recent examinations have painted a different portrait of the CAP in the many localities where poor people struggled to participate in programs that aimed to end poverty. UMOS, like many CAP organizations, survived the often controversial and turbulent community-control activism of the late 1960s and the demise of OEO, and it continues to thrive to this day.[5]

The problem of defining the role of migrants in the CAP program grew from the law that had created the War on Poverty. In 1963, the Kennedy administration, reacting to growing concern for the plight of

America's poor, began planning for a new poverty program. Research submitted to the administration that summer found that "33 to 35 million Americans were living at or below the boundaries of poverty in 1962."[6] Despite the prosperity enjoyed by many Americans, the administration had proof that poverty continued to burden the lives of countless others.[7] In 1964, President Lyndon Johnson pushed a domestic antipoverty bill as a component of his legislative agenda that included several revolutionary rights programs. He further extended coverage to migrants and the underserved ethnic Mexican population of the Southwest. Johnson, after all, was a Texan and a former schoolteacher who taught Tejano children in LaSalle County.[8]

On August 20, 1964, Congress passed the Economic Opportunity Act (EOA), which included the concept of "community action" as an essential component of the law. The language of the act gave the impression that the responsibility for, and management of, poverty programs like UMOS would fall to poor people themselves. The purpose of the law was to "provide stimulation and incentive for urban and rural communities to mobilize *their* resources to combat poverty through community action programs."[9] The CAP was to rely on individual Community Action Agencies "developed, conducted, and administered with the maximum feasible participation of residents of the areas and members of the groups served."[10] This language resonated with poor communities nationwide, yet few planners knew quite what to expect.

The ways Tejanos and migrants in Milwaukee defined themselves into the local "community" provide a needed corrective to overgeneralizations that dominate the history of both the War on Poverty and the various rights movements that flowered in the late 1960s. In Wisconsin, the farm labor movement led by OU and support for the UFWOC grape boycott, together with the activism of urban "Latin Americans," combined in the name of panethnic community control at UMOS, an event that led to community control movements at most Latino social service agencies in Milwaukee after 1968. Once employed by UMOS, former migrants and progressive Wisconsinites built a community organization that also became the center of a variety of cultural, personal, and political networks while continuing to serve the needs of migrant workers seeking to "settle out" in Wisconsin.[11] Their activism emphasized the needs of migrant workers in a national and transnational Tejano, Chicano, and Latin American context, and their vision of politics

Bill Smith (left) and Ernesto Chacon (right) in a fruit-boycott picket line, Milwaukee, Wisconsin, July 1969. Photo courtesy of David Giffey.

expanded Mexican Americanism to encompass community control, ethnic pride, and the remaking of UMOS as a migrant-centered social and political space.[12]

Tejano migrants did not build the community they sought to institutionalize at UMOS out of whole cloth. In fact, migrants from places like Crystal City were expanding a social world that they had established on the foundation of an agricultural labor network that for much of the twentieth century had moved Tejanos and others across the continent each year in search of work. Economics brought Tejanos north and kept them circulating. These often localized labor flows relied for the most part on networks tied to workers' particular sending regions, small towns, and cities. Often very distinct local communities joined as people moved across these networks. Within this translocal labor world, migrants also incorporated a variety of social service agencies and institutions founded for the benefit of migrants by resident nonmigrants. At midcentury, these had primarily been missionary aid societies, religious organizations, labor placement centers, and various ad hoc groups established at the local level to assist migrants; in such agencies, the migrants were not often active in program management. When the War on Poverty formally embraced the rhetoric of community control, the relationship between migrants and the agencies founded to help them shifted significantly, so that by 1968 activists had once again altered the democratic impulse of Mexican Americanism to support the participatory mandate of the EOA.

In Milwaukee, Tejano migrants became part of a broader Mexican-ancestry community. Just ninety miles north of Chicago, Milwaukee attracted migrants from the larger metropolis to the south, as well as direct migrants from the southwestern United States and Mexico. A significant population of Mexican immigrants had settled in Milwaukee in the early 1920s, mainly laboring in the industrial section of the city near the Menomonee River in tannery, steel, and railroad work. Many of these migrants came directly from Mexico after working in rail and other industries as they traveled north. This first wave of Mexican immigrants stayed on and established many of the city's earliest Mexican community and religious institutions on the Near South Side of Milwaukee, where they lived alongside the city's heterogeneous immigrant and ethnic working class. Experiencing some decline in population during the Great Depression, the Mexican-origin population rebounded during and after World War II as Mexicans and Tejanos moved to Milwaukee. Specific population numbers for Latinos are hard to come by, but the census reported less than five thousand Spanish speakers in the city in 1970. Scholars of Milwaukee have estimated that the actual number of Latino residents was much higher and included a highly mobile population of between eight and thirty thousand people, the majority being from Mexico, Texas, and Puerto Rico.[13]

Tejano migrants who settled in Milwaukee after 1950 found a diverse Latino community experiencing a political and cultural renaissance in the middle 1960s. Puerto Ricans settled in Milwaukee in large numbers during and after World War II, and several community groups engaged in a variety of outreach and social service activities to receive them and ease their transition to life in Milwaukee. Many traveled directly from Puerto Rico, with others settling in Milwaukee after living in New York or Chicago. Several of the Puerto Rican activists of the 1960s came from Chicago and maintained connections with that city's large chapter of the Young Lords organization in the Near Northwest Side barrio. In Milwaukee, Puerto Ricans lived on both the Near South Side among the larger Mexican American community and in a small barrio in the Riverwest neighborhood alongside the predominantly African American North Side community. In the late 1960s, a small group of well-educated Latin American students joined social reform movements and community organizations following graduate work in the United States. The large population of Puerto Ricans and the vanguard of well-educated Latin Americans added to the diversity of Latino influences in the city. This multilayered panethnic activist population led the first social movement to help migrants and Latinos take control of UMOS as a community institution, an act that paved the way toward community control of nearly all Latino-serving agencies and developed into a sustained movement for a place within other local institutions.[14]

Several economic factors drew Latinos to Milwaukee in the postwar period. The eleventh-largest city in the United States in 1960, Milwaukee was home to abundant entry-level manufacturing jobs at wages higher than those available to agricultural workers, a primary factor in attracting the mainly working-class Tejanos and Latinos who settled there. Employers advertised in the city's bilingual newspapers and recruited workers through social service and religious agencies in the barrio community. With a population of 741,324 in the city and a

Map 4. The Mexican American/Latino, African American, and Puerto Rican neighborhoods of Milwaukee

metropolitan population of over 1 million, Milwaukee was a vast metropolis compared to the cities of South Texas or the farming communities of Wisconsin, which often housed fewer than 15,000 people. In Milwaukee, religious groups and organizations such as UMOS played an increasingly important role in recruiting settlers and assisting them as they adjusted to city life, sought out community resources, and found employment in a community of Tejanos, Mexicans, and Puerto Ricans.[15] Yet such organizations only facilitated an already established migrant stream bringing workers from the agricultural regions of Wisconsin to the city of Milwaukee and nearby cities of Kenosha, Racine, and Waukesha in search of year-round employment.

The Tejano and Latino activists who entered Milwaukee came to a city with an active and well-organized African American protest movement linked to political and social movements at the regional and national levels. By the mid-1960s, Milwaukee was playing a prominent role in national militant activism and had earned the moniker "Selma of the North." Home to an aggressive civil rights movement that sought to improve conditions for African Americans, the city had witnessed several years of direct action protest, arrests, a high-profile desegregation case, demonstrations, and marches. Led by the Congress of Racial Equality, NAACP attorney Lloyd Barbee and a number of politicians, as well as the Commandos, a Black Power group that emerged from the NAACP Youth Council directed by Italian American Catholic priest James Groppi, a well-developed network of activists, attorneys, and religious leaders pushed to end racial discrimination in the city. Although tensions sometimes arose between the city's mainly African American North Side and its Latino Near South Side over resource allocation, these two groups, including many moderates and elected officials, increasingly worked together when it came to street demonstrations, the California grape boycott, employment discrimination, welfare reform, and other local issues of mutual concern. UMOS, as an organization that relied on the assistance and support of workers of all races, played an important role in bringing the two minority communities together to demand social, racial, and economic justice at the local and national level.[16]

Milwaukee and the state capital at Madison had well-developed movements protesting the war in Vietnam. While the history of New Left protests led by the Students for a Democratic Society (SDS) and other groups on the University of Wisconsin–Madison campus are part of the mainstream history of the 1960s, the city of Milwaukee and the University of Wisconsin–Milwaukee campus also became sites for anti-war movements, which grew in tandem with the nationally recognized activism based in Madison. SDS activists at the UW–Milwaukee campus staged mass rallies and sit-ins against Dow Chemical and the CIA, as the city's East Side neighborhood became a center for large-scale public protests. Latinos attending the university, some of whom were veterans of the armed services or the war in Vietnam, participated in these movements. The two movements traded activists and tactics back and forth throughout the 1960s. In 1968, as Tejanos and Latinos organized for community control on the South Side, antiwar activists led by Catholic priests burned 10,000 draft cards, youth activists staged large demonstrations downtown, and the SDS staged overlapping protests at the UW–Milwaukee and UW–Madison campuses.[17]

Although set within an increasingly complex social movement milieu, UMOS was not opposed to social reform or civil rights and in fact supported such efforts through many of its programs. For many Tejanos and farmworkers, UMOS served both as a social movement center and often as a personal outpost on this northern frontier of migrant life. From its founding, UMOS sought to improve education, training, and working conditions for individual migrants as it encouraged them to consider settlement in urban Wisconsin.[18] Its programs helped real people to achieve personal mobility. Migrant workers such as Alberto Avila, who already knew several dozen successful earlier migrants from his hometown of Crystal City living in Milwaukee, described how he relied on UMOS to enable his settlement: "I told my wife, 'Let's see if we can settle down in a place so we don't have to go back and forth to Texas . . . every year.' We decided to stay here and see if we could make it over here [in Milwaukee]. The first thing that we did was go to UMOS, and they found us an apartment, and they gave us welfare. . . . they helped us out, and I went as a student in UMOS."[19] After several weeks in 1969 as an adult student making $64 a week, Avila found a job with Rexnord Corporation in its foundry. Over the next three decades, Avila held various jobs and, despite layoffs, became a homeowner who was able to send some of his children to college. Avila was only one of many Tejanos from Crystal City and other migrant labor centers who had long lived and worked across this northern frontier of Mexican American life, and he was able to join the ranks of the urban working class with the help of government intervention—an intervention increasingly directed and managed by other Tejanos and fellow migrants after 1968.

UMOS and the Birth of the Migrant War on Poverty

Committed from its founding to helping migrants like Avila settle in urban Wisconsin, UMOS had its origins in the service mission of Wisconsin-based religious organizations already providing aid and assistance to migrants under the auspices of the Wisconsin Welfare Council Migrant Committee in the 1950s. These resident religious and social service advocates greeted the passage of the EOA with much optimism. As early as 1963, Wisconsin religious leaders, most prominently Rev. Ralph Maschmeier, a Lutheran minister from Waukesha, and Fr. John R. Maurice, a Catholic priest from Milwaukee, along with the Wisconsin Council of Churches, initiated discussions to identify funding sources to establish a statewide program that would provide aid and training to migrants and bring some of the existing programs together under one roof.[20] Incorporated as a not-for-profit agency in 1965 with assistance from former migrant and Crystal City resident Genevieve Medina to seek monies from the newly created Economic Opportunity Act programs, UMOS received its first grant of $31,000 in OEO funds to operate day care centers in small southeastern and south-central Wisconsin agricultural areas where many migrants worked.[21] These programs provided transitional learning experiences that enabled migrant children to prepare for elementary school, attain English-language proficiency, improve their health, and, according to planners, "extend the child's horizons and interests, stimulating interest in learning."[22] Most important, perhaps, the UMOS schools allowed the children to leave the fields in order to learn and play.[23] UMOS employees, white and Tejano alike, hoped that these day care programs would bring parents to the school, where they might take advantage of job training programs.

Day-to-day contact with migrant children provided local white UMOS staff with firsthand knowledge of the astonishingly poor health and material conditions of migrant children, an experience that often strengthened their resolve and desire to expand the program to serve the entire migrant family. Many migrant children suffered from tuberculosis, malnutrition, dental disease, and other serious yet preventable conditions. After receiving its initial OEO funding, UMOS sought to broaden its program in 1966.[24] One early recruitment effort was the "roving counselor" program, which used former farmworkers from Texas to contact potential participants and bring them into the program. UMOS formalized the policy by increasingly hiring former migrants. These counselors entered migrant camps and communities during the harvest season to inform, educate, and recruit participants for UMOS programs, serving as its main point of contact with the community. UMOS programs sought "to provide in-camp education in citizenship, community organization, money management, health, homemaking, and child care," as well as referrals to service agencies and resources for those recruited to settle in Milwaukee. Many of the roving counselors played a role in the growth and development of Obreros Unidos and Milwaukee-based Latino activism, strengthening the activist network as they moved between UMOS offices, activist organizations, and the labor camps. In some ways, they made up a radical internal community of mainly young men from Texas at UMOS.[25]

Those who created UMOS did not envision the organization as an activist agency. Officially it sought to "avoid problems with employers" and stay neutral in the areas of civil rights and labor relations so that it could focus on migrant welfare and settlement from season to season.[26] As a progressive social service agency, UMOS sought only to "make it possible for the migrant to break out of the cycle of poverty and enter a new and better life now enjoyed by the vast majority of Americans." To maintain the fragile relationships among the state, agriculture, and migrant workers, management declined to take sides when it came to the political issues affecting migrants. This neutrality paid off, as UMOS experienced significant success and the support of government, academic, and business leaders: the organization soon became the clearinghouse for all OEO-funded migrant poverty, training, and child welfare programs in Wisconsin.[27]

Despite this middle-ground policy, the world around UMOS underwent significant change after 1966. As detailed in the preceding chapters, Mexican American labor and political activism emerged in the southwestern United States and spread to Wisconsin in the summer of 1966 following the farmworkers' march to the capital at Madison. As UMOS worked at establishing a presence among migrant farmworkers, a small group of former migrants and a team of graduate researchers were busy collecting data on migrant workers for the University of Wisconsin after 1964—an experience that would transform them into activists.[28] The completed research revealed that migratory cucumber harvesters earned less than $4.00 per day in Wisconsin.[29] Upset by these findings, in August of 1966 Jesus Salas, Manuel Salas, and Salvador Sanchez, together with several graduate students assigned to the research project, organized and led the march to Madison to shed light on the suffering of migrants in Wisconsin. In response to these events, the Wisconsin-based management team at UMOS worked to maintain neutrality while expressing some support publicly. That UMOS failed formally to support the union at the same time many of its "roving counselors" were unofficially doing so suggested just how rapidly the bond between the mostly white resident reformers and the young Tejanos was beginning to come apart.

In some ways, the organization of UMOS guaranteed the minimum participation of migrants. It allowed the management to maintain maximum control, a practice its managers apparently saw as being in line with the federal mandate for "maximum feasible participation."[30] UMOS's founders did not expect management to pass rapidly to migrant workers but rather created several administrative layers between the local, white, mainly religious leadership and resident managers, on the one hand, and the growing number of Tejano migrant and former-migrant employees, on the other. In order to achieve success with their program, however, UMOS reserved the grassroots positions for Tejanos, which empowered the roving counselors, making them the public face and voice of the organization. And these counselors worked the same camps as those seeking to establish OU and the same neighborhoods of Milwaukee that were becoming radicalized as panethnic Latin American activism grew during the 1966 and 1967 harvest seasons.[31]

Roving counselors were not only central to the success of UMOS's programs, but they also carved out their authority as community leaders by filling the need for bilingual outreach workers who understood migrant life. Some may have in fact participated in the founding of OU, as many were from the same towns or regions in South Texas as the union workers. In fact, the manager of the UMOS roving counselors was Carlos Salas, union founder Jesus Salas's older brother.[32] Thus, Tejanos may not have had much input in UMOS management, but they were on the front lines of the OEO-funded effort, where many migrants saw them as the face and voice of the organization. This position gave the roving counselors stature within the community, since they were mainly former migrants who had family members working in the fields, facts that enabled them to persuade migrants to consider UMOS programs; and when the organization provided real benefits, it was the counselors the migrants thanked. UMOS both needed and benefited from the roving counselors, who used their position on the inside of migrant life to attract migrants to the organization.[33]

While Tejanos worked at the grassroots level, the structure of the UMOS board limited the participation and management role of migrants by a set of restrictive internal administrative rules. This organizational law included rules that allowed migrant representatives only three board positions, with two of the three chosen by existing board members and the third chosen by a vaguely defined "migrant advisory committee." This institutional structure restricted migrant access to the board by limiting input to an outside "advisory" committee with little power.[34] In various documents submitted to the OEO, "migrants" were listed last on the UMOS list of "communities" served by or participating in the agency, after groups such as "interested citizens," "public agencies," and "growers and canners." The bylaws cited the "maximum feasible participation" requirement, but it appears that UMOS read this language as divisible into two parts. The first group included "residents of the areas," which meant the mostly white Wisconsin nonmigrants, including canners, growers, religious leaders, and bureaucrats; a second included Tejanos and other migrants.[35] Apparent from the details of the organization's bylaws is that UMOS management saw itself as working for migrants rather than with them.

In August 1967, the OEO made a point of informing UMOS of the important role migrants should play in its programs. The OEO, perhaps aware of the underrepresentation of migrants in administration, reminded UMOS administrators of the "close link" between adult basic education instruction and day care and the overall program goal to "help people help themselves out of poverty." It instructed: "Steps should be taken to ensure the participation of the people being served in the planning and operation of the local program." Further, the OEO suggested that migrants be involved in advising UMOS on issues related to day care and that "aides hired by the program *must* be from the group to be served." In fact, the OEO created the day care aide position so that the migrants would "have an opportunity to have job experience, education, and a chance at advancement through increased skill."[36] Although "participation" was central to compliance with OEO guidelines, the difference between "management" and "participation" provided UMOS with wide latitude in achieving the goal of farmworker involvement.

Some within the organization felt that change needed to come, perhaps in response to activism within the Mexican American community. In 1967, a group of board members pressed UMOS to begin to promote current Tejano and Latino employees to management positions. Despite this move, the administration sought to maintain control over the choice of staff selected for promotion. The UMOS executive committee resolved, for example, that "as soon as OEO approves the program change, the personnel committee is requested to promptly interview and promote such present Spanish-speaking staff members as *they* believe will satisfactorily fill the positions of Area Program Coordinators for the Milwaukee and Kenosha-Racine area." Although a step in the right direction, this resolution allowed whites to serve as a filter for Tejano and Latino hires and in so doing to maintain control of administrative positions. Tejanos already working for UMOS were to become eligible for promotion from front-line positions as roving counselors to "area program coordinators." Although these were promotions, they were not management positions, but rather lower-level supervisory positions subordinate to the all-white management. The problem of Tejano and Latino participation continued to be a weakness in UMOS operations under the EOA.[37]

Social Networks, Movement Activism, and UMOS

The growing civil rights and labor rights activity of Mexican Americans in Wisconsin began to affect UMOS more directly after it moved operations from the medium-sized town of Waukesha to the heart of Wisconsin's largest barrio on Milwaukee's South Side at 809 Greenfield Avenue. By early 1968, the OU farmworkers' union movement and affiliated California grape boycott had won the support of the state AFL-CIO and many Wisconsinites, and Tejanos supporting these labor movements played an increasingly vital role in Milwaukee's Mexican American and broader Latino community. Moving its headquarters to Milwaukee in 1968 placed the UMOS agency at the center of a Mexican American and Latino community experiencing a wave of labor and political activism. In fact, the OU/UFWOC boycott office was only blocks away from the new UMOS headquarters. The farmworkers' movement had brought many people into a pan-Latino activist environment, and UMOS placed itself at the center of this community, taking over the large, imposing Saint Vincent's orphanage from the Milwaukee archdiocese.[38]

Other social service agencies existed on the South Side to assist Latinos in Milwaukee. Most prominently, the Spanish Center, established by UMOS cofounder Fr. John Maurice, began as an English-as-a-second-language program serving Latinos as well as Polish immigrants and others. As activism increased, Fr. Maurice took the lead filing complaints against the Milwaukee public schools for discrimination against Latino children, establishing the Bruce Guadalupe grade school, and ushering in a variety of programs managed by Latino professionals. "The Spot," established by the Milwaukee Christian Center, also served the needs of Latino youth through its recreation and after-school programs meant to provide alternatives to gang life. In 1968, with funding from the Labor Department, the city established the South Side Concentrated Employment Program (CEP) office, with a mandate for community participation, in the same building that housed UMOS, providing yet another source of community support.[39]

African Americans and Latinos were increasingly working together in the civil rights arena, linking the three main areas of minority settlement in Milwaukee through crosstown coalitions. In May, a contingent of UMOS employees joined African American, Puerto Rican, and other Milwaukee civil rights activists as they chartered busses to transport people to the Poor People's March on Washington. In the summer of 1968, a number of community meetings brought together members of the NAACP Youth Council, UMOS employees, and Puerto Rican activists to discuss employment discrimination at the South Side's landmark employer, the Allen-Bradley Company. Including "recently returned Vietnam veterans, college students, Puerto Rican ex-gang leaders, and recently arrived Chicanos from southwest Texas turned on to the politics of the sixties," the meeting held in the storefront offices of the Spanish Center brought together activists who decided to sponsor a march and protest. Fr. Maurice, director of the Spanish Center, stepped aside as a "gringo priest," did not participate in the meeting, and called on Latinos to take more control of meetings and programs.[40] Joined by the

In 1969, Ezequiel Guzman (center), of Crystal City, Texas, visited the offices of *La Guardia*, a bilingual newspaper established in Milwaukee during the late 1960s. Photo courtesy of David Giffey.

NAACP's Youth Council led by Fr. James Groppi, three hundred protesters marched and led a demonstration outside the large landmark Allen-Bradley factory famous for its four-faced clock, the largest in the world, and located in the heart of the South Side community. Struggling at first to bridge the racial divide, these multiethnic and multiracial protests gained media attention and linked the civil rights movements of African Americans, Puerto Ricans, and Mexican Americans. These three groups, together with the United Electrical, Radio, and Machine Workers, Local 1111, bargaining agent for current employees, demanded that Allen-Bradley, a federal contractor, hire more than a few dozen minorities in a plant that employed thousands and was located in the center of a Latino neighborhood.[41]

Following the protests at Allen-Bradley, a core of activists from the Mexican American and Puerto Rican communities founded the LAUCR to implement community control across the Latino neighborhoods of Milwaukee and to protest discrimination generally. The focus of the group was to gain control of agencies offering social services to the poor; push for institutional change at the state, city, and community levels; and engage in electoral politics, police reform, and education activism. Led by UMOS employee Ernesto Chacon, the organization linked settled, long-term Mexican Americans, young Latinos, former migrant workers from Texas, and Puerto Ricans led by Rev. Orlando Costas, a pastor at the South Side's Evangelical Baptist Church. With its large budget and federal funding independent of city control, UMOS was the first and most likely target for the newly formed protest group, which gave rise to Milwaukee's Brown Beret chapter, a body that also included Puerto Ricans and people of Mexican ancestry under an inclusive Brown Power banner.[42]

Riding this wave of panethnic community control activism, in the winter of 1968 a group of Latinos and Tejanos sought to implement "maximum feasible participation" under the EOA at UMOS. Jesus Salas, already well known for his leadership of the OU labor union and the California grape boycott, joined Ernesto Chacon, Mexican immigrant and longtime community activist Dante Navarro, and fellow OU organizer and UMOS employee Salvador Sanchez in the effort to win control of UMOS.[43] In 1967, while still heading OU, Salas had criticized UMOS for serving as merely "an educational program" and for failing to take public action for enforcement of state laws related to "workmen's compensation and housing code violations."[44] Salas recalled the reluctance of UMOS to get involved with the striking workers:

> UMOS's offices were in Milwaukee and I had problems. Between '67 and '68 . . . six hundred workers and their families lost their jobs. Many of them didn't know that until they were already here. In '68, when these [union] workers start coming in [to settle in Milwaukee,] I go and talk to the UMOS staff and I tell them, "We gotta do something, these people have just lost their jobs because of the strike action" . . . and I said, "You gotta provide some services." To make a long story short, they denied us. They said they didn't want to get involved with strikers because they were afraid of how the growers and the processors would receive that involvement. . . . So then, I started going to the UMOS meetings and getting involved.[45]

Salas and Chacon began to challenge the authority of UMOS in the migrant community. They argued that the white managers did not allow for effective representation of and participation by migrants. According to Salas, the EOA's maximum feasible participation provision "meant [that] advocacy [should be] directed by participants, both migrants and ex-migrants."[46] Because of his established leadership position among migrant workers and his internal family and personal network at UMOS, which was based on ties to South Texas, Salas was able to take control of the push for Tejano and migrant control of the agency.

The takeover at UMOS grew from meetings held by several different Latino activist groups in Milwaukee. In November of 1968, after private discussions with influential Tejano employees, including labor union cofounder Salvador Sanchez, now a UMOS field operations coordinator, and Ernesto Chacon, the group formed an informal committee to pressure UMOS to hire more Tejanos and Latinos as managers and administrators. After submitting "12 points" of criticism, the call for affirmative action on behalf of "concerned south-side citizens" mentioned at the outset of this chapter, Salas and others pushed for control of the agency and for the ouster of the white management team.[47]

The protesters felt that their demand for migrant management was in line with government policy and that the time had come for community control. UMOS managers, on the other hand, apparently thought that they would be able to phase in migrant control over a number of years and were not yet ready to respond to these demands. In reply to the protests, Director Kruse said there was no "question or argument about Latinization of the staff," yet he argued that asking for the resignation of the white administrators with so many grants pending in the spring might harm the agency, a view seconded by Auxiliary Catholic bishop Jerome Hastrich of Madison. Fellow board member Dante Navarro complained that despite the goal of Latinization, the program "never went into effect."[48]

By late 1968, the OEO increasingly sought to implement community control at Community Action Agencies (CAAS) nationwide. As part of this policy, the OEO released a series of instructions to assist agencies in including greater levels of participation in CAP operations on the part of poor people.[49] According to the OEO, "CAP grantees have a responsibility to broaden the scope of opportunities within their own agencies . . . for participation of the poor, and to help the poor equip themselves to take advantage of these opportunities."[50] Responding to these pressures from the federal government, the Tejano community, and their own board, UMOS managers felt confident that they were increasing the involvement of former migrants in the agency's programs and administration.[51] Commenting in 1968, UMOS founder and board chair Fr. Maurice remarked, "Probably the greatest headway was the increasing involvement on the part of migrants and ex-migrants . . . [which] gave better direction and meaning to the whole project. This increased involvement and concern on the part of migrants and ex-migrants will hopefully continue to deepen in the year ahead."[52] Despite Fr. Maurice's intentions, the scope of participation did not expand into management under Kruse. Between 1966 and 1968, UMOS reported that in two primary employee groups, "Administrative and Field" and "Teaching" employees, "Latinization" had taken place, which presumably meant that Tejanos and other Latinos were taking these jobs. Tejanos and a small number of Latinos comprised 73.3 percent of workers in the former category and 35.8 percent in the latter. Yet "Administration," when viewed apart from "Field" work, remained nearly lily-white in 1968, and Tejanos, despite "Latinization," remained the lowest-paid employees.[53]

Following the protest, members of the UMOS board supported a rapid transition to migrant and Tejano management. In the winter of 1968, the board, led by chairman William Koch, a professor at the University of Wisconsin–Madison, supported the appointment of several migrant representatives to new board seats.[54] After the expanded board took control, it voted to meet the demands of the protesters. This migrant takeover of the board with the assistance of supportive white board members prompted the immediate resignation of UMOS's white managerial staff, a move perhaps meant to cause confusion and disruption in UMOS programs. In April, the board, again led by Koch, supported the appointment of Jesus Salas to direct UMOS and requested that the OEO provide a leadership transition consultant to assist the new management in making the change. Rather than polarization, a focus on "migrant" control resulted in a high level of cooperation between supportive white and migrant board members and protest leaders. By working together, whites, Tejanos, religious leaders, university faculty, and others committed to UMOS supported the "Latinization" of the organization.[55]

Not all received the news that Salas now directed a program with a budget of over one million dollars with happiness. The placement of labor union founder and activist Salas at the head of UMOS led to a backlash as Wisconsin's agricultural industry sought to have UMOS funds cut. Much of the opposition to Salas came from the same Waushara County vegetable growers and processors who had fought the Obreros Unidos labor union, including future Wisconsin Supreme Court judge Jon Wilcox, then the county's Republican assembly representative and a cucumber grower.[56] The agricultural interests, in their effort to discredit Salas, made the contradictory argument that the two years Salas had spent leading and organizing a migrant farmworkers' union in fact disqualified him from holding a leadership and organizational position assisting migrants. Wilcox moved to amend the state's antitrespass law to prevent workers from organizations such as UMOS from entering the fields and migrant housing camps.[57] Despite this effort, UMOS benefited from the coordinated support of Wisconsin's Senate delegation, several Milwaukee- and Madison-area Congress members, and a number of nonprofit agency heads.[58] The OEO, now managed by Donald Rumsfeld under the Nixon administration, approved the 1969 UMOS operating grant.[59] By 1969, Tejano migrant control was a reality at UMOS, beginning a trend to expand the role played by Latinos in a number of other service organizations on Milwaukee's Near South Side.

Further complicating matters, in the late summer of 1969 Jesus Salas engaged in direct action protests together with African American alderwoman Vel Phillips and Fr. James Groppi. Organizing what was soon dubbed the "Welfare Mothers' March on Madison," Salas joined long-time community activist Phillips and Groppi, a charismatic Catholic priest known nationally for his aggressive approach to civil rights in Milwaukee. Fitting for a protest beginning in Milwaukee, the home of Harley-Davidson, a group of bikers led this caravan of cars and busses full of Latinos, whites, and African Americans to the state capitol at Madison where students of the University of Wisconsin swelled the ranks of protesters. Merging the long-standing African American and Latino civil rights movements in Wisconsin, the marchers engaged in a sit-in at the state capitol, causing state representatives to flee, and took over the assembly chamber. In a photograph, Salas is standing arm in arm with Fr. Groppi. Police arrested both Salas and Groppi under an antiprotest statute banning "misconduct on public grounds and in public buildings." Salas phoned the OEO after his arrest to inform them that he had not been "employed" at the time of his arrest, but had been "on leave" to participate in the march—a definitional turn that would keep him out of trouble with the state and the OEO.[60]

After Salas's arrest, the issue of violations of OEO instructions regarding employee participation in direct action activities arose. One irate Wisconsinite complained that Salas was using the "taxpayer's money . . . against us." In response to this letter, Wisconsin OEO director Robert Neal Smith wrote that "as an advocate of the poor, an Office of Economic Opportunity Employee or agency may take part in direct action as long as lawful means are employed," and he pointed out that Salas was on leave and that if he was found to have engaged in criminal activity, the state of Wisconsin did "not have any direct control over OEO Title III-B grants."[61] The OEO and UMOS refused to oust Salas.[62] Despite the turbulence of the first year of Salas's management, UMOS programs continued and were the cause of little controversy.[63] No longer seeking the middle ground, UMOS employees like Salas became increasingly active in politics and social concerns across the state and within the Milwaukee Latino community.

In late October, Salas submitted his 1969 report to the UMOS board of directors. He lambasted the administration that preceded him for having "been too selfish and fearful" and for failing to allow "the indigenous . . . population" a place in the decision-making process. Salas called on local whites still on the board to "put the cards on the table."

He proposed having board meetings in "Spanish and translated into English" to make them more accessible to community members. Salas also made it clear that he wanted to establish a policy of providing a "ladder within the program for the staff to climb, either economically or in responsibility" so as to keep good employees at UMOS and provide opportunities for migrants and Tejanos.[64]

Soon after the report, Salas resigned, paving the way for longtime migrant activist and UMOS employee Salvador Sanchez to take over UMOS management. In so doing, he remarked that it was "time for a change and for the development of more Mexican American indigenous leadership."[65] More broadly, Salas commented, "Additionally, I leave because the political and economic situation in this country is daily worsening for the poor and much has to be done in the fields and streets in organizing for change. I feel I can more effectively attempt to create this change with the guidelines set by the self-determination of the people instead of those presently involved in misdirecting our country. *Viva la Causa!*"[66]

As the director of UMOS, Salas had succeeded in continuing UMOS programs without disruption despite nearly constant attacks on the organization. Upon his departure from UMOS, he left an organization that from its large building on Greenfield Avenue on Milwaukee's South Side offered courses for adults and a day care center and maintained several branch offices around the state. Under Salas's direction, UMOS provided services to all migrants regardless of nationality. Salas also helped to establish local migrant councils at the branch offices to allow for a greater degree of migrant participation in UMOS's affairs at the various county and city centers across the state, a step that made migrant councils important consultative bodies. In addition to encouraging a higher level of migrant participation at all levels, Salas made sure that young Tejanos gained experience in program management. In the process, UMOS went about creating a cadre of activists, some of whom later broke with Salas and left the organization, yet continued to serve Milwaukee's migrant community.

Salvador Sanchez's leadership of UMOS included a heightened commitment to direct action. As UMOS director, Sanchez led and organized several marches on Madison between 1971 and 1974 to demonstrate the failure of the state of Wisconsin to enforce its own laws related to migrants.[67] Before joining UMOS as a roving counselor in 1967, Sanchez had been a labor activist, and he saw UMOS as an activist agency: "We came to realize that our responsibilities as staff were much more complex, that in fact we were not just out to 'recruit' families and bring them to the cities. There were problems to deal with in the fields: housing code violations, minimum wage violations, unemployment problems, workmen's compensation, and innumerable others. It was our responsibility to do all that we possibly could to find solutions to the problems, including making legal complaints." Sanchez noted that "because of the emphasis staff placed on serving the total need of the farmworker, both rural and urban, services improved."[68] As an activist organization, UMOS continued to operate programs with much success and relatively little scandal. Maintaining its commitment to the settlement of migratory farmworkers, the program settled 108 families in Milwaukee for program year 1970–71 and extended its educational programs into rural areas, where it offered training courses at satellite campuses near migrant work areas.[69]

On August 24, 1971, Salvador Sanchez and UMOS supporters completed a nine-day march to Madison, where they filled the capitol building with protesters in a massive sit-in. Sanchez's 1971 march made many of the same demands as the 1966 marchers had made: "Enforcement of equal employment opportunity (EEO) legislation; . . . Amendment of State Civil Service regulations to ensure equal opportunity for Latinos; an affirmative action program to remedy problems between police and the Latin communities; enforcement of [Wisconsin's] protective laws; action to correct problems within . . . Wisconsin's Spanish speaking communities; [and] creat[ion of] an inspection and enforcement division . . . on the Housing Code."[70] Much like the marchers of 1966, UMOS protested what it considered the failure of the administrative state to execute the laws of Wisconsin related to migrants and minority groups. For this reason, Sanchez asked many of the state's department heads to meet the marchers before the protest began.[71]

In early 1972, UMOS underwent an independent review by an outside agency. The review criticized the strong commitment of staff to "ethnic movements," a charge rebuffed by UMOS:[72] "UMOS employees came to work for the program in support of their belief for change and betterment of conditions for migrant farm workers and all poor people. We do not expect our employees to disengage themselves from commitments they have outside the agency; on the contrary, participation

Migrant march to Madison from Milwaukee organized by UMOS, August 1971.
Courtesy of United Migrant Opportunity Services, Inc., Milwaukee.

is encouraged and vital to the growth of the community as a whole."[73] Under Tejano control, UMOS firmly supported its employees' right to participate in the Tejano and related social movements. At last, UMOS was an activist agency controlled by the Tejano migrant community.

Between 1965 and 1973, UMOS received steady funding from a number of sources in addition to the OEO and maintained a budget that fluctuated between $1 million and $1.3 million per year. Following nearly a decade of expansion, UMOS offered an increasingly rich body of programs serving the health, nutrition, housing, vocational, educational, day care, and job placement needs of Wisconsin's migrant workers. By 1973, UMOS had expanded its service area to include thirty-two Wisconsin counties, and as the provisions of the OEO evolved, it adapted to the revision of federal funding sources so that its employees could continue to engage in sustained direct action on behalf of migrant farmworkers. In 1974, Salvador Sanchez resigned, leaving a funded organization now known for its commitment to migrant advocacy and for producing dynamic Tejano leaders. Sanchez's dynamic leadership marked the end of OEO funding for UMOS and the end of charismatic Tejano activism on the part of UMOS directors, yet it paved the way for continued Chicano control and the survival of the organization.[74]

In 1974, Lupe Martinez assumed control of the UMOS directorship, a position he has held for over thirty years. With the activist period of the late 1960s at an end and the OEO in decline, replaced for the most part by the Comprehensive Employment and Training Act and other programs after 1973, UMOS has nonetheless continued to play a significant role in Milwaukee's migrant and Latino community. During Martinez's tenure, UMOS expanded its service mission and began to promote a number of important community events, including a Cinco de Mayo festival, a Hispanic Awards banquet, and other annual community celebrations. For over thirty years since the resignation of Sanchez, UMOS has played a leading role in Wisconsin's Latino community and has increased its mission to include activities in Texas and other midwestern states. After its period of activism and protest, UMOS and the migrants who ran the organization entered the mainstream.[75]

Conclusion

For the translocal migrant activists who protested the management of UMOS in 1968, the experience of interstate labor migration, recent participation in the farm labor unionism of Obreros Unidos, the California grape boycott, and the general trend of social movement activity in Milwaukee all played a role in setting the activist agenda for Tejano and migrant community leaders. By the late 1960s, this mobile social world had expanded to embrace an activism with particular emphasis on the specific needs of migrant workers who sought to relocate to the city. In Milwaukee, migrants became part of an emerging national and transnational Chicano and Latin American worldview, benefited from the need for bilingual workers, and encountered other Latinos and Latin Americans. In this process of social change, interstate migrants constructed a vision of politics that expanded Mexican Americanism to encompass community control, ethnic pride, and a trans-Latino worldview and in the process remade UMOS as a migrant-controlled social and political space that embraced the Tejano roots and ethnic politics of the majority of migrants.

The UMOS case demonstrates the broader successes of a single Community Action Agency that served migrants who expanded their own definition of community. By allowing for the participation of the poor—in the UMOS case, migrants—in the management of OEO programs, moreover, the Economic Opportunity Act enfranchised a group of workers long denied the rights, benefits, and protections of U.S. citizenship within the interstate migrant world in which they lived. In this sense, the OEO and UMOS allowed for the "maximum feasible participation" of a group of formerly disenfranchised poor people. Indeed, consideration of the many local War on Poverty agencies like UMOS within the national context reveals how many CAAs experienced a cycle of controversial protest followed by a transition to community control and program evolution. This revisionist history is in sharp contrast to the collapse forecast in early sociological writing and documented in some historical examinations of the EOA and the Community Action Program.[76] Tejano activists had once again shown that a pragmatic approach to social movements, the state, and educational institutions yielded power and results in a world defined by a migrant ethic of self-reliance and community control. Some of the leaders trained at UMOS and in the surrounding pan-Latino activism of Milwaukee's barrio sought to carry the practical experience and management skills they learned at UMOS and in social movement organizations more generally back to Crystal City, where so many of Milwaukee's movement activists came from, when the town reignited in the late 1960s as a center of Mexican American protest—a status it maintained into the 1970s.

5

Circular Activist Flows and the
Rise of La Raza Unida Party in Texas

As Mexican American and U.S. Latino activism became national in scope in the late 1960s, a variety of movements emerged from within the Mexican-ancestry community and the urban trans-Latino communities of the Midwest. As it had in the past, the migrant stream linking Crystal City to Wisconsin and other locations continued to facilitate the development of transregional activism; those who traveled back and forth brought a constantly changing set of ideas and fellow travelers with them as they turned the wheel of labor migration to serve the needs of political mobilization. This continuing and adaptive thread of activism shows some of the ways the national effort to expand Mexican American—and, increasingly, Latino—civil rights evolved in a specific community. Its story challenges common notions of how the local and national movement evolved within the broader social movement context of the late 1960s and early 1970s.

Teens and young adults led the second Mexican American uprising in Crystal City. As the labor movement in Wisconsin declined and La Raza Unida Party (RUP) arose from the ashes of past failure in Texas, the labor activism of Wisconsin and the renewed political activism in Crystal City dovetailed with and assisted one another. Ties maintained and constructed by leading activists based in Wisconsin, those attending college in Texas, and those working in California formed the nucleus of a newly emergent translocal and transregional activist community. Through these networks built on the frame of the Tejano diaspora, a vanguard of Crystal City activists once again borrowed and shared ideas, tactics, and people from a number of places to build a locally rooted social movement.[1]

The spark that galvanized the second Crystal City revolt in 1969 emerged out of a conflict over the role of young Mexican American women on the cheerleading squads rather than from any mobilization for electoral office. Young Cristaleños took the broader civil rights movements of the 1960s and fashioned their own school-based movement focused on equality in the selection of cheerleaders. This push for civic equality in the schools led by young women eventually brought about the well-known transformation of Crystal City from home of the failed 1963 Mexican American political revolt to the most vibrant local manifestation of what many came to call the "Chicano movement."

This chapter reconsiders the second Crystal City revolt by examining the role transregional migrant activists played in its success. Although the history of Crystal City's dual uprisings is well known, no scholar has yet considered the transregional movement component, despite a long recognition that over 80 percent of the Mexican-ancestry population engaged in interstate migratory labor. By linking Crystal City's second revolt to the transregional community of migrants that supported it, this chapter places one of the most important moments in ethnic politics in the United States in its local, national, and migrant contexts for the first time. Crystal City's labor-based social network allowed young people to hear of and test new ideas, strategies, and resources across the Tejano diaspora throughout a period of sustained activism in both Texas and Wisconsin. The second revolt is also notable for the increased leadership of women and young people with a high level of education and experience. Like the earlier movements in Crystal City and Wisconsin, this revolt, too, revealed the possibilities and limits of community activism.

The politics that emerged in Crystal City in the late 1960s reveal the national shift from the liberal Mexican Americanism common across the Southwest and Great Lakes after World War II to the more militant Americanism of the Chicano movement's ethnic nationalism, embodied by leading activist movements in Texas, Colorado, and California.[2] Clearly influenced by the African American civil rights movement, the farmworkers' movement, anticolonialism, and the broader counterculture of the late 1960s and early 1970s, the Chicano movement emerged as a hybrid, concerned with civil and social rights, and functioned within the terrain of American pluralism. Even at their height, many Chicano organizations remained dependent on the basic architecture of state-centered liberalism as they called for Aztlán on behalf of "La Raza."[3]

Although the Chicano movement lacked the institutional foundation of the African American civil rights movement, several key centers of political and ideological thinking developed in the middle and late 1960s. Central among these radical voices was Reies López Tijerina of the *Alianza Federal de Mercedes* (Alianza), who called for the restoration of land grants to Spanish and Mexican heirs in New Mexico. Like César Chávez and others who marched as a form of protest, Tijerina brought national attention to these claims by leading a group of marchers from Santa Fe to Albuquerque in 1966. A Christian preacher by training, the Texas-born Tijerina was a gifted speaker who mixed his speeches with Christian iconography and fiery irredentist rhetoric. Adding to his mystique, Tijerina led an armed "courthouse raid" in New Mexico that embodied an assertive, albeit masculine, style of Chicano radicalism for many young activists. Jailed for his activities, Tijerina was both a revolutionary and a martyr to a cause.[4]

Another model of militant activism developed in the urban barrio of Denver, Colorado, where a farmworker's son and former boxer, Rodolfo "Corky" Gonzales, established the Crusade for Justice (Crusade) in 1966 as a grassroots organization committed to social change. Like César Chávez and Tijerina, Gonzales was born in the 1920s and was older than those he inspired and led. Rejecting accommodation and his past relationships with government programs, Gonzales by the late 1960s pressed for self-determination for Chicanos and soon became a spokesman for the radical voice in Mexican American politics. If Tijerina had engaged in armed rebellion and Chávez in peaceful protest, Gonzales merged the rhetoric of rebellion with the cooperative grassroots activism of the farmworkers' community-focused struggle. Gonzales expressed the anger and hopes of the movement in his poem, "Yo Soy Joaquin," which resonated with Mexican American youth living as in-between people in the United States. The Crusade, moreover, through sponsorship of the Chicano Youth Liberation Conferences, served as an important meeting ground for Chicano and other activists from across the country. The Crusade became increasingly irredentist in rhetoric, an evolutionary step embodied in the *Plan Espiritual de Aztlán* (1969) which informed and defined cultural nationalism for many in the movement, and for some, expressed the soul of the Chicano Movement itself.[5]

In Texas, the Mexican American Youth Organization (MAYO) became the primary Chicano militant organization led by a younger leadership cadre. Much like the Crusade, it became a central gathering place and training ground for young activists committed to cultural nationalism, yet was focused much more than its Denver counterpart on participatory politics, and its founders were all born during and after World War II. Well educated and part of the youth generation, the founders of MAYO looked to organizations led by older leaders such as Chávez, Gonzales, and Tijerina, as well as parallel movements among African American youth, when formulating their strategies and plans of action. Although it failed to embrace the term "Chicano" in its name, the leadership, led by José Angel Gutiérrez of Crystal City, often referred to Anglos as "gringos" and to Mexican Americans as "la raza," embracing the rhetoric and militant style of Chicano nationalism as it maintained a commitment to community organizing and electoral politics.[6]

Though movement leaders and participants in Texas and elsewhere often spoke in nationalist terms and used inflammatory rhetoric, the actual practice of the movement tended toward a pluralist or self-help politics. In this way, Aztlán was more than a nationalist goal. It was a practical effort across the United States for youth of Mexican ancestry to win respect for their long history in North America and the Southwest and a broader role for their community in the mainstream of American society and politics.[7] As the movement pressed for a radical departure from accommodation and borrowed a militant imaginary from the black power and anticolonial movements of the era, many groups within it focused on federal or other governmental support for community programs and educational reform or engaged in electoral politics in an effort to establish virtual homelands in cities and barrios across the United States. This policy of militant rhetoric and interest-group politics allowed what became the third-party movement of RUP in Crystal City to maintain a practical radicalism in the context of Americanist engagement.

High School Cheerleaders and the Birth of "Brown Power" in Crystal City

Across much of America, and Texas in particular, high school football teams and cheerleading squads were institutions of great significance inside the school and among the broader community of parents and local supporters. In Crystal City, the racialized nature of local society added another dimension to the place of football and cheerleading squads within the landscape of local power relations. There was more to football than the game, since it served as a primary gathering point for adult and teenage men, women, and families; honors on the field often brought off-field honors to the players and cheerleaders and increased the prestige of families.[8] Cheerleading and the rituals of homecoming queen played an important role in female social prestige and honor. In Crystal City, teachers, along with Anglo alumni (or "exes," as they are often known in Texas), played an active role in the selection of school honors and institutions important to female students. They maintained most prestige positions for Anglo girls at a high school now overwhelmingly serving Mexican American teens.

With a faculty of ninety-seven Anglos and thirty Mexican Americans, the school appeared to be making some progress in instructional diversity. For over a decade, Mexican American teens had held most elective prestige positions, since fewer than four hundred Anglo children attended school in a district of nearly three thousand students. In sports, the school opened the door to Mexican American participation in most boys' and girls' teams. At the level of football sideline participation, however, there were never more than two Mexican American cheerleaders selected for the squad, even as Mexican American boys played an ever larger role on the team. As a result, some Mexican American parents and students clearly felt that a de facto quota restricted Mexican American girls' participation or excluded them altogether.[9]

Off the gridiron, yet tied to the football season, an all-Anglo high school alumni association selected the homecoming queen and court. The association had never crowned a Mexican American girl homecoming queen in a school now overwhelmingly comprised of Mexican Americans. The practice of restriction on the cheer squad and what some considered the discriminatory homecoming queen selection process convinced Mexican American students and parents that a conspiracy of Anglo parents and faculty members (often members of prominent local families) worked to limit Mexican American women's participation in prestigious school activities.[10]

In an environment of rising expectations of civil rights and social rights in Texas, Wisconsin, and the Southwest, these restrictions on women's participation in the schools seemed outdated to Mexican

American teens and parents. Mexican American girls coming of age in the late 1960s continued the push for student control and participation in all aspects of student life that others had begun in the middle 1950s. Severita Lara, the leading student activist in 1969, explained:

> Cheerleading and [being voted] "most popular" and "most beautiful," all of those were very important to some of us in high school. We began to see that even though we were 90 percent Chicano here at school, it was always three Anglos and one Mexican American cheerleader. And we said, "Why does this have to be this way?" We started questioning, "Well how is it done?" And, then we started looking at the process . . . and that's when we started questioning, and then we started looking at the whole system and started looking and saying, "Did you notice that the 'most beautiful' is always an Anglo? The 'most representative,' the 'most likely to succeed,' and all of these things?" And we said, "Why . . . is [a Mexican American] never there?"[11]

In 1969, two Anglo cheerleaders graduated, leaving vacancies on the squad. This gave students like Lara an opportunity to challenge the quota by convincing Mexican American women to try out.

The challenge to the quota system at Crystal City High School involved all the components of high school women's social life and provided a group of young women with a first entry point into the world of protest and negotiation. In the spring of 1969, Diana Palacios, a popular young Mexican American woman, tried out for one of the vacant cheerleading positions and failed to win a spot. In response, Mexican American students protested the operation of an ethnic quota limiting Mexican American women to a minority position on the team.[12] Palacios had tried out the year before but felt the teachers did not select her because "she didn't get along with Anglos."[13] Mexican American students led by Lara and Palacios began discussions regarding the cheerleading quota and other forms of discrimination practiced by Anglo teachers, coaches, and alumni groups within the Crystal City public school system.[14] The students decided not to boycott the schools in the spring of 1969 because of a concern that protests so close to the end of the year might not yield results and could jeopardize graduation for seniors. Instead, they circulated petitions that provided a set of issues for discussion as student leaders and the school superintendent sat down to consider the complaints. The superintendent expressed a willingness to alter school policy, giving Lara and the other student leaders hope, as they began summer break, that the school might democratize the cheerleading and homecoming selection process when they returned for their senior year.[15]

As these efforts progressed, MAYO cofounder and intellectual leader José Angel Gutiérrez returned to Crystal City from San Antonio with his wife, Luz. His immediate purpose was to establish a federally funded Head Start program. The arrival of the Gutiérrezes set the stage for possible future political activism. The couple quickly befriended the high school activists, most prominently Severita Lara. As the president of MAYO, Gutiérrez had gained notoriety traveling across Texas to call on Mexican Americans to challenge discrimination, segregation, and "gringo" control, while others within his group helped organize successful protests and school walkouts.[16]

MAYO in San Antonio was a broadly focused social movement organization that utilized its internal youth leadership and foundation funding as it worked to make barrio residents activists. Within just a few years of its founding, MAYO directly challenged the status quo in racial and ethnic politics in San Antonio. As historian David Montejano has shown, MAYO established programs for barrio gang members and sought to overcome the divisions that had fostered intra-ethnic gang warfare among Mexican American youth gang members. MAYO's aim was to educate, inform, and radicalize the barrios of San Antonio. MAYO also challenged the leadership of people like Texas congressman Henry B. Gonzalez by backing candidates who were liberals and who rejected the ethnic moderation of leaders like Gonzalez. By creating flux, MAYO threatened the seemingly settled consensus politics of South Texas and in so doing drew the fire of Gonzalez, who fought the organization's supporters and leadership without restraint.[17]

While at the center of this San Antonio–based controversy over MAYO, Gutiérrez completed his master's thesis in political science at Saint Mary's University that argued for the political reorganization of several South Texas counties where Mexican Americans comprised the majority population. This thesis became official MAYO policy as the "Winter Garden Project," which worked on registering voters and bringing majority politics to South Texas and Zavala County.[18] Gutiérrez, leaving MAYO's operations in San Antonio to its cofounders, moved back to Crystal City just as the social movement led by teenage women provided the spark for community mobilization that MAYO needed.

That summer, the Anglo-majority school board rejected the agreement made between the students and the superintendent. The board denied the existence of any quota system or favoritism toward Anglo women in the selection process for the cheerleading squad or for school honors.[19] Following another of the migrant streams centered at Crystal City, Lara spent the summer visiting family members in California, where she learned of the Mexican American school walkouts held in Los Angeles the year before. According to Lara:

> During the summer of '69 . . . my sister and I went to . . . San Jose, California, and we met some people there and we started talking about school . . . and Los Angeles had had a "blow out" [student walkout] because of all the discrimination that was going on, and we heard what had happened and how they did it, and then . . . Armando Trevino . . . who had already graduated was in California [working] at that time, and we happened to meet at one of my uncles' homes in Gilroy, California . . . and we started discussing this . . . planning . . . and it kind of started there.[20]

While her immediate family no longer participated in the migrant stream, Lara traveled with other family members who continued to migrate to the agricultural areas around San José, California, each year. This time in California allowed Lara to gain access to, and an understanding of, the developing Chicano movement in California from her settled family members while never leaving the broader Tejano diaspora.[21]

When students returned to school in Crystal City, they came as witnesses to the school board's rejection of the settlement offer presented by the superintendent, and they prepared themselves for confrontation. The movement expanded to challenge the discriminatory selection process for the homecoming queen. In October 1969, the Crystal City High School Ex-Students Association announced that the annual homecoming queen competition required that at least one of the candidate's parents be graduates of Crystal City High School. Enraged at this clear effort to manipulate the selection rules, young Mexican American women began public protests aimed at challenging the role of the Ex-Students Association in conferring this important student honor.[22]

To level the playing field, the students called on the school to place the election of homecoming queen in the hands of current students rather than alumni. Severita Lara and other students organized protests and distributed information informing their peers about the issues. The school promptly suspended Lara for unauthorized soliciting and leafleting on campus. Students wore brown armbands in protest, a demonstration of their increasing affinity with the Chicano movement—and perhaps as a result of consultations with Luz and José Gutiérrez. Gutiérrez, with the help of the newly formed Mexican American Legal Defense and Educational Fund (MALDEF), compelled the school to reinstate Lara.[23] In early November, the student activists, Gutiérrez, and Crystal City high school graduate and attorney Jessie Gamez brought the student complaints to the school board.

On the other side of the issue, Anglos, and the Mexican American moderates who governed with them, reacted negatively to the renewed social protest. The local newspaper became the main outlet for criticism directed at the activists. Resident Larry C. Volz complained that the demands represented the wishes of only a "small fraction of the student body . . . the trash that demand and demonstrate for their rights, rather than earn them as most of us have." He called on the school board to reject the student demands and further characterized the student effort as one that sought to "dictate, with the threat of violence, the administration of our school affairs."[24] In a section presumably aimed at José Angel Gutiérrez and Jesse Gamez, Volz called on the community to reject the leadership of a group of "disturbed young men whom Crystal City has been good to." One self-described "German American" belittled the desire of the Mexican American students for a curriculum that incorporated the history of the Spanish and Mexican legacy in Texas. Another Crystal City high school graduate argued that by requiring that the homecoming queen and court be the daughters of graduates, alumni merely sought to encourage "putting forth extra effort and finishing" high school.[25]

The following week, Mexican American students and parents responded by writing letters to the editor. Noelia Martinez, the mother of several Crystal City graduates, asked the Anglo community whether it was "possible, repulsive as the idea seems to the majority of us, that there are influences within the administration and policy forming groups of the school district that are racist . . . always insisting that the selected cheerleader or twirler groups must not have more than one Spanish-surnamed girl?" Luis Gonzales reminded the public that the students demanded instruction in the history of Spanish and Mexican Texas because "we played a major role in the forming of our great Southwest." Gonzales concluded that "this country needs . . . aggressive, intelligent young men like Angel" (the name that local residents used for José Angel Gutiérrez) and that if African Americans had "Martin Luther King," then Mexican Americans needed "our Angel Gutiérrez." Trinidad Rubio, a 1966 graduate of the high school, hoped that an end to the discriminatory treatment of Mexican Americans would make Crystal City a "better town in which its citizens [could] live in peace." Student leader Severita Lara chimed in, adding, "We are equal—don't push us down" and reminding readers that "the majority rules in a democracy." Many of the letters detailed personal histories of agricultural labor migration and military service, and they asserted that through labor and service, Mexican Americans had earned their place in local society.[26]

Young Mexican American women organized to respond to the Ex-Students Association's new rules. A poll of Mexican American female students revealed that only one teen met the parental graduation requirement. She did not run for the position of homecoming queen, however; rather, Mexican American students organized a protest against the selection process. Severita Lara circulated a petition with "probably about fifty or sixty signatures of girls" protesting the homecoming queen selection procedures and submitted it to the principal. The principal responded that the schools had no power to act, since the Ex-Students were an outside group.[27]

Although an "external" group selected the queen and court, the coronation and dance took place on school property, a fact that enabled a possible legal challenge. Changing their focus, the students then protested the use of school property by a private group that engaged in a discriminatory selection practice. Under threat of litigation, the school board rejected the request of the alumni association to use public school property for its homecoming ceremony. In response to this decision, the alumni group elected two Mexican Americans to its executive board, but the school board did not alter its decision, forcing the Ex-Students to hold the homecoming coronation and dance in a farm shed owned by a local rancher.[28]

Although the homecoming queen controversy ended in a victory for the student activists, the board continued to reject their demands, prompting a student walkout across the school district. Mexican American students formed the Youth Association, pledged to "total school reform" in Crystal City, and led the walkout under this banner.[29] The students and their families picketed the schools, with nearly five hundred students on strike the first day. The protests expanded each day, bringing national television and press reporters once more to Crystal City when the boycott population reached sixteen hundred students. In response to these protests and the media attention, the school board invited representatives of the Texas Education Agency (TEA) to visit the district. The board continued to reject student demands for a meeting yet agreed to a brokered meeting of the board, parents, and the TEA representatives.[30] The students feared that the board meant to coerce or silence parents, a concern that led the parents to reject the invitation.[31]

Using networks developed as the leader of MAYO, Gutiérrez organized a student activist trip to Washington, D.C., where the students could draw national attention to the crisis in Crystal City and put outside pressure on the school board. High school student leaders Severita Lara, Diana Serna, and Mario Trevino met in Washington with Texas senator Ralph Yarborough, Massachusetts senator Edward Kennedy, and Chris Roggerson, deputy director of the Department of Health, Education, and Welfare's (HEW) civil rights office, to discuss the situation in Crystal City. After Roggerson's meeting with the students, the agency decided to send investigators to Crystal City to determine whether the schools were violating the civil rights of the Mexican American students—a move that put federal funding for Crystal City schools at risk. At the time, Severita Lara commented that the boycott aimed at the withdrawal of federal funds, "because that's one way to hurt them and get them to start promoting the proper action."[32]

The boycott brought the people into the streets and reignited a local movement culture in the city, as protest meetings and rallies featuring prominent Mexican American political figures became a part of daily life. Under Gutiérrez's leadership, MAYO had assisted student boycotts and walkouts in Texas, Michigan, and other states across the Southwest, and in this case it provided tactical and strategic advice to the boycott leadership.[33] For much of December, the Mexican American community supported the children as more students boycotted the schools across all grade levels. Supporters came into town to help the students catch up with their homework and other lessons over the holiday break. Other activists helped organize "tutor-ins" and "liberation schools" similar to those used in Black Panther school boycotts in 1967 and the Young Lords Harlem sit-ins in 1969.[34] Converting dance halls and Catholic parish hall rooms into schools, outside activists helped students continue their educations.[35] That the boycott was tactically planned to limit missed school days and continue protest efforts and teaching during the holiday break convinced many to participate in an effort to resolve the issue on return after the break.

The presence of federal investigators in Crystal City put pressure on the school board and forced a resolution of the conflict. The federal government and supportive parents pressed the students' claims. The boycott ended on January 6, 1970, after federal mediators brokered a deal that allowed the boycotting students to return to school without penalty. It was not a clear victory for the student activists, since the school board agreed only to consider an expanded set of student goals that now included bicultural and bilingual education, better testing of Mexican American student ability, and election of student body positions and most honorary positions by majority student vote.[36] Nonetheless, the New York Times declared a triumph for "brown power" and "Chicano" activists, a movement that, it pointed out, began in Crystal City in 1963 and had spread to East Los Angeles and Denver by 1970.[37] In response to these efforts in South Texas, Los Angeles Times reporter Ruben Salazar commented in February 1970 that Chicanos were "merely fighting to become 'Americans' . . . with a Chicano outlook."[38]

Transregionalism and La Raza Unida Party

During and after this period of student activism, Crystal City activists living outside the state returned home to participate in what became a broader movement for community control. According to Gutiérrez, the events of 1969 set in motion the merger of the youth activists of 1963 with the new student activists: "The important difference was that we had a memory. We knew the mistakes we made in 1963. We knew how we fell apart. . . . We learned how to do it better in '69. The issues . . .

were different. You had the political generation that was involved in '63 still involved in '69, all the wiser, and you had the component of young people who were not involved in '63. . . . That is part of the metamorphosis of the politics . . . all the disenfranchisement, the poor, the women, the young people took leadership."[39]

According to Severita Lara, the school boycott led to an influx of supportive local and other Mexican American activists from Texas, who joined the movement and organized the community. Returning activists came home with experience in politics and institution building after having held leadership roles in social movements in Texas and Wisconsin. They were aware of the problems that led to the collapse of Los Cinco, and they sought organizational unity and the recruitment of activists able to resist Anglo economic pressure. In early 1970, Gutiérrez took a managing role in the Youth Association and created a framework for a second and more permanent political takeover in Crystal City.[40]

Local activists moved quickly to counter past weaknesses. They formed a community group even before the RUP, Ciudadanos Unidos (Citizens United, CU), that emerged soon after the Youth Association boycott took shape. The CU organized activists and parents into a strong grassroots organization. Gutiérrez remarked that CU "sought out members who stood for Mexicano social justice" and the "protection of one another against the gringo" to "collectively limit the power of the gringo over La Raza."[41] Julian Salas, Jesus Salas's uncle, later an RUP municipal judge, explained, "When Ciudadanos Unidos was organized, La Raza Unida was actually born."[42] The CU operated as a "board of directors" for the party and created a forum for community input and party accountability.[43]

Following the successful school boycott, Gutiérrez resigned the presidency of MAYO and began the process of building the CU as a base to support what became the RUP in Crystal City and Texas. To succeed in appealing to the local population of migrants, the RUP drew candidates from across the transregional migrant stream and among those who lived and worked as activists in Wisconsin. Reaching out across the Tejano diaspora to select candidates, the RUP began the process of retaking control of the city government and laying the foundation for winning county government posts as well, while blunting critics' common refrain of "outsider influence."[44] Arturo "Turi" Gonzales explained how news of the revolt brought him back to Crystal City: "I think I was working in Hartford, Wisconsin, when a friend of mine from Carrizo [Carrizo Springs, Texas, about ten miles from Crystal City], he filled me in on what was happening; things with José Angel Gutiérrez, and my organization, the Mexican American Youth Organization, and that brought me right back."[45] Arturo Gonzalez joined the CU as an organizer after gaining ample experience as a UMOS employee and OU union activist. Gonzalez shared several common friendship connections to Crystal City natives and Wisconsin migrant activists, including Rodolfo Palomo, Francisco Rodriguez, Ezequiel Guzman, Jesus Salas, and José Angel Gutiérrez.[46]

The ebb and flow of migration from Crystal City to Wisconsin continued as several recent high school graduates settled in Milwaukee to work or attend college. Economic reality led teenage boycott participants and migrants such as Raul Rodriguez and Geraldo Lazcano to leave Crystal City and settle in Milwaukee after graduation, where they carried news from their hometown to friends and family members. Around the same time that Arturo Gonzalez left UMOS and Wisconsin for Crystal City, Rodriguez found employment at UMOS using similar friendship networks.[47] Lazcano took a bus to Milwaukee, where he lived with family members, enrolled in college, and later found work in a factory.[48] By the late 1960s, UMOS had transformed the Tejano diaspora into a vehicle to serve the economic needs of Crystal City migrants and other Tejanos seeking to "settle out" in Milwaukee and other Wisconsin cities. UMOS was also an activist training center engaged in a two-way flow of talent, as some employees migrated home to Texas to assist the RUP mobilization in Crystal City and others came north looking for work.

In early 1970, the RUP established itself in Crystal City as a viable political party and helped organize several other South Texas county party operations. By selecting candidates with activist experience, a migrant background, or independent financial resources for the upcoming April school board elections, the RUP fielded candidates who had little dependence on local Anglos. Moreover, migration to Wisconsin and possible public- or grant-funded local employment served to protect candidates and activists. The CU selected José Angel Gutiérrez, Arturo Gonzales, and Mike Perez, a radio announcer for the popular KBEN radio station and the owner of the Pan American Club, a dance hall, as the first RUP school board slate. The RUP candidates easily won, thanks

Participants at a La Raza Unida Party meeting held in Milwaukee gather at a South Side tavern (c. 1970). Pictured are Pedro Ortiz of Crystal City, a Brown Beret and member of LAUCR; José Angel Gutiérrez of Crystal City, later president of the national RUP; Antonio Torres, a member of LAUCR and UMOS; Ernesto Chacon, former UMOS staff member and founder of LAUCR (front row); Ramona Villarreal, a Brown Beret from San Juan, Texas; Mario Avila of Crystal City, a member of LAUCR; and an unknown woman (back row). Courtesy of United Migrant Opportunity Services, Inc., Milwaukee.

to the well-organized precinct and campaign organization established by Gutiérrez and Virginia Musquiz with the assistance of MALDEF, which monitored the election.[49]

By the summer of 1970, the RUP had established itself as a successful electoral organization and community-based group. Unlike in 1963, the Texas Rangers did not militarize the city, and the police, while present, did not initiate dramatic confrontation. News of the victory spread across the nation in both the pages of the mainstream press and the many new Chicano newspapers, as well as in *La Guardia*, based in Milwaukee, whose editorial staff included many from Crystal City and South Texas, some of whom returned to play a role in the RUP government.[50]

The RUP also established a local newspaper, *La Verdad* ("the Truth"), featuring news sections that highlighted events across the Tejano diaspora. The news was markedly political, informing local readers of national political events within the Mexican American community and of the growth of RUP affiliates across the nation. *La Verdad* reported on the growth of the Crusade for Justice and the Colorado RUP led by Rodolfo "Corky" Gonzales. The paper also covered midwestern developments, such as the establishment of the RUP in Ohio by Texas native Enrique Gonzalez and an RUP organization in Saginaw, Michigan, a central receiving city for Tejano migrant sugar beet workers from Crystal City and South Texas. The paper offered an advertising outlet to the Mexican American businesses of the barrio, including some that advertised in the mainstream *Zavala County Sentinel* as well. *La Verdad* also provided a public service by highlighting news important to farmworkers, such as information on a variety of migrant service organizations operating child care and health centers across the Midwest and South Texas.[51] It functioned as a movement and community newspaper, reflecting the growth of the local movement within the context of the Tejano diaspora and the farmworking community that served as the foundation for the RUP in Crystal City.

The social networks of the Tejano diaspora played a significant role as the RUP went about selecting candidates for elective office and appointing others to bureaucratic posts from among those experienced in the labor and political efforts in Wisconsin. In December 1970, when the RUP tried to take control of the city's urban renewal program, RUP council members asked José Angel Gutiérrez and Rodolfo Palomo to run the organization. Palomo, a native of Crystal City with experience as an organizer for OU and the UFWOC grape boycott organization in Wisconsin, had close ties to both labor and activist social networks based in Wisconsin and Texas as a close friend of Arturo Gonzalez and Jesus Salas. He spent much of his time between 1968 and 1970 organizing Tejano migrant workers with Jesus Salas's brother Manuel and Bill Smith in Wisconsin cannery and field harvest operations under the auspices of OU. City council candidates Roberto Gamez and Jose Talamantez, both Crystal City High School graduates, also worked organizing migrants in Wisconsin before returning home to run for office as RUP candidates.[52] Thus, the social movements of Crystal City–based Tejanos in Wisconsin trained and prepared activists and organizers for the RUP in Texas.

The social networks linking Crystal City and Milwaukee allowed activists to play a significant role in politics and protest activities in both places. On September 16, 1970, Mexican American and Puerto Rican students at Milwaukee's South Division High School and Kosciusko Middle School, with the assistance of the Brown Berets, led their own walkout and march to the headquarters of the Latin American Union for Civil Rights. Celebrating Mexican Independence Day in Milwaukee, the LAUCR and the Brown Berets held a rally and a *teatro* performance by a Brown Beret ensemble featuring "Jeep" Mendoza, a poet and former farmworker from Crystal City. The Milwaukee walkout, like many of the student protests taking place in Mexican American communities across the nation, aimed at bringing culture and educational equity to the curriculum at South Division, the Latino-serving high school then undergoing a demographic shift from being a primarily Euro-American school to serving more Latinos and Tejanos each year. Several of the same Milwaukee activists who assisted the students in the walkout traveled to Crystal City to work on the RUP election campaign.[53] In just a few days, groups of activists traveled in cars between Milwaukee and Crystal City when organizers were needed—a pattern that continued throughout the 1970s.

As the RUP established its grassroots base in Crystal City, the party simultaneously began to expand its power into the surrounding, predominantly Mexican American, counties of the Winter Garden District and build the foundation for a statewide and perhaps national movement. The party won school board, city council, and mayoral successes in nearby Carrizo Springs and Cotulla and supported the development of the RUP across Texas. Fifteen of the sixteen RUP candidates balloted were elected to the offices they sought. One San Antonio–based politician opined that the emergence of the RUP brought a "democratic revolution" to South Texas. The RUP had put the state's nearly 750,000 Mexican-ancestry voters in play for the first time in an open challenge to the Democratic Party's long hold on a key swing vote. It also appeared that the victory of the RUP led the Mexican American Political Association (MAPA) in California to endorse a Mexican American for governor and pushed Corky Gonzales to step up his effort to bring the RUP to Colorado.[54]

As they attempted to place the party on the county ballot in three Winter Garden counties, RUP officials faced the daunting challenge of learning how to build a third party without a formal state organization. The entrenched opposition of county officials and powerful county judges, as well as the fact that the party consisted of young, inexperienced activists rather than seasoned political operatives, limited the ability of the party to win a place on the ballot. Unschooled in the procedural formalities of election law, the RUP was denied a place on the ballot in Zavala, Dimmit, and LaSalle counties for failure to follow a rule that required the naming of specific candidates for any political party that did not seek ballot status across Texas. The RUP took the case to court, prompting the Texas attorney general to issue an opinion that upheld the denial of a ballot position; the secretary of state, rejecting this view, wrote in support of the RUP candidates. In October 1970, the Supreme Court of Texas, siding with the attorney general, decided that the RUP, without a statewide organization, failed to meet the requirements of election law and refused to order the county-specific balloting of its candidates.[55]

Forced to operate a write-in campaign, the RUP drew volunteer workers from across the nation in support of the infant third-party movement. Fifteen volunteers from Milwaukee, some of them editorial board members at La Guardia, Milwaukee's only bilingual paper, returned "home" to Crystal City to work on the campaign. These returned migrants went about the grassroots effort of organizing block meetings in supporters' homes to explain the write-in campaign to voters.[56] To counter the grassroots efforts of RUP's write-in campaign, the county Democratic machine focused on absentee ballots, a tactical move that helped defeat RUP's effort, since the RUP had forfeited the absentee campaign as a matter of law. According to an anonymous participant from Milwaukee, the RUP lost the election but entered 1971 better organized and with the knowledge to secure a ballot position for its candidates as a statewide rather than county political party. In *La Verdad*, Esteban Najera published "Corrido de las Elecciones" ("Song of the Election"), which lamented the fact that *"errores muy pequeños"* (very small errors) had cost RUP the election. The RUP learned from its mistakes and entered 1971 focused on making the party "statewide" to allow it to take advantage of looser rules that guaranteed it a place on the ballot in every Texas county.[57]

The success of the struggle to establish the RUP inspired activists across the Tejano diaspora and in large cities like Los Angeles, where some tried to emulate the Crystal City efforts. In South Texas, the party expanded its control in nearby cities and counties that also had significant interstate migrant farmworker populations. The transregional nature of community life encouraged José Angel Gutiérrez to prompt activists in northern and western communities fed by the Tejano diaspora to extend the RUP. In midwestern states like Michigan and Ohio, current and former farmworkers from Texas often served as local founders and party activists. In Milwaukee, for example, the LAUCR worked to put Latino candidates on the ballot and establish an RUP branch in Wisconsin. In California, following the Chicano Moratorium protests against the Vietnam War and the subsequent police riot, longtime activist Bert Corona discussed the formation of a party in East Los Angeles that would resemble the Crystal City RUP.[58]

Even as the struggle to expand the party beyond Crystal City continued, the RUP peopled Crystal City's various governmental and political offices with locals from across the transregional migrant network. The first RUP city council selected Milwaukee resident Francisco "Panchillo" Rodriguez, a Crystal City native, former UMOS employee, OU organizer, and union cooperative manager, to serve as the first RUP city manager. Rodriguez, a political science student at the University of Wisconsin–Milwaukee, remembered the surprised responses of his professors to his questions about city management. When his faculty mentors realized that the RUP had in fact appointed Rodriguez city manager, they helped him gather information before he left the university to become the first Mexican American city manager in Crystal City since Los Cinco lost power in 1965.[59]

The RUP established a practical activism within the local Mexican American community. RUP's leaders had little interest in building a machine or establishing themselves as typical South Texas bureaucrats or lifetime political bosses. After all, the RUP had criticized the Anglo candidates and Anglo-supported candidates they intended to replace in 1963 and 1969 for operating an antimajoritarian political machine. Most of the young men who formed the core of the RUP's group of candidate-activists had attended or graduated from Crystal City High School in the late 1950s and early 1960s, attended some college, and participated in the farmworkers movement in Texas and Wisconsin. Continued migration from Crystal City to Milwaukee and back provided a key transfer of talent as increasingly well-educated and experienced former migrants returned to occupy positions in the local government and party. Other Chicanos flowed in from the cities and small towns of the Southwest, as MAYO and the Volunteers of Aztlán program brought young people then active in Austin and Los Angeles to Crystal City.[60]

From the start, despite the large role played by men as elected officials, women of all ages strove to make the RUP a more inclusive organization. Luz Gutiérrez and several other local women rejected "Women's Auxiliary" status and successfully demanded leadership roles in CU, the political policy committee, and neighborhood groups that operated in ways similar to ward machines in a large city. Some, like longtime Crystal City resident activist Virginia Musquiz, who had played a role in the Los Cinco coalition and continued to work in voter registration and campaign efforts between 1965 and 1969, now took on leading roles in the grassroots operation of the RUP. Activists from other cities moved to Crystal City to join the RUP. MAYO member Viviana Santiago, for instance, played an important role in the decision-making apparatus of the party. As women pressed for change across the United States, this trend increasingly played a role in the broader development of the RUP.[61]

In 1972, the demonstrated successes of the RUP in Crystal City cast a long shadow over Chicano America, and civil rights leaders met to unite the many state groups and select a national leadership for the party. This national conference grew out of Chicano Youth Liberation Conferences organized by Corky Gonzales in Denver, Colorado, beginning in 1969. Representing the more radical position among Mexican American radicals, Gonzales rejected the "integration" of this minority into the dominant society and insisted on celebrating the independent culture and history of Chicanos.[62] Several RUP activists from Milwaukee, including Ernesto Chacon, founder of the LAUCR, attended the first Denver meeting, which adopted the "Plan de Aztlán," a nationalistic program that laid out the basic contours of "Chicano" nationalism in a form that borrowed heavily from anticolonialist language. The document, attributed to Gonzales, read in part, "We declare the independence of our mestizo nation. . . . We are a union of free pueblos, we are Aztlán." At the 1970 meeting, Milwaukee Brown Beret founder, Vietnam veteran, and Laredo, Texas, native Juan Alvarez read a poem titled "La Chicana," celebrating Chicano women's activities, with El Teatro Urbano of San Jose, California, as a musical accompaniment. The convention, much like past conferences held by Gonzales, gave Chicano artists, poets, and nationalists a space to come together and share ideas, art, and political strategies. For a brief time in 1971, there was even speculation that Jesse Jackson's Chicago-based Operation PUSH might organize African Americans, Chicanos, and Puerto Ricans into a single coalition. Gonzales had long led the way in arranging for these annual events, but in 1972 a coalition of leaders called for a meeting of the many state RUP groups established before and after the rise of the RUP in Crystal City to establish a national political party.[63]

The 1972 party meeting contrasted the approaches of the Texas and Colorado activist communities and placed the pragmatic radicalism of Gutiérrez in contention with Gonzales's brand of third-party nationalism. Since the victory of the RUP in Crystal City had placed radical Chicano politics on the national agenda, Gutiérrez had committed the Texas RUP to ballot box "revolution," yet he also thought the party should remain open to serving as a broker between the Democratic and Republican parties in places where it lacked the strength to win elections. Gonzales saw the party as independent and felt there was no place for such a pragmatic approach. These two visions of the RUP as a national organization came together at the 1972 national conference in El Paso, Texas, as activists met to map out the future of the party.[64]

The national meeting of the RUP drew Texas delegates and participants from across the Tejano diaspora and from Tejano networks within large states like California and across the Midwest. The diasporic connection to Texas influenced the makeup of delegations to the 1972 convention from the midwestern states of Illinois, Michigan, and Wisconsin, since these were largely comprised of former migrant workers from South Texas. Indeed, Gutiérrez used the network of former Tejano migrants to lobby for the presidency of the national RUP at the conference.[65] At the convention, he met with representatives from Wisconsin and other midwestern, migrant-receiving state delegations to plan his election strategy. Through shared friendships and organization networks, he knew many of the delegates from the Great Lakes states with largely migrant Mexican American populations. Gutiérrez kept abreast of national and local developments across the diaspora by reading leading Chicano newspapers from Milwaukee, Denver, Delano, and other locations. When it came time to elect a national president, it was Wisconsinite and UMOS employee Dante Navarro, together with Ernesto Chacon, who seconded the nomination of Gutiérrez and called for the convention floor vote.[66] With the aid of Texas migrants and their allies in the various state groups, Gutiérrez won the full support of the delegations from Washington, D.C., Oregon, Indiana, Kansas, Maryland, Texas, and Wisconsin, as well as majorities of the delegates from Arizona, New Mexico, Washington, and Utah. California, torn between the two ideological positions, split its vote between Gutiérrez and Gonzales. With this backbone of support, Gutiérrez became the first president of the national RUP, an organization most newspaper reporters credited him with founding in Crystal City, Texas.[67]

This outcome of Gutiérrez's organizing the Tejano diaspora apparently surprised Rodolfo Gonzales, yet this key social network had its roots in migrant labor streams similar to those that had brought most Mexican Americans to places like Colorado, Wisconsin, and the Midwest in the first place. Denver-based and representing a settled urban community of Mexican Americans, the Crusade for Justice leadership perhaps underestimated the vastness of the Tejano diaspora and its political potential. According to Gutiérrez, Gonzales believed that the midwestern delegates were only Crystal City "plants," not representatives of important, settled communities of migrants.[68]

Gutiérrez summed up the Tejano migrant support system as it functioned in Crystal City:

You know if you get beat up you're going to call on your brother and your family for assistance. . . . You're not going to call on strangers who don't know or understand you. . . . So, if you're already organized around *La Familia* unit, when you look for help you know where to find it . . . in friends, relatives, or people who are family to you . . . and these people will have another set of people who are family or relatives that are blood to them. And, in this way you can organize in a very natural way because you're expanding your relationships from the bottom that are not artificial or contrived, it's a very natural bond.[69]

Aware of the political potential of such a network, Gutiérrez used it not only to gain control of the National Raza Unida Party but also to raise funds for the RUP in Crystal City from Cristaleños now settled in the Midwest: "I made it my job to find them because that was my fund-raising avenue. I'd go and make them feel guilty, and they'd give me money. I'd say, 'You *cabrones* left, and I'm holding the bag! If you're not gonna help, you've got to give me money!' And they would. They also became more militant outside of Crystal City."[70] These words ex-emplify the link that Gutiérrez and other activists perceived between Crystal City and the evolution of the RUP across the translocal migrant networks that tied Texas to a vast diaspora. Traditional interpretations of politics in Crystal City from the Los Cinco revolt of 1963 to the rise of the RUP after 1969 have only seen this movement within a limited local and southwestern context, but it clearly inspired and assisted other or-ganizing across a translocal Tejano diaspora.[71]

The 1972 RUP conference was both the beginning and the end of the RUP as a national organization. After the conference, the party seemed to die outside of South Texas and Los Angeles, as Gonzales increasingly withdrew from the group. One month after the RUP conference, Gon-zales rejected activist Reies López Tijerina's invitation to a land-grant conference in New Mexico, stating, "I want no type of alignment with political prostitutes."[72] The two men had once been close, and in 1967, on behalf of their respective organizations, had signed a "cooperation" pact with Elijah Muhammad's Black Muslims. In March 1973, perhaps indicating that Gonzalez's organization, or some part of it, now fully embraced irredentism, a gun battle took place pitting armed individuals inside a Crusade for Justice building against the Denver Police Department.[73]

Crystal City and the Decline of La Raza Unida

Although the RUP never materialized as a national political party, connections between the Texas RUP and activists in Wisconsin and other midwestern states continued. Mexican Americans in the Midwest and other migrant communities of the United States maintained a connection to Texas and the broader Chicano movement through the same networks that initially facilitated and sustained labor migration. Gutiérrez visited Michigan, Wisconsin, and other midwestern cities several times after 1969 to assist Tejano organizing efforts and visit friends from Crystal City, and he continued this movement across a migrant stream linking Texas to the Midwest, Pacific Northwest, and California.[74]

The connection to Wisconsin was perhaps the most enduring, as the party sent activists back and forth each year well into the late 1970s. In a letter written on September 27, 1973, to Pedro Ortiz, Gutiérrez stated, "It is always a good feeling to have brothers and sisters or yourselves eager and willing to promote *el Chicanismo familiar*."[75] RUP officer Carlos Reyes of Los Angeles, California, when working as a party official in Crystal City, often wrote and phoned former city manager Francisco Rodriguez after his return to Wisconsin in 1973. Reyes and Mario Compean, past president of MAYO, both eventually found work in Madison, Wisconsin, with UMOS before attending or working for the University of Wisconsin.[76]

In an effort to expand the relatively weak economic development initiatives put forward by the RUP in the period after 1970, the party called on activists from Wisconsin to spearhead a new program in 1975. To accomplish this goal, two leading migrant activists from Wisconsin—Jesus Salas and Miguel Delgado—returned with Alejandro Nieri to help jumpstart the many failed economic development efforts of Zavala County and Crystal City under the newly created Zavala County Economic Development Corporation (ZCEDC). In 1975, they wrote grants for funding from the Community Service Administration (CSA), heir to the Office of Economic Opportunity program. Salas, Nieri, and Delgado had several years of experience as employees of OEO-funded programs in Wisconsin, with Salas having served as a program director. This training and expertise in Wisconsin's OEO programs meant that all three worked with the CSA and its predecessor organizations at a variety of levels and had extensive grant-writing experience. In one example of a truly transregional effort, a Milwaukee-based credit union established by former farmworkers held organizational funds until the RUP and other organizations could establish a credit union in Crystal City. Between 1975 and 1976, this Wisconsin team received over $1 million in federal grants for economic development and established smaller ventures to import goods from Mexico for sale in Wisconsin and the Midwest.[77]

The RUP and Gutiérrez used the network of friends and families that connected the Midwest to Crystal City to recruit qualified Chicanos for government posts and candidates for elective office, drawing heavily upon those employed at UMOS and other Milwaukee migrant service agencies. Gutiérrez described these Cristaleño informal networks as providing a "job information system . . . mutual benefit society . . . insurance company . . . a communication network—you name it," to which the RUP "added the political dimension."[78] Jesus Salas described the transfer of Cristaleño activists between both cities: "Former organizers for the farmworkers union and people who had been involved here in Wisconsin go back and help out the movement in Crystal City. . . . We never saw it as two different things. For us it was the same. The politics were tied together, and the leadership developed in tandem. I went back in the mid-seventies after the takeover of [Zavala] county, and I stayed down there helping organize Raza Unida Party."[79]

Despite these old friendships, tensions developed as Crystal City became a major recipient of federal funds and a community with many overlapping agencies, each controlling well-paid jobs in a rural county where jobs were scarce and the majority of residents had limited education. Tensions arose that pitted local leaders, often with limited education yet controlling a lot of political influence, against outsiders and the educated managers of grant-funded programs.[80] Several former migrants led by Arturo Gonzales, Rodolfo Palomo, and Guadalupe Cortinas, all former residents of midwestern states, and others remade the Barrio Club as a group opposed to Gutiérrez and Ciudadanos Unidos. This development pitted old friends against one another as the two groups fought for the spoils of Crystal City politics.[81]

Conclusion

The RUP held control of Zavala County from 1969 to 1979, and in this period South Texas witnessed the transformation of its political system under state and national scrutiny. In Zavala County and across the region, Mexican Americans, some in opposition to the RUP, now ran most South Texas counties where they comprised a majority. In the urban centers of the Southwest and Midwest, Mexican Americans built coalitions with African Americans, Puerto Ricans, and others, even as tensions between and within minority groups also surfaced.

By 1979, the process of political collapse within the RUP at the local, state, and national levels was complete. Never a real political force in California, Colorado, or any other state for that matter, the RUP failed to survive as a national or even a regional party. At the local level, a disagreement with the local gas company led to the loss of natural gas service in Crystal City after 1977. Crystal City and the RUP made national news as local residents began cooking with Korean War–era surplus wood-burning stoves, which Jesus Salas, head of the ZCEDC, helped distribute.[82] Salas, Delgado, and others won a CSA grant for a cooperative farm but then had to fight against President Jimmy Carter to receive the funding. Tensions between conservative Democratic governor Dolph Briscoe, a prominent Uvalde executive and rancher who had labeled the ZCEDC grant an effort to establish "a little Cuba" in Texas, and José Angel Gutiérrez apparently compelled President Carter to cut funding for the grant. Carter, who supported "open government" in the wake of Watergate, claimed executive privilege for memos discussing the ZCEDC grant. Many in Zavala County were certain that Briscoe called in a political favor and that these political realities were the subject of discussion in the memos. Others felt that if Gutiérrez had removed himself from the ZCEDC project, Carter and Briscoe might have funded it. With no one willing to change position, the Carter administration decided not to release the nearly $900,000 grant.[83] The RUP continued to make the national news, but none of it was good. In 1979, political allegiances were so splintered that many of the people recruited by Gutiérrez, including Miguel Delgado and Jesus Salas, ran in opposition to the RUP candidates and former allies and friends now entrenched in the Barrio Club, including former OU volunteers Arturo Gonzales and Rodolfo Palomo.[84]

Because of the split at the local level, few of these old schoolyard and migrant stream friendships lasted, and the networks built in the social space of migration and within the migrant neighborhoods in the 1950s and 1960s collapsed. Several of Gutiérrez's childhood friends from the aspiring Mexican American middle class, including Jesse Gamez and Guadalupe Cortinas, both attorneys, challenged him in court. By 1979, political life in Crystal City had become little more than a fight over the dwindling economic spoils in a small town many migrants saw as home yet now sought to escape permanently. The same young men and women who once pushed for civil rights in Crystal City fought one another, and the RUP, splintered and torn, turned inward on itself before disappearing completely in the years after white flight and capital flight drained the city of most of its businesses and middle-class residents.[85]

The victories of RUP were inspiring but short-lived. Its young activists brought ideas and tactics learned while in San Antonio, cities and towns in Wisconsin and California, and other places they migrated to as students and workers and applied these lessons to the problems of South Texas. Their accomplishment in creating the RUP inspired other Mexican Americans across the nation to activism, service, and a politics of engagement in California, Texas, and the Midwest. Within the national movement, Crystal City was a central location for Chicano activist development, but more than this, the Tejano diaspora, which once sent migrant laborers north, now sent activists in a circular movement that outlived the RUP. In Crystal City and Milwaukee, the tone and rhetoric of politics shifted from Mexican Americanism to Chicano (and Latino) nationalism; yet the RUP and related movements nationwide maintained a focus on electoral politics and community development as they pursued local, state, and federal funding for worthwhile programs serving Tejanos and Latinos. This form of nationalist-informed Chicano Americanism clearly emerged from the radicalism of MAYO and Milwaukee-based organizations and is evident in the practical steps activists took. Even as activists sounded the call of Chicano self-determination, they applied for federal and state grants to create their version of Aztlán, which, although it was transnational and often looked to Mexico and Cuba for inspiration, still sought economic and educational grant funding from the government. This practical, pluralist politics demonstrated by the actions of the RUP in Crystal

City shows how the actual policies of the Chicano movement embraced many Americanist principles.

Local and Texas politics, together with the general economic stagnation present in agriculturally dependent Southwest Texas, conspired to limit the successes of the experiment in Chicano governance in Crystal City. Local Texas politics increasingly made pariahs out of both the RUP and Zavala County as a whole. Interestingly, as the 1970s and 1980s progressed, many of the local activists themselves returned to places like Wisconsin to continue work in Latino and migrant-serving agencies. Other nonmigrant activists who had worked in Crystal City for the RUP also joined the "brain drain" heading north. Mario Compean, a cofounder and former state director of MAYO and a leading force in RUP politics, became a student at the University of Wisconsin–Madison and director of the newly established Chicano Studies Department. Carlos Reyes, also an RUP official, moved to Wisconsin to work for UMOS and the University of Wisconsin–Madison. Jesus Salas, after several years working for the ZCEDC, also abandoned Crystal City to return to Milwaukee for employment. After the final collapse of the RUP in the early 1980s, José Angel Gutiérrez likewise entered this migrant stream, moving to Oregon. Others fled Crystal City for Austin, San Antonio, and Dallas–Fort Worth.

Many working-class Cristaleños now left Crystal City, diminishing the circular flow more with each year that passed, and community members settled out in the West, Northwest, and Midwest, as well as in many medium and large Texas cities. By the 1980s, they would return to Crystal City only for the occasional baptism, wedding, or, more commonly, funeral. Crystal City, a once vibrant ranch town with a bustling Mexican American district, became a ghost town full of empty houses, abandoned commercial buildings, fading RUP murals and Mexican statues, and potholed streets first paved after the rise of the RUP.

Conclusion

OF DIASPORA, POLITICAL ECONOMY, AND THE POLITICS OF MEXICAN AMERICA

Looking down the main street of Crystal City in the early twenty-first century, there is little sign that this was a center of radical politics or even that it was the economic center of the Winter Garden District. Many of the storefronts are empty or occupied by marginal businesses; most of the national chains have pulled out, and few of the palm trees that once graced the parklike center of town remain, replaced by empty parking spots. As one drives around the city, abandoned and vacant homes owned by residents of other parts of Texas, as well as Wisconsin and places as far away as Oregon, dot the landscape. In the driveways and grocery store parking lots during the Christmas holiday, license plates hail from Wisconsin, Illinois, Minnesota, California, as well as Texas and Mexico, as the town swells briefly. In the late 1990s, the majority of subscriptions to the *Zavala County Sentinel* were sent out of the county to Dallas and other large cities in Texas, as well as Wisconsin, Michigan, California, and other states across the diaspora. After the "revolution" brought on by La Raza Unida, many Anglos, Anglo-owned businesses, and Mexican Americans moved away to Uvalde and nearby Carrizo Springs following the loss of natural gas service in the late 1970s. In many ways, the radical decade ended with a whimper and the election of Ronald Reagan in 1980.

While Crystal City experienced decades of stagnation and decline, Tejanos played an increasingly important political and social role in the manufacturing-based economy of Milwaukee. Even as that city underwent the deindustrialization common to the large cities of the Midwest and Northeast, Tejano and other Latino migrants increasingly settled in and found jobs there and in surrounding areas. Perhaps most important, Tejanos experienced mobility in Milwaukee, as many from Crystal City and South Texas found work as managers at social service agencies and small businesses and in politics as representatives and activists for a diverse Latino community. As that community grew larger in Wisconsin, it continued to struggle with issues of discrimination and poverty and increasingly confronted immigration issues. Yet, even as Milwaukee struggled with its own postindustrial condition, it was a city where people of more than a dozen ethnic and racial groups celebrated their culture at a variety of annual festivals held in a lakefront park dedicated to such fêtes under the shadow of a river-spanning bridge named for a Socialist mayor.

The activists of the 1960s often became bureaucrats and Democratic Party workers focused on issues related to the Latino and Tejano communities. Jesus Salas, for example, served on the University of Wisconsin System Board of Regents along with several other Latinos and continued to play a role in statewide politics. Many others involved in Crystal City and Milwaukee migrant politics, among them Ernesto Chacon, Carlos Reyes, and Francisco Rodriguez, also worked for the state of Wisconsin or the University of Wisconsin. Former MAYO and Texas RUP president Mario Compean worked for UMOS, attended the University of Wisconsin, and later moved west to Minnesota, then Washington State as he revived a connection to his own migrant past. Many nonactivists likewise followed these same streams to find work and make new homes as Tejano migrants in a national diaspora.

This book has tried to shed light on the continuity and contradictions of Mexican Americanism and of the Tejano diaspora that served as its foundation by viewing the period between the Second World War and the early 1980s through a lens focused on that portion of the migrant stream operating between Texas and Wisconsin. Through an examination of events at key locations in these two states, it has considered the many ways an ethnic and racialized group embraced the ideology and practice of Mexican Americanism and adapted it to community needs in an active and dynamic process. Migrants maintained a variety of identities as workers, activists, and citizens who, perhaps more than anything else, sought economic stability at one and sometimes both ends of the migrant stream.

What does the Crystal City, Texas–Milwaukee, Wisconsin, case tell us of translocal and transregional politics in an age of transnational and interstate movement? First, that it is important to recognize that in a world defined by these global flows of capital, culture, and people, translocal currents continue to operate and to link regions within the nation-state. International flows likewise sometimes travel internal migrant streams blazed by domestic migrants of the same ethnic or racial group. This is true of the Mexican workers who first entered the midwestern states, the Tejanos who followed, and the Mexican and Latin American migrants who now move northward, eastward, and westward in the United States along well-established rural and urban labor pathways often rooted in the Tejano diaspora.

At one end of the diaspora, the RUP as a third-party movement collapsed in Texas under its own weight. Yet despite its short life, the RUP and the movement that took root in Crystal City helped change politics in the Mexican American–majority borderlands. First, it brought Mexican Americans into the political sphere in a way denied them in the past. The RUP showed how everyday people could support a movement, draw Mexican American voters to the ballot box, and define themselves and their politics publicly and aggressively. Even after the collapse of the RUP, the party's electoral success compelled the Democratic and Republican parties to consider different models as they sought the votes of Mexican Americans and recruited candidates.

In places where the RUP never took hold, moreover, Mexican Americans in Texas and across the Southwest elected ethnic representatives. Anglos in many places sought to avoid another Crystal City "revolution" by accepting the inevitability of participation, and a militant, yet moderate, politics took hold in a number of Mexican American–majority counties and cities. This led to a demographic revolution across Texas that forever changed the face of the two dominant political parties and of local government agencies, police departments, and fire departments. In many ways, the radicalism of the RUP, which in Texas always borrowed heavily from the language and rhetoric of Americanism, forced the hand of racial and ethnic reform across Texas, even as its own power as a viable party waned.

When one looks north to Milwaukee and Wisconsin more generally, the story of integration and acculturation is quite pronounced. Despite the small overall population of Mexican Americans and Latinos in the state, the organizations founded by Latinos and Tejanos in the 1960s continued to serve the community and produce trained leaders for other organizations well into the twenty-first century. Obreros Unidos may have disappeared after the failure of union organizing in Wisconsin, but the activism of OU brought many of the shed and cannery workers into labor unions, and these unions increasingly responded to the needs of Mexican-ancestry seasonal workers. In both of Wisconsin's major cities, Milwaukee and Madison, organizations like UMOS thrived after the formal end of the War on Poverty, offering programs under a variety of state and federal agencies. UMOS became one of the largest migrant service organizations in the United States, operating nationwide, linking migrant workers from South Texas and Wisconsin to programs from coast to coast. This expanded mission made sense, since the activism that developed across the translocal migrant stream tied migrant communities together in ways that enabled the crosspollination of activism, ideas, and leadership. These tangible results flowed from a highly fruitful mix of political wisdom that farmworkers had gained in resisting domination by Anglos in Texas, the continued force of progressive labor traditions in the Midwest, the New Left, and the experiences of Tejano activists and institution builders in Wisconsin.

The Texas migrant networks highlighted here provided material resources as well as the ideological inspiration necessary to transform local migrant networks into a viable foundation for sustained translocal civil rights and labor rights activism. Recognizing the importance of these linkages is a first step toward a more accurate rendering of the nationwide Tejano diaspora and its impact on Mexican American history. Crystal City migrants adapted indigenous community resources, kinship networks, state and federal legal protections, national institutions of the Great Society, and their own life of migration in South Texas and Wisconsin to the needs of a civil rights movement that was national in scope and local in execution. In this swirl of activity, the interplay between crosscurrents of social solidarity across a Tejano and later Latino diaspora mixed with Americanist ideology and ethnic pride to allow for a flexible reworking of migrant culture within the contours of translocalism.

Was the "Chicano movement" a success in this case? Certainly, many migrants and nonmigrants watched as Crystal City became one of the centers of the many Chicano movements that developed in the Southwest and Midwest after 1963. After 1969, Crystal City became the de facto capital of the Chicano movement's political efforts and the site of one of the most controversial cases of minority governmental control in the nation in ways that highlighted the strengths and weaknesses of the RUP, Chicano nationalism, and the Chicano movement more broadly. The people of this small city in South Texas gained much from their brief moment as a national center of political development and controversy—yet this did not stem the tide of small-city decline.

What was lost? Perhaps the city itself was lost. Crystal City is now nearly a ghost town in a South Texas border region experiencing economic expansion across the Highway 83 corridor, of which Crystal City is a part. Perhaps it is true that many of the whites were racists, since so many shut down their businesses, sold their homes, and pulled their children out of the schools after 1969. After the rise and fall of the RUP in Crystal City, the town is perhaps more remote than ever before, with no natural gas power, no economic development, and no viable commercial district. Other nearby towns have also experienced rural decline as residents move to cities like San Antonio—but these are sleepy towns with natural gas connections.

Crystal City, one might argue, was always poor; its people were mainly interstate migrants, and whites, while powerful, were a minority population for most of the twentieth century. The RUP did not alter these social and economic realities. Moreover, migrant workers sought out economic stability and upward mobility through permanent settlement in Wisconsin, California, Minnesota, Michigan, Oregon, Washington, and other states, creating a number of transplanted towns like Crystal City that maintain community and kinship ties. Those workers and activists who settled out of the migrant stream learned political lessons and, as I have argued, took these with them as they moved across the nation. As a result of the quiet victories that resulted from activism in Texas and Wisconsin, Tejano children stayed in school longer, found better jobs within the working class, and, as time went on, entered colleges and universities at both ends of the diaspora.

The migrant activists also learned that they could not go home again. For some, this meant that what they had learned from life in the North and the multiracial and multiethnic social practices they exercised in these states did not translate well on the U.S.-Mexico border in a racialized society divided between Mexicans and Anglos. Many activists left

Crystal City in the 1970s never to return, even after committing themselves to making their hometown a better place. Yet some of these individuals, having settled elsewhere, maintained their families' historic homes in Crystal City as a reminder of their roots and as a place to stay when attending reunions, funerals, and community events.

In Wisconsin, on the other hand, the diversity of communities, the acceptability of ethnicity in a city of strong ethnic groups, and opportunities at the city, state, and county level worked to lessen intragroup tensions. It was in the North that migrants experienced greater freedom and flexibility—a fact that reinvigorated the migrant stream as Tejanos increasingly moved north and west in search of opportunity, much as their grandparents had done following the Mexican Revolution of 1910.

In the end, civic nationalism of the sort learned in school and practiced in the Midwest, rather than Chicano nationalism as practiced by the RUP, brought lasting success to the Mexican American migrants and citizens who forced open the door of participatory democracy at both ends of the Tejano diaspora. Too often, historians blame the Mexican Americans of the past for lacking the vision to reject the theoretical privilege of citizenship in favor of a transnational space of coethnic Mexicano pride, or derisively assume they internalized the prevailing view of whiteness held by many Mexican American elites when they should have been building bridges with African Americans and Mexican nationals. Certainly, Tejano migrants built, crossed, and maintained bridges between peoples, but they also suffered segregation, racism, and the negative aspects of transnational labor competition. These American citizens, as the GI Forum often lamented, were forced north across the migrant stream by a mix of economic factors and most importantly by the unrelenting flow of Mexican labor into Texas. In this sense, Greater Mexico grew at quite a personal cost for the domestic farmworker.

At the start of the twenty-first century, some American nativists consider Mexican-ancestry residents in the United States a problem and a challenge to the American nation. Nativism is nothing new. As scholars have pointed out, Mexican American citizens in the nineteenth and twentieth centuries fought against a social position as aliens or foreigners in the United States, a place that was for many their homeland and birthplace. Often, these same Mexican American citizens complained of the problems resulting from a nearly open border with Mexico and the competition resulting from the inflow of so many Mexican nationals. Because of these struggles for a place within the American community, Mexican American history has suffered from a common tendency to mischaracterize efforts at Mexican American citizenship in an effort to support transnationalism as an ideal. Mexican Americanism was, however, more than a false consciousness, more than the unfortunate result of shortsighted, restrictive, citizenship-based discrimination or an adoption of whiteness politics. Mexican Americans adapted their lives to the many identities and ideologies in the United States, and many clearly identified themselves as U.S. citizens even as they lived in transnational and transregional cultural and social worlds defined by interactions with both Mexican international and Tejano interstate migrant life. The particular Tejano diaspora detailed in this book is evident each November when Crystal City celebrates its annual Spinach Festival, an event that brings tens of thousands of former residents and tourists to town for music, family, and school reunions. In Milwaukee, the Fiesta Mexicana, held each August on the shore of Lake Michigan, serves the same purpose, as it also brings the Crystal City diaspora together, in a multigenerational celebration of family and shared memory, and demonstrates the ways migrant communities live on and thrive in the twenty-first century.

Notes

Abbreviations of Sources

APC   *Appleton Post-Crescent*
LAT   *Los Angeles Times*
LVM   *La Voz Mexicana*
MJ   *Milwaukee Journal*
MJS   *Milwaukee Journal-Sentinel*
MS   *Milwaukee Sentinel*
NYT   *New York Times*
TVOH   Tejano Voices Oral History, Center for Mexican American
       Studies, University of Texas at Arlington Library
WP   *Washington Post*
WSJ   *Wall Street Journal*
ZCS   *Zavala County Sentinel*

Introduction

1. The main contours of Mexican and Tejano northward and westward migration parallel those of African Americans in the United States in that the demand for workers in the urban manufacturing and agricultural industries of the North and West led to recruitment and the establishment of migrant streams to the cities of those regions. Unlike African Americans, Tejanos, and to a lesser degree Mexican migrants, continued to circulate between the U.S.-Mexico border and the North. On the operation and permanence of the African American great migration's settlements and institutions, see Grossman, *Land of Hope*; and Best, *Passionately Human*. The Tejano experience with its constant circularity was closer to that of Italian transmigrants detailed by Gabaccia in her pathbreaking study, *Militants and Migrants*.

2. My conception of "Mexican Americanism" is influenced by the work of Gerstle, *Working-Class Americanism*; and Mario Garcia, *Mexican Americans*, 20. I do not subscribe, however, to a generational approach, but rather see this form of Americanism as a shifting transgenerational and intergenerational ideology

and practice that, like many ethnic identities, is the result of hybrid and contested negotiations in particular social and political spaces, as demonstrated in the seminal work of Neil Foley, *White Scourge*; David Gutiérrez, *Walls and Mirrors*; Montejano, *Anglos and Mexicans*; and George Sanchez, *Becoming Mexican American*. Mexican Americanism changed over time, shaped by the local, translocal, and transnational milieus that defined life where Mexican-ancestry people lived.

3. Alma Garcia, *Chicana Feminist Thought*.

4. Although most often rooted in Jewish studies, what might be termed "diaspora studies" now considers the variety of transnational and translocal communities often tied together by nation, religion, kinship, and community ties across or within nations. In this book, I will refer alternatively either to a "Mexican American diaspora" or more particularly to a "Tejano diaspora." Under the term "Tejano," I include not only those with ties to Spanish and Mexican colonial settlements in Texas but also more generally the bulk of Texas residents who settled before and after the Mexican Revolution of 1910 and who became "Tejanos" as they increasingly saw themselves as such within the interstate migrant labor stream. Most government publications referred to them as "Texas-Mexicans." On the broader Southern diaspora, see Gregory, *Southern Diaspora*. Gregory's data-rich study shows that after World War II, the out-migration of Tejanos and settlement in other regions doubled each decade, so that by 1970 there were nearly half a million Hispanics born in the South (mainly Tejanos) settled outside their home state. This out-migration grew more pronounced in the 1960s, when nearly four hundred thousand left, mainly from the state of Texas. Although most Tejanos went to California, the Great Lakes were the second-most-common destination. For examples of diaspora studies across disciplines, see Cohen, *Global Diasporas*; Braziel and Mannur, *Theorizing Diaspora*; and Gabaccia, *Italy's Many Diasporas*. For examples of Latino diaspora research, see Robert Smith, *Mexican New York*; and Whalen and Vazquez-Hernandez, *Puerto Rican Diaspora*. See also my own argument for considering transnational and internal migration as sharing key facets in Marc Rodriguez, *Repositioning Migration History*. On the impact of transnational cultural transmission, see Limón, *American Encounters*.

5. For some interesting essays on the need for and practice of transnational labor history, see Van der Linden, *Transnational Labour History*. For anthropological research that takes translocal practices into account, see Yamashita, introduction to *Globalization in Southeast Asia*; Nederveen Pieterse, *Globalization and Culture*; and the rich ethnographic work of Copeland-Carson in *Creating Africa in America*. In *Repositioning Migration History* and "Movement of 'Young Mexican Americans,'" I argue that translocal internal migrant networks and labor streams operating in the United States must become a part of the broader field of diaspora and migration studies. For an example of a study that considers translocal activist transmission, see Blackwell, "Contested Histories."

6. For one of the more perceptive studies of Chicano nationalism, see Ernesto Chavez, *¡Mi Raza Primero!* And for a reflection on the meaning of identity imagining among Mexican Americans and Latinos, see Torres, prologue to *Miner's Canary.* For some of the histories of the movement and Chicano history generally written by participants or from a Chicano nationalist perspective, see Acuña, *Occupied America* (1972 ed.); Munoz, *Youth, Identity, Power*; and Navarro, *Mexicano Political Experience.* For a somewhat critical interpretation limited to the Southwest, see Guzman, *Political Socialization.* For a reflective intellectual history of the movement, see Ignacio Garcia, *Chicanismo*; and Ramón Gutiérrez, "Internal Colonialism," "Community, Patriarchy and Individualism," and "Aztlán, Montezuma, and New Mexico." For a policy-oriented analysis, see Marquez, *Constructing Identities.*

7. For information on Mexican immigration, internal migration flows within Texas, and the culture of the region of South Texas, see Arreola, *Tejano South Texas*; Montejano, *Anglos and Mexicans*; McWilliams, *Ill Fares the Land*; and Vargas, *Labor Rights Are Civil Rights.*

8. See, generally, Vargas, *Labor Rights Are Civil Rights.*

9. On migration and labor in the Midwest, see the now-classic Valdés, *Al Norte*; and Senate Subcommittee on Migratory Labor, *Migrant Farm Worker*, which details the routes as well as migrant sending and receiving regions and places this annual migration in geographic and economic context.

10. See also arguments linking communities of artists and writers operating across the Mexican American Midwest/Southwest diaspora in Goldman, "Iconography of Chicano Self-Determination"; Delgadillo, "Exiles, Migrants, Settlers, and Natives"; and Cummings, "Cloth-Wrapped People."

11. For a better understanding of the acculturating aspects of Mexican Americanism and the variety of tactics and limitations of Americanist ideology, see Mario Garcia, *Mexican-Americans*; Allsup, *American G.I. Forum*; David Gutiérrez, *Walls and Mirrors*; Neil Foley, "Becoming Hispanic"; Guglielmo, "Fighting for Caucasian Rights"; and Blanton, "Citizenship Sacrifice."

12. Manuel Martinez, *Countering the Counterculture*; Johnson, *Revolution in Texas.* For earlier manifestations of this tendency, see Christian, "Joining the American Mainstream."

13. On Mexican American citizenship and patriotism during and after World War II, see Naomi Quiñones, "Rosita the Riveter"; Peter Carroll, *Felix Longoria's Wake*; David Gutiérrez, *Walls and Mirrors*; and Mario Garcia, *Mexican Americans.*

14. On the ideology and practice of the Chicano movement, see generally Juan Quiñones, *Chicano Politics*; Munoz, *Youth, Identity, Power*; Montejano, *Quixote's Soldiers*, and Ignacio Garcia, *Chicanismo.*

15. Texas Education Agency, *Texas Public Schools*, 60–64. For a survey of the problems faced by Mexican American schoolchildren in the United States, see Gilbert Gonzales, *Chicano Education*; Manuel, *Education of Children in Texas* and *Educational Problem*; Kibbe, *Latin Americans in Texas*; Blanton, *Strange Career*;

Works, *Texas Educational Survey Report*, 207–16; and Patrick Carroll, "Tejano Living and Educational Conditions."

16. On the limited success of pre–World War II official "Americanization" campaigns in California, see George Sanchez, *Becoming Mexican American*; and Menchaca, *Mexican Outsiders*. On the somewhat different case in Texas, see San Miguel, "Roused from Our Slumbers"; Donato, *Other Struggle for Equal Schools*; and Blanton, *Strange Career*. For research into the importance of schooling for upward mobility, see Thernstrom, *Other Bostonians*; Gleason, "American Identity and Americanization"; Olneck, "Americanization and the Education of Immigrants" and "Immigrants and Education"; Lieberson, *Piece of the Pie*; and Perlman, *Ethnic Differences*.

17. For more information on the concept of "segmented assimilation," see Portes and Zhou, "New Second Generation"; and Portes and Rumbaut, *Legacies*. I contend that for Mexican Americans in Texas, this same sort of process took place well after the "second generation" and overlapped the generations due to the high level of social, educational, and political isolation faced by Mexican-ancestry people in Texas. See also Alma Garcia, *Chicana Feminist Thought*; and Barrera, *Beyond Aztlán*, for discussions of the essence and contradictions of Mexican American and Chicano/a identity.

18. On the GI Forum, see Ramos, *American GI Forum*; and Allsup, *American G.I. Forum*. On citizenship and its requirements, see Macedo, *Liberal Virtues*; Berkowitz, *Virtue and Modern Liberalism*; and Sewell, "Le Citoyen." On the concept of liberal citizenship and what he terms the requirement for "civility" or "decency" between citizens—an understanding and learning process I see as key to an understanding of one's self as a rights-endowed person—see Kymlicka, "Ethnic Associations," as well as *Multicultural Citizenship* and *Politics in the Vernacular*; and Brilliant, *Color Lines*.

19. Perea, "Black and White Binary Paradigm." Jones, in *Selma of the North*, an otherwise exhaustive study of civil rights activism in Milwaukee, almost completely neglects the important role of Latinos in the broader civil rights movement of that city. Exemplary studies of civil rights history in the North, such as Sugrue's ambitious and insightful *Sweet Land of Liberty*, sadly continue to downplay the widespread activism of Latinos in the North and West as the efforts of small, insignificant populations, an omission that distorts the significant role played by Latino activists in Illinois, Ohio, Michigan, New York, and Wisconsin. In the 1960s and 1970s, Tejanos, Mexicans, and Puerto Ricans boycotted schools, marched alongside African Americans, and staged sit-ins that disrupted city and state politics from California to Wisconsin to New York City and altered the nature of politics in these cities. In important correctives, Valdes, *Barrios Norteños*; Johanna Fernandez, "Radicals in the Late 1960s"; and Lorrin Thomas, *Puerto Rican Citizen*, show how Latino politics played an increasingly significant role in northern civil rights efforts.

20. For a discussion of Latino "cultural citizenship," see Flores and Benmayor, introduction to *Latino Cultural Citizenship*; and Rosaldo and Flores, "Evolving

Latino Communities." There are, of course, limits to "cultural" citizenship within a juridical regime of limited rights in the United States, and other countries for that matter, since "cultural" citizenship is by itself no replacement for the rights and responsibilities of "real" citizenship. Some recent scholars have imagined that this might become an alternative to state-centered citizenship regimes, but it is hard to imagine the decline of the state anytime soon. It is my contention that the Mexican American activists and ordinary people in this book wanted both cultural and legal citizenship rights within the United States.

21. For a traditional history of these events, see Shockley, *Chicano Revolt*.

Chapter 1

1. Richard G. Santos, "Daughter Seeks Info. on Father, Ernesto Herrera," *ZCS*, July 17, 2003.

2. Across the Midwest and California, the migration of Tejanos led Latino-serving newspapers to cover Texas news and events, and many of these migrants brought Texas-based organizations, such as LULAC and the AGIF, with them to their new homes in places like California. Pitti, *Devil in Silicon Valley*, 94, 107, 124–30, 166–83; "Start Fund for Gonzalez, Candidate for Senate," *Latin Times* (Chicago), Mar. 10, 1961. For examples of Texas-based organizations that grew across the diaspora, see Allsup, *American G.I. Forum*; and Kreneck, *Mexican American Odyssey*.

3. Grebler et al., *Mexican-American People*, 106. For an insightful look at the strategies, practices, and worldview of those at the upper echelons of LULAC and the GI Forum, see Neil Foley, *Quest for Equality* and "Becoming Hispanic." For more general histories of these organizations, see Allsup, *American G.I. Forum*; and Kaplowitz, *LULAC*. On the long history of race relations in Texas, see Montejano, *Anglos and Mexicans*.

4. Nationally oriented studies with some local coverage include Allsup, *American G.I. Forum*; Mario Garcia, *Mexican Americans*; David Gutiérrez, *Walls and Mirrors*; and Ramos, *American GI Forum*. On the local impact of national changes in Mexican American culture, politics, and labor, see Pitti, *Devil in Silicon Valley*.

5. This pattern of development and social separation is similar to that in Southern California's company- and industry-dominated cities and counties. See, most recently, Gilbert Gonzalez, *Labor and Community*; Menchacha, *Mexican Outsiders*; Matt Garcia, *World of Its Own*; and Alamillo, *Making Lemonade*.

6. Montejano, *Anglos and Mexicans*, 129–45; Arreola, *Tejano South Texas*, 45–63. On border politics and society generally, see Anders, *Boss Rule*; Hinojosa, *Borderlands Town in Transition*; and Zavala County Historical Commission, *Now and Then*.

7. Crystal City Festival Association, "Crystal City Celebrates," 4–7; "Winter Garden District Most Favorable Spot in the U.S. Says San Antonio Paper," *ZCS*, Jan. 4, 1935; June Broadhurst, "From Tents to the Present Tense," and

Ben Jackson, "Townbirth," n.d., Crystal City Vertical File, Center for American History, University of Texas at Austin; Arreola, *Tejano South Texas*, 50–54; Montejano, *Anglos and Mexicans*, 174–78; Pastrano, "Industrial Agriculture," 235–50; Vargas, *Labor Rights Are Civil Rights*, 18–27; Valdes, *Al Norte*, 5 1–60.

8. Douglas Foley, *From Peones to Politicos*. Foley masked the names of the borderland cities under study. His work on the Winter Garden District gives an accurate portrayal of the segregated society of the area and refers to Zavala County as "Aztlan." On segregation and the rationale behind it in the Winter Garden District, see Paul Taylor, *Mexican Labor*. For one of the few available promotional pamphlets, see Missouri Pacific Railroad Company, *South Texas*. On the general history of Zavala County, see Holdsworth, *History of Zavala County*; Tate, "History of Zavala County"; and Zavala County Historical Commission, *Now and Then*.

9. Application to the Department of Housing and Urban Development, pt. 1, p. 1, Office of the City Manager, Crystal City, Tex.

10. Alberto Sanchez, interview; Amalia Aguillar, interview.

11. T. C. Hill, interview. Also, the Chamber of Commerce sponsored "Bargain Festivals" to showcase the "Heart of the Rich Winter Garden Trade" at Crystal City, "the home of Popeye," with games, prizes, and a cakewalk. See *ZCS*, Feb. 27, 1953.

12. Hill, interview. For an idea of the types and number of businesses, see various advertisements, *ZCS*, Jan. 19, 1951, and various listings in the *Crystal City Telephone Directory* (Southwestern Bell Telephone Company, 1958). On the Winter Garden District generally, see Tiller, "Some Economic Aspects of Vegetable Production."

13. Alberto Sanchez, interview; Bernard Leeper, interview; Aguillar, interview. I refer to this neighborhood as either "Mexico Grande" or "barrio" because those interviewed used these terms interchangeably, as well as "Mexico Viejo." The local press referred to this area as the Mexican "colony" or Mexican "section." I chose to use the names given by Mexican American locals.

14. Gloria Cuellar, interview.

15. Larry Goodwyn, "Los Cinco Candidatos," *Texas Observer*, Apr. 18, 1963, 5; *ZCS*, Mar. 13, 1953. The many taverns of the barrio sometimes hosted more than good times and beer drinkers, as was the case on February 21, 1953, when Martin Castaneda shot Dominigo Varcenas with a .22-caliber weapon. The distinction between a barrio, as a large, urban, Mexican and Mexican American district, and a colonia, as a small, rural, Mexican and Mexican American district, seems important only in the largest metropolises of the United States. Crystal City was an urbanized community home to several distinct "Mexican" districts across this city of less than ten thousand people. The area I refer to as the "barrio" is the largest of these neighborhoods and was the primary center of commercial life for residents of Mexican ancestry.

16. See the following in ZCS: Among the many articles on tuberculosis, "Country Nurse Talks Health at Rotary," May 16, 1941; "Chest X-Ray Survey Due," May 17, 1957; "Special Nurse Hired for TB Work," Oct. 11, 1957; "TB Association: Seals on Sale Friday," Nov. 15, 1957; "TB Nurse Needed," July 26, 1957; "Protect Children from TB," May 1, 1959; "TB Committees Listed," May 22, 1959, Feb. 19, 1960; "Chest X-Ray Results Told," Feb. 26, 1960; "TB News," Mar. 25, 1960. On migration see "Aqui y Alla," July 2, Oct. 5, Oct. 15, and Dec. 10, 1954; "Migrants Start Trek North," May 24, 1957; "In Wisconsin: Two Girls Drown," Aug. 16, 1957; "Tribute Paid Garcia Family," Nov. 8, 1957; "En Gratitud," Mar. 11, 1960. On desertion see "District Court Busy," Mar. 25, 1960. The "Aqui y Alla" section of the ZCS tracked the many migrant settlements across the United States.

17. Cuellar, interview.

18. Mercedes Gatica, interview. The Montgomery Ward department store employed Mr. Gatica in its Crystal City catalog store in the 1960s, and he remembered Chicano clerks working during the 1950s. Oscar Cervera, interview, June 21, 1999. According to Cervera, there were limits to the interaction allowed within these Anglo stores, and the Chicano employees knew that they were to defer to Anglos and address them as "Sir" or "Mrs." See also "Rifas de Las Firmas Comerciales," ZCS, Apr. 23, 1954; and "Former Resident Receives College Honor," ZCS, Dec. 20, 1957.

19. Cervera, interview, June 21, 1999. See also advertisements in the ZCS, Jan. 2, 1953.

20. Miguel Delgado, interview, Feb. 20, 1997; Jesus Salas, interview, Feb. 9, 1998.

21. Classifieds, ZCS, Jan. 30, 1953.

22. ZCS, Feb. 6, 1953.

23. Aguillar, interview.

24. Arturo Gonzalez, interview.

25. Cervera, interview; José Gutiérrez, Making of a Chicano Militant, 34–35; Rivera, Earth Did Not Part (1992; all citations are to this edition, unless otherwise noted.), 92–96. Cervera, Gutiérrez, and Rivera, all former residents of Crystal City, each clearly mark out the lines of segregation that at an early age separated adolescent relations among Anglos and Chicanos.

26. For a fictional account of how difficult Mexican Americans found navigating the public space of the market, see Rivera, Earth Did Not Part, 130–34.

27. Francisco Rodriguez, interview, July 29, 2000. The "De Aquí and De Allá" appeared in the Feb. 27, 1953, edition of the ZCS as a counterpart to the "Here and There" section in the main paper. Written in Spanish by Mrs. Irene Trevino, this section of the paper reported on births, deaths, and marital news, as well as religious and business events. For news on local Mexican American military personnel wounded in Korea, see, for example, ZCS, Feb. 16 and Mar. 2, 1951.

28. José Gutiérrez, Making of a Chicano Militant, 24. In his autobiography, Gutiérrez said that it was "illegal" to join such groups. It is doubtful that it was

illegal to join, but within the local segregated social system it appears that Anglos considered few Chicanos worthy of membership.

29. Zavala County Historical Commission, *Now and Then*, 85; Shockley, *Chicano Revolt*, 228.

30. Zavala County Historical Commission, *Now and Then*, 83–84; Rubel, *Across the Tracks*; Ozzie Simmons, "Anglo-Americans and Mexican-Americans," 152. Rubel and Simmons found exceptions to strict segregation in which elite Mexican Americans maintained power in several counties along the Mexican border with the United States.

31. "Church News: Sacred Heart Church," *ZCS*, May 14, 1954. See also the following in *ZCS*: "Angela Rubio Crowned 1954 GI Forum Queen," May 28, 1954; "Junta Del Ladies Auxiliary Club," July 2, 1954; "Reunion de la Ladies Aux. Club," July 23, 1954; "Study Club Comulgo El Domingo," Aug. 6, 1954; "Study Club Principiara Nuevo Proyecto," Aug. 26, 1954; "Study Club Tuvo Baile," Aug. 27, 1954; "La Study Club Tiene Baile" and "Los Christophers van a la Convención," Oct. 1, 1954; "New Woman's Club Formed," Apr. 5, 1957; "C.W.C. to Sponsor Bazaar Next Sunday," July 17, 1959; "Miss Rodriguez Elected Miss KBEN" and "Girls Club Observes Anniversary," Apr. 8, 1960; "Miss Rodriguez New C.W.C. Prexy [sic]," Mar. 18, 1960.

32. The Del Monte Corporation had originally established its operations in Crystal City as the California Packing Corporation. Locals, even after the shift to the Del Monte brand, referred to the plant as "Cal-Pack." Tiller, *Texas Winter Garden*, 76; "4-15-52 Calpak produced 1 Millionth Can of Spinach" in "1952 Was an Average Year, Files Reveal," *ZCS*, Jan. 2, 1953; "Millionth Can of Spinach Canned," *ZCS*, Mar. 20, 1953.

33. See Ngai, "Braceros."

34. Jesus Salas, interview, Feb. 9, 1998; Tiller, *Texas Winter Garden*, 76.

35. Santos, "The Old México Grande of Crystal City," *ZCS*, June 29, 2006; Rosa Martinez, interview. All that remained of these taverns in 1997 were old signs, raised bar sections, and the crumbling assembly pieces of floor-mounted barstools that sat on concrete slab foundations overlaid with colored ceramic tiles. In most cases, the brick or sheet metal walls had long disappeared, but some buildings still displayed fading painted tavern signs and cracked tile floors. In Southern California, the influx of braceros had the same impact on the city of Santa Paula, which experienced a boom as the Mexican section catered to the bracero trade. See Menchaca, *Mexican Outsiders*, 97–99.

36. Zavala County Judge's Criminal Docket Book 5:119, 200. On July 26, 1954, the court found Adolfo De Leon guilty of selling beer on election day and fined him one hundred dollars. On December 22, 1958, the court fined Manuel Sambuano one hundred dollars and costs for selling beer during prohibited hours. These prohibited hours for beer sales and sales to minors were quite common. For an interesting look at women and the Texas-Mexican cantina, see Villarreal, "Cantantes y Cantineras."

37. See Zavala County Criminal Docket Book 5–6 (Dec. 1952–Jan. 1964). For many of these cases in the middle 1950s, the court fined citizens between one and twenty dollars and deported the aliens for minor violations. In an extreme case, the court found Ignacio Garcia guilty of aggravated assault upon José Gonzales. The court sentenced Garcia, an alien, to time in jail plus an additional sixty days in jail and then deported him. See Docket Book 6:38. It does not appear from the docket book that the tension between braceros and citizens was unusually high, since the fight pattern indicated that Mexican-ancestry aliens and citizens often fought.

38. Miguel Delgado, interview, Feb. 4, 1997; José Gutiérrez, *Making of a Chicano Militant*, 21–22. The bracero trade created an opportunity for Delgado's mother, who operated a tavern in Mexico Grande to earn enough money to support her family.

39. José Gutiérrez, *Making of a Chicano Militant*, 20; "Cal Pak Farm Has Tour," *ZCS*, Oct. 18, 1957; "The Barker," *ZCS*, Mar. 13, 1959.

40. José Gutiérrez, *Making of a Chicano Militant*, 20. For a discussion of opposition to the Bracero Program, see Allsup, *American G.I. Forum*; and American G.I. Forum of Texas and Texas State Federation of Labor, *What Price Wetbacks?* Although the preceding title speaks of "wetbacks," there is coverage of some of the worst living conditions in the Winter Garden. The broader policy of labor importation for this period is examined in Copp, *"Wetbacks" and Braceros*.

41. See discussion of the tensions between Mexican Americans and braceros in Matt Garcia, *World of Its Own*, 160–61. For good discussions of the politics and economic impact of the Bracero Program, see Menchaca, *Mexican Outsiders*, 90–92, and Martin, Abella, and Kuptsch, *Managing Labor Migration*, 94–95.

42. Oropeza, *¡Raza Sí! ¡Guerra No!* 29. In fact, Oropeza shows the many elements of a highly masculine gendered postwar patriotism that grew from the wartime experiences of Mexican American men in the armed forces. She also highlights the ways the military experience had brought them into intercultural and interethnic relations, where they were treated as the equals of other ethnics, while African Americans were still segregated. In the 1950s, GI Forum members perhaps included Korean War veterans who may have served in the rapidly desegregating military after 1948. For minority and Mexican American expectations, as well as the politics and impact of the desegregation effort in a Cold War context, see Takaki, *Double Victory*; and Dudziak, *Cold War Civil Rights*, 85–87. More generally on the role of militarism in American society before and after World War II, see Sherry, *In the Shadow of War*.

43. For more on what they term "Latino cultural citizenship," see Flores and Benmayor, introduction to *Latino Cultural Citizenship*; and Rosaldo and Flores, "Evolving Latino Communities."

44. Geraldo Saldana, interview. Saldana, local secretary of the Crystal City American G.I. Forum (AGIF), now in his early nineties and living in San Antonio, Texas, would speak for just a few minutes, but he did say that "many of the

local Anglos considered our organization [AGIF] a subversive group, because they didn't understand what we were doing."

45. For a compelling example of veterans' activism after World War II as a grassroots local struggle that operated with the same intent yet without much financial or other support from the National Association for the Advancement of Colored People (NAACP), see Dittmer, *Local People*. More grassroots research of this sort needs to be done to fully explore the extent to which Mexican American activists in the 1950s and early 1960s embraced the ideologies of the leadership of organizations like the GI Forum, the League of United Latin-American Citizens (LULAC), or the Community Service Organization (CSO) or made their own movements at the local level. On Americanism, see the revised edition of Gerstle, *Working-Class Americanism*. Political sociologists argue that "vigorous citizenship" often emerges out of grassroots activism and social movements that make demands on the state at its various levels for an active-participatory democracy. See Bellah et al., *Habits of the Heart*, 212.

46. José Angel Gutiérrez, who remembered Muñoz as a boy, provided the description of him. In particular, Gutiérrez remembered his large policy book and uncommon necktie. Interview, Sept. 26, 2003.

47. Muñoz to Barden, Aug. 18, 1951, folder 147.9, Dr. Hector Perez Garcia Papers, Special Collections, Bell Library, Texas A&M University–Corpus Christi; "E. C. Muñoz Asistió a Junta en Del Rió," *ZCS*, July 16, 1954.

48. See David Gutiérrez, "Migration," 494. As Gutiérrez points out in reference to the interwar period, some went about "consciously cultivating a primary political identification as 'Americans.'" My point here is that unlike the period between the wars, the 1950s reveals a more sustained engagement with life outside the barrio or colonia, especially on the part of returning veterans and later youth. On the theory of the "third space," see Bhabha, *Location of Culture*. The key early works utilizing various forms of barrioization theory (closely related to the ghettoization theory of Kenneth Kusmer and others) are Camarillo, *Chicanos in a Changing Society*; Del Castillo, *Los Angeles Barrio*; Romo, *East Los Angeles*; and Ríos-Bustamante and Castillo, *Illustrated History*.

49. I borrow this term from Werbner and Yuval-Davis (introduction to *Women, Citizenship, and Difference*), who introduce the concept of an "aspirational politics" of citizenship among women political actors. The same aspirational focus defined the politics of Mexican Americans, in that they sought a future in which the ideals of citizenship and American freedom would be available in South Texas. On the long history of school desegregation in Texas, see San Miguel, *"Let All of Them Take Heed."*

50. Lyndon B. Johnson, "Your Senator Reports," *ZCS*, May 14, 1954.

51. Pycior, "Henry B. Gonzales," 299–302.

52. Tushnet, *Making Civil Rights Law*, 34; Ramos, *American GI Forum*, 19–31; Blanton, "George I. Sanchez," 588. On the AGIF more generally, see Allsup, *American G.I. Forum*.

53. Eduardo Idar to E. C. Muñoz, Aug. 25, 1953, loc. 141.9, Dr. Hector Perez Garcia Papers, Special Collections, Mary and Jeff Bell Library, Texas A&M University–Corpus Christi. Eduardo Idar Jr. was the son of the LULAC founder and part of an important Tejano family. For more on the Idar family, see Meier and Gutierrez, *Mexican American Civil Rights Movement*, 111–13.

54. Idar to Muñoz, Aug. 30, 1953, loc. 141.4, Garcia Papers.

55. "Petition with Signatures," Aug. 3, 1956, loc. 56.14, Garcia Papers. This petition demanding the removal of braceros claimed to represent "American citizens of Mexican origin."

56. Idar to Hipolito Martinez, Mar. 3, 1952, and Idar [unsigned] to Gus Garcia, Mar. 17, 1952, loc. 141.12, Garcia Papers. Idar wrote Martinez apologizing and promising that he did not "want them to think the Forum is letting them down." In the letter to Garcia, Idar complained that Garcia's failure to file an appeal in a case in Carrizo Springs led the AGIF to lose "a great amount of prestige not only in Asherton, but in Carrizo Springs, Crystal City, and even as far away as Eagle Pass, and Cotulla." He reminded Garcia that accomplishments on the state and national level are important but those local matters, if they "trip up," can cause severe harm.

57. See the following in *ZCS*: "Agua en el Cemetario," June 1, 1951; "GI Forum Local Enviara Delegados a Houston," July 2, 1954; "Miss Galvan Represents Crystal City as Queen of American GI Forum," July 4, 1951; "American GI Forum Opening Austin Office," Oct. 26, 1951; "GI Forum Sponsors Inauguration of New City Patio," May 21, 1954; and "El Club GI Forum Hace Proyecto Para Ayudar La P.T.A.," July 30, 1954.

58. "Mexican Chamber Sponsors Free Circus," Mar. 22, 1957; "Mexican Chamber: Street Sweeper Needed," July 5, 1957; "Mexican Chamber Gives Scholarship," June 5, 1959, all in *ZCS*.

59. Post and Smith, "Clergy," 39–40. Other organizations such as the Masons had segregated lodges in Crystal City and, in the case of the Ignacio Zaragosa Lodge no. 5, had meetings with fellow Masons from Piedras Negras, Mexico, and elsewhere. There is no record of these groups playing a role in politics. "Zaragosa Lodge Has Meeting," Apr. 17, 1959; "Zaragosa Lodge Fetes Visitors," May 1, 1959, both in *ZCS*.

60. Douglas Foley, "Transition of Early South Texas," 60–61. On the 1953 pool scandal, which also seems to have involved the AGIF, see Idar to Mr. W. P. Brennan, Acting Mayor, City of Crystal City, July 18, 1953, and Idar to the Mayor, Municipal Building, Crystal City, Texas, June 25, 1953, both in Zavala County Discrimination File, Texas Good Neighbor Commission, Records, 1943–87, Archives Division, Texas State Library, Austin.

61. Hector P. Garcia to E. C. Muñoz, Feb. 23, 1951, loc. 147.11, Garcia Papers.

62. "An Unfortunate Affair" (editorial), *ZCS*, Mar. 30, 1951.

63. Although no copy of the entire original letter exists, those opposed to its distribution published portions of it in English and Spanish in an adver-

tisement. "Advertisement: Has There Been a Defamation of the Dead?" *ZCS*, Mar. 30, 1951.

64. "An Unfortunate Affair" (editorial), *ZCS*, Mar. 30, 1951.

65. "Raymundo Astran," *ZCS*, Mar. 2, 1951; "If One of Us Should Not Return," *ZCS*, Apr. 14, 1951.

66. "Anuncio Politico," *ZCS*, Apr. 23, 1954. In the "El Noticiero" section of the paper, G. C. "Bodee" Daugherty announced his candidacy for sheriff and solicited the vote of Latin Americans by promising to promote an interest in "la raza," its business, and families, and to assist the church. For other candidate appeals in Spanish, see various political advertisements for the sheriff's race in *ZCS*, July 23, 1954. E. B. English, the incumbent, won, as reported in "1794 Votes Cast in Primary Election," *ZCS*, July 30, 1954. Winning the Democratic primary meant winning the election in South Texas.

67. For information on the Veterans' Land Board scandal, see Cox, "Land Commissioner Bascom Giles."

68. "Land Probe Here," *ZCS*, Jan. 21, 1955.

69. "Five Sued on Land Deals," Feb. 4, 1955; "Mayor Sued," Feb. 18, 1955; "Judge Sued," Feb. 25, 1955; "Attorney General's Office Will Help Prosecute Violators of Veterans' Land Act," Mar. 4, 1955; "Mayor Offers to Repay State," Mar. 11, 1955; "State Takes Civil Depositions," Apr. 1, 1955; "Shepperd Lists Land Actions," Apr. 1, 1955, all in *ZCS*.

70. Jose and Marta M. Ledesma, interview. Ledesma and his family were forced to leave behind the new ranch home they had recently purchased in the primarily Anglo section of Crystal City.

71. Shockley, *Chicano Revolt*, 19; Walter Smith, "Mexicano Resistance," 162–63; "School Districts Set Elections," *ZCS*, Mar. 11, 1960. On the similar practice of benevolent or aspirational citizenship among African Americans and women in antebellum America, see Ryan, *Grammar of Good Intentions*. It is also worth noting that these activists were not making overt public claims for what Flores and Benmayor have defined as "cultural citizenship," but rather to public participation within the existing framework of liberal citizenship in the postwar era. See Flores and Benmayor, *Latino Cultural Citizenship*.

72. *ZCS*, Apr. 8, 1960; Crystal City Independent School District, School Board Minutes, Apr. 4, 1960, Crystal City, Tex. The four top vote getters, all Anglo incumbents, were elected; E. C. Munoz was not. There were several other write-in votes for Spanish-surnamed residents.

73. Walter Smith, "Mexicano Resistance," 163.

74. Biographical information taken from Handbook of Texas Online, s.v. "Aldrete, Cristóbal (1924–1991)," ⟨http://www.tsha.utexas.edu/handbook/online/articles/AA/falwl.html⟩ (accessed July 2, 2006).

75. Crystal City ISD, School Board Minutes, July 11, 1960.

76. Ibid., May 9, 1960, and July 14, 1960. At the May 9 meeting, the school board considered closing the De Zavala School, one of two "Mexican" schools

in Crystal City. At the July 14 meeting, the board did away with the language-specific elementary schools and converted these to "migrant" schools.

77. Ibid., Aug. 8, 1960.

Chapter 2

1. One such example of this encounter is profiled in the front-page story "Essay Winners Told," ZCS, Feb. 27, 1959. The winning essay, written by a Mexican American high school student, discussed the link between citizenship, civic duty, and conservation.

2. Texas Education Agency, "Report of Pupils," 4–6; U.S. Congress, Hearings before the Special Subcommittee on Bilingual Education of the Committee on Labor and Public Welfare, United States Senate, Ninetieth Congress, First Session on S. 428, part 2, June 24 and July 21, 1967 (Washington: U.S. Government Printing Office, 1967), 669–81. More generally, see Manuel, Education of Children in Texas; and Grebler, Moore, and Guzman, Mexican-American People, 142–55.

3. On the growth of Spanish-surnamed students in Texas schools, see Texas Education Agency, "Report of Pupils." For an expansion of the theory of "game play" among high school social groups, see Ortner, New Jersey Dreaming, 112. On the way Mexican American majorities altered local conditions in the school, see Post and Smith, "Clergy." On the way oppositional politics among African Americans has similarly sought to find a place within and sometimes disrupt preexisting space and institutions, see Kelley, Race Rebels.

4. On the international dimensions of education policy in Texas and at the federal level, see Kibbe, Latin Americans in Texas; San Miguel, "Let All of Them Take Heed," 91–103; Manuel, "Progress in Inter-American Education"; Little, "Texas Good Neighbor Commission"; and Kingrea, First Ten Years.

5. There is a long history of legal contestation over the issue of Mexican American school segregation. For this history and related cases, see Rangel and Alcala, "Project Report"; and Wilson, "Brown over 'Other White.'" See also Jesus Salvatierra v. Inhabitants of Del Rio Independent School District, 33 S.W.2d 790 (Tex. Civ. App. 1930). On pedagogical segregation, see Blanton, Bilingual Education, 70–71, 112–13. See also Westminster School District v. Mendez, 161 F.2d 774 (9th Cir., 1947). The segregation of Mexican-ancestry "migrants" did not become the subject of litigation, but it became a political issue in the late 1960s when federal funding of migrant education programs increased. Research studies showed that districts, when they provided any special programs at all, often continued to segregate migrant from nonmigrant students. See "Migrant Classes Called Stinted," NYT, Mar. 20, 1971.

6. See Texas Education Agency, Texas Public Schools, 60–64; Gilmer-Aikin Committee on Education, To Have What We Must; and Samford, "Gilmer-Aikin Committee."

7. Walter Smith, "Mexicano Resistance," 174–76. The majority of the school district budget went to the maintenance and expansion of school facilities serving Anglo students. Where Mexican American students were concerned, minimal upkeep of the several rundown "Mexican" elementary schools was the rule, and few of these students were expected to attend the high school, which could not adequately hold them if they did.

8. Walter Smith, "Mexicano Resistance," 151. On the assimilation policies of Texas, see Thomas Simmons, "Citizen Factories."

9. Texas Education Agency, "Report of Pupils," 3; Harding, "Migrant Pupils"; Mellenbruch, "Let's Teach Spanish"; Grimm, "Texas History Seldom Told"; Hill and Vickers, "Sorry, No Hablo Español"; Poulos, "They Learn Basic English."

10. Severita Lara De La Fuente, interview; Trujillo, "Community Empowerment," 132; Walter Smith, "Mexicano Resistance," 151.

11. Shockley, *Chicano Revolt*, 9; De La Fuente, interview.

12. Paul Taylor, *Mexican Labor: Dimmit County*, 385. This study features the establishment of this type of school in Dimmit County, which borders on Zavala County. This school was similar in curricular focus to the Mexican government's "Mexicanization" school efforts, examined in George Sanchez, *Becoming Mexican American*, 116–18.

13. "Doña Hermania L. Sifuentes—Wife, Mother, Teacher," ZCS, Sept. 30, 1982; Jesus Salas, interviews, July 27, 1992, and Feb. 9, 1998; Francisco Rodriguez, interview, July 25, 1998; Jose Herrera, interview; José Gutiérrez, *Making of a Chicano Militant*, 46; Trujillo, "Community Empowerment," 132–34.

14. Francisco Rodriguez, interview, July 29, 2000.

15. Gutiérrez, interview, Apr. 19, 1995; Francisco Rodriguez, interview, July 25, 1998; Jesus Salas, interview, July 27, 1992. Similar communities and schools took shape in California. For example, see the discussion of similar barrio schools in Matt Garcia, *World of Its Own*, 72–73.

16. See Kreneck, *Mexican American Odyssey*; San Miguel, *"Let All of Them Take Heed"*; "Doña Hermania L. Sifuentes—Wife, Mother, Teacher," ZCS, Sept. 30, 1982; and Francisco Rodriguez, interview, July 25, 1998. There was also another such school run by Suzy Salazar. For a similar primer school example, see Manuel, *Spanish-Speaking Children*, 84; and Poulos, "They Learn Basic English."

17. Pridgen, "Survey and Proposed Plan," 35; Alway, *Will You Make a School?*; Grebler, Moore, and Guzman, *Mexican-American People*, 18, 152. At the local level, overcrowding had been an issue since the 1930s, and across Texas low levels of post-elementary education for Mexican Americans was the norm.

18. José Gutiérrez, *Making of a Chicano Militant*, 24. Some scholars consider this form of segregation another element of the "internal colonialism" applied to Mexican Americans in the southwestern states. On internal colonialism generally, see Blauner, *Racial Oppression in America*; Acuña, *Occupied America* (1972 ed.); and Moore, "Colonialism."

19. Crystal City Independent School District, School Board Minutes, Aug. 30, 1948, and Aug. 1, 1955, Crystal City, Tex. With growing pressure to end segrega-

tion based on race, the school district began a program of open transfer that allowed those Mexican Americans selected by Anglo administrators entry into the traditionally Anglo schools. Shockley, *Chicano Revolt*, 20.

20. Quoted in Trujillo, "Community Empowerment," 134; Walter Smith, "Mexicano Resistance," 185. It appears that the number of "tracks" fluctuated with the number of Mexican Americans in each grade.

21. Ortner, *New Jersey Dreaming*, 92. See also her more extended discussion of high school society and categories in "Burned like a Tattoo."

22. Ortner, *New Jersey Dreaming*, 116, 176. For information on the greater participation rates of Mexican Americans in high school activities prior to the Los Cinco revolt of 1963, and the student activism of 1969, see the *Crystal City High School Javelin*, 1958–69. For some years, the only information available was the graduation photos that hang in the high school lobby. These indicate that after 1955, Mexican American youth came to dominate the overall school population. Class photos before the 1950s show the occasional Mexican American graduate yet begin to show, as Smith has pointed out, an increase each year in Mexican American students' enrollment, if not graduation, beginning in the 1940s.

23. Salas, interview, Feb. 9, 1998; Oscar Cervera, interview, June 21, 1999; Walter Smith, "Mexicano Resistance," 195.

24. On Texas high school life, see Douglas Foley, *Learning Capitalist Culture*; Foley, Mota, and Lozano, *Early South Texas Society*; and Smith and Foley, *Transition of Multiethnic Schooling*. Foley and his many graduate students did several studies of South Texas school, religious, and political life in the early 1970s, and much of this field research captures everyday life and memory in the Winter Garden District and the Rio Grande Valley.

25. Walter Smith, "Mexicano Resistance," 177–79. "Bloc voting" was a common practice among Mexican American youth after 1955. Smith documents a teacher's call for "proper democratic behavior" aimed at breaking up the growing trend toward bloc voting.

26. "Homecoming," in Zavala County Historical Commission, *Now and Then*, 66.

27. "1957 Graduates: Crystal City High School," ZCS, May 24, 1957; Miguel Delgado, interview, Feb. 10, 1997; Francisco Rodriguez, interview, July 29, 2000; "Literary Events: School Wins Trophy," ZCS, Apr. 24, 1959; "The Crystal City Javelin Band Presents Spring Concert," ZCS, May 15, 1959.

28. Teacher-selected honorees, including "Most Beautiful" and "Most Representative," continued to be Anglos through the late 1960s. Post discusses this disturbing practice across the several Winter Garden counties in "Ethnic Competition," 183.

29. Francisco Rodriguez, interview, July 29, 2000; José Gutiérrez, *Making of a Chicano Militant*, 47; *Crystal City High School Javelin*, 1958–62. See also the early success of various Mexican American athletes reported in the county newspaper, e.g., "Eagle Pass Plays Javelins Tonight," ZCS, Jan. 26, 1951, detailing the success of Rubin Rodriguez, who made two free throws to win the game against rival Eagle Pass for the varsity basketball team, or "A"-team.

30. "Introducing New Teachers," *ZCS*, Oct. 18, 1957. Rivera joined Mary Medellin, a Crystal City graduate, as a Spanish and physical education teacher.

31. Francisco Rodriguez, interview, July 29, 2000; Cervera, interview, June 21, 1999; "Javelins Win Five," *ZCS*, Mar. 22, 1957; "Javs Still Win," *ZCS*, Apr. 5, 1957; "Javelins Win 6–0" and "Crystal High Lights," *ZCS*, Nov. 1, 1957; "Javs Lead District" and "District Track Meet," *ZCS*, Apr. 24, 1959; "Javelins Are District Champs," *ZCS*, May 8, 1959. Outside the school system, Little League baseball likewise highlighted teams sponsored by local businesses that featured Mexican American players on nearly every team. It appears that Little League integrated before the schools and prepared players for the school teams. See Little League team photos in *ZCS*, July 2 and 16, 1954.

32. "Five Girls Named Cheer Leaders," *ZCS*, Apr. 19, 1957; "Photo: Crystal City High School Marching Band," *ZCS*, Sept. 6, 1957; *Crystal City High School Javelin*, 1958–69; "Cheer Leader Tryouts Held," *ZCS*, May 1, 1959. It must be remembered that cheer, twirl, and other such squads were important activities for high school girls in the decades before girls' sports teams.

33. "Homemakers Hold Garment Review," *ZCS*, May 21, 1954; "La Booster Club Local Presentara 'Prevista de Modas,'" *ZCS*, Aug. 6, 1954; "HE Classes Have Fashion Show," *ZCS*, May 29, 1959.

34. Crystal City High School Student Council (Hector Nevarez, president) to Mr. R. C. Tate, Superintendent, and the Board of Trustees, Crystal City Independent School District, School Board Minutes, Oct. 12, 1959.

35. Francisco Rodriguez, interview, July 29, 2000. For example, according to Rodriguez, high school English remained a difficult subject for many Mexican American students, yet the school mainstreamed them with the Anglo students. Alternatively, when Anglos took Spanish class, the school separated Mexican Americans into "native" speaking sections and allowed Anglos to attend segregated introductory sections.

36. Jesus Salas, interview, Feb. 9, 1998. In elections, Mexican American students were making headway in the mid-1950s. For the 1957–58 school years, Mexican American class presidents and officers predominated for freshmen, sophomores, and juniors. The senior class president was an Anglo, yet Mexican Americans held all other posts. "Crystal High Lights," *ZCS*, Oct. 11, 1957.

37. Larry Goodwyn, "Los Cinco Candidatos," *Austin Observer*, Apr. 18, 1963; Shockley, *Chicano Revolt*, 37; José Gutiérrez, *Making of a Chicano Militant*, 51.

38. Goodwyn, "Los Cinco Candidatos."

39. Francisco Rodriguez, interview, July 25, 1998. Francisco Rodriguez, a schoolmate who had attended elementary, middle, and high school with both José Angel Gutiérrez and Jesus Salas, two prominent future activists, was the emcee that night in charge of making sure the speakers were on the stage on schedule. He remembered that Cornejo saw himself as a messianic character and preferred to enter the stage from the crowd to symbolize his role as a man of the people. This dramatic entry seemed a bit much to Rodriguez, who was trying to keep the speeches on schedule, and it hinted at problems to come.

40. On the support provided by the Teamsters and PASSO, as well as controversies related to this support, see "Both Crystal City Slates Predict Election Victory," *San Antonio Express*, Mar. 27, 1963; "S. A. Group Deep in Crystal City Race," *San Antonio Express*, Mar. 29, 1963; Brown, "Crystal City: Symbol of Hope" and "Crystal City: New City Council"; "Crystal City Gave PASO Pilot Project It Needed," *Dallas Morning News*, May 7, 1963; "Shock Waves from Popeye Land," *Texas Observer*, May 16, 1963, 6–7; "A Comment," *Texas Observer*, Apr. 18, 1963, 10; Hart Stilwell, "Another Comment," *Texas Observer*, May 16, 1963, 8. My focus is on student activism, yet the support of the Teamsters and PASSO cannot be overstated. In March 1963, the federal government entered the voting rights fray to protect the rights of African American voters in Greenwood, Mississippi, as it dispatched agents to Crystal City to investigate claims of racial discrimination and voter harassment.

41. Two labor historians, Vicki Ruiz and Thomas Dublin, demonstrated the close connection between laboring in industrial settings and the continued maintenance of community and migrant networks, the creation of new workplace communities, and the transformation of these to suit a variety of new purposes. See Ruiz, *Cannery Women, Cannery Lives*, xvi, xviii, 32; and Dublin, *Women at Work*, 41–48.

42. Shockley, *Chicano Revolt*, 24–25; Navarro, *Cristal Experiment*, 26.

43. Juan Cornejo, interview; Brown, "Crystal City," 16; Shockley, *Chicano Revolt*, 24–25; "Antagonism Splits Texas City," *NYT*, Apr. 14, 1963; Navarro, *Cristal Experiment*, 26. Cornejo contested his labeling by Shockley as a "*jefe*" and rather viewed himself as a committed trade unionist who "had been organizing . . . politically, within the working class" before the rise of activity in 1963. Cornejo, interview.

44. On Del Monte Corporation, see Braznell, *California's Finest*; and Eames and Landis, *Business of Feeding People*. On Del Monte's operations in Crystal City, see U.S. Senate, Committee on Commerce, *Federal Trade Commission Oversight*, 104–5.

45. Carlos Conde, "Crystal City Gave PASO Pilot Project It Needed," *Dallas Morning News*, May 7, 1963. On Viva Kennedy and PASSO, see generally Ignacio Garcia, *Viva Kennedy*; and "Mayor Denies Charges," *ZCS*, Mar. 29, 1963.

46. Delgado, "Fraternization," 5; José Gutiérrez, *Making of a Chicano Militant*, 41–42.

47. José Gutiérrez, *Making of a Chicano Militant*, 36–39; Delgado, "Fraternization," 6.

48. José Angel Gutiérrez, videotaped interview, in *Chicano!: History of the Mexican American Civil Rights Movement*, vol. 4, *Fighting for Political Power* (Los Angeles: National Latino Communications Center, NLCC Educational Media, 1996); José Gutiérrez, *Making of a Chicano Militant*, 36–39.

49. Albert Peña Jr., interview by José Gutiérrez, July 2, 1996, CMAS 15, TVOH.

50. José Gutiérrez, interview, Apr. 19, 1995; Ezequiel Guzman, interview; "How Mexicans Swept an Election in a Texas Town," *National Observer*, Apr. 4, 1963.

51. José Angel Gutiérrez's comments taken from interview with Joaquin Jackson by José Angel Gutiérrez, Lawrence Clayton, and Susan Allen, Aug. 1, 1996, transcript, p. 4, TVOH.

52. Guzman, interview.

53. Francisco Rodriguez, interview, July 29, 2000.

54. José Gutiérrez, *Making of a Chicano Militant*, 36.

55. Guzman, interview.

56. Delgado, "Fraternization," 5.

57. Francisco Rodriguez, interview, July 29, 2000. I replaced his words with the term "teenagers" in this quote. He said, "We were only seventeen," when in fact most of the Crystal City high school class of 1962, including Mr. Rodriguez, was eighteen. It apparently was a slip of the tongue. José Gutiérrez, *Making of a Chicano Militant*, 35–42.

58. Shockley, "Crystal City, Texas," 476, and *Chicano Revolt*, 26; Navarro, *Cristal Experiment*, 31.

59. Cornejo, interview; Shockley, "Crystal City, Texas," 66.

60. *Dallas Morning News*, July 28, 1965.

61. "Mexican Chamber Says 'No Politics,'" *ZCS*, Mar. 29, 1963.

62. "The Struggle for P.A.S.O.," *Texas Observer*, June 14, 1963, 5; "Attn: Walsh (With Crystal City)," Zavala County Folder, John B. Connally Papers, Lyndon Baines Johnson Presidential Library, Austin, Tex. The lack of education among Los Cinco continued to be an issue even after the election. Since Juan Cornejo had been central to the effort, it is no surprise that he was one of the candidates. Los Cinco were Juan Cornejo, a third-grade dropout and veteran who had completed some remedial education in the military; Manuel Maldonado, a clerk at a local hardware store with a fourth-grade education; Antonio Cardenas, an oilfield worker, truck driver, and migrant with a fourth-grade education; Reynaldo Mendoza, a barrio photographer and migrant who completed ninth grade; and Mario Hernandez, a fledgling real estate salesman known for flashy suits with a tenth-grade education.

63. Shockley, *Chicano Revolt*, 27–28; "Revolt in Texas," *WSJ*, Sept. 9, 1963.

64. "Interest High in Council Race," *ZCS*, Mar. 29, 1963.

65. See various campaign advertisements in the *ZCS*, Mar. 29, 1963; and Shockley, *Chicano Revolt*, 21–34.

66. On Ranger captain Allee, see *Handbook of Texas Online*, s.v. "Allee, Alfred Young," ⟨http://www.tsha.utexas.edu/handbook/online/articles/AA/fal97.html⟩ (accessed July 19, 2006); Samora, Bernal, and Peña, *Gunpowder Justice*; De la Garza, *Law for the Lion*; O. W. Nolen to John Connally, May 1, 1963, Zavala County File, Connally Papers; Jackson and Wilkinson, *One Ranger*.

67. Albert Peña Jr., interview by José Angel Gutiérrez, July 2, 1996, CMAS 15, TVOH.

68. José Gutiérrez, *Making of a Chicano Militant*, 43–44, 53–57; "Mayor Denies Charges," *ZCS*, Mar. 29, 1963.

69. Shockley, *Chicano Revolt*, 38; U.S. Senate, Committee on Commerce, *Federal Trade Commission Oversight*, 104–5.

70. "Latin Ticket Wins Council Race," *ZCS*, Apr. 5, 1963; "New Council Takes Office Apr. 16," *ZCS*, Apr. 5, 1963; Cuellar, "Social and Political History," 59; *Texas Observer*, Apr. 18, 1963, 7.

71. Crystal City resident H. L. Hackey, quoted in "Antagonism Splits Texas City," *NYT*, Apr. 14, 1963; M. Dale Barker, "The Barker," *ZCS*, Apr. 12, 1963; "Crystal City in TIME," *ZCS*, Apr. 12, 1963.

72. Irl Taylor to John B. Connally, Apr. 30, 1963, Connally Papers.

73. "Tom Allee to WOAI-TV," letter published in the *ZCS*, Apr. 12, 1963.

74. Navarro, *Cristal Experiment*, 38–39; "Council-Elect Says 'Business as Usual' Is Plan," *ZCS*, Apr. 12, 1963.

75. "Texas Rangers Hit by 'Pistol Rule' Charge," *LAT*, May 3, 1963; "Rangers Patrol Texas Community," *NYT*, May 5, 1963.

76. "Local Group Asks That Rangers Stay," *ZCS*, May 3, 1963.

77. Among the many Ranger-sympathetic letters, see Mexican Chamber of Commerce (Frank Guajardo, president) to John Connally, Apr. 29, 1963; Crystal City Chamber of Commerce (Bill Briscoe, president) to Connally, Apr. 29, 1963; Irl Taylor to Connally, Apr. 30, 1963; Lloyd E. Goff Sr. to Connally (handwritten letter), May 3, 1963; Jerry Greene to Connally (telegram), May 8, 1963, all in Zavala County Folder, Connally Papers.

78. "New Councilmen Take Office," *ZCS*, Apr. 19, 1963.

79. "Races: Revolt of the Mexicans," *Time*, Apr. 12, 1963, 25; "The Anglo Minority," *Newsweek*, Apr. 29, 1963, 26; "The Texas Giant Awakens," *Look*, Oct. 6, 1963, 71–75.

80. Dr. J. A. Garcia, Dr. Hector Garcia, and Dr. Oleo Garcia to John Connally, May 1, 1963, Zavala County Folder, Connally Papers.

81. George I. Sanchez to John Connally, May 2, 1963, Zavala County Folder, Connally Papers.

82. Tomas M. Rodriguez to John Connally, Apr. 30, 1963, Zavala County Folder, Connally Papers.

83. John Connally to Tomas M. Rodriguez, Apr. 30, 1963, Zavala County Folder, Connally Papers.

84. Dick Meskill, "In the Shadow of San Fernando," *Alamo Messenger* (San Antonio), Apr. 12 and 19, 1963.

85. Ibid., May 3 and 10, 1963.

86. "Crystal City Expected to Affect More Elections," *Dallas Morning News*, May 9, 1963; "Dissenting Passo Group Scores Crystal City Coup," *Alamo Messenger*, Apr. 19, 1963; "Pena, Ploch Trade Oral Jabs over Crystal City," newspaper clipping dated May 10, 1963, Zavala County Folder, Connally Papers.

87. "Council Names New Manager" and "George Ozuna Assumes Manager Post," *ZCS*, May 3, 1963; José Angel Gutiérrez, interview by George Ozuna Jr., Sept. 23, 1997, CMAS 139, TVOH.

88. Juan Cornejo, interview by José Angel Gutiérrez, Jan. 14, 2000, transcript, p. 29, TVOH.

89. Ruben Salazar, "Mexican American Tells of Holding Texas Office," *LAT*, May 27, 1963; Ruben Salazar, "Mexican TV: Latin-Americans Eye the American Dream," *LAT*, June 5, 1963; Ruben Salazar, "Hoffa Help Pledged to Latin Group," *LAT*, Nov. 11, 1963.

90. Shockley, *Chicano Revolt*, 79.

91. Organizations that opposed Los Cinco, such as the Mexican American Chamber of Commerce, were willing, when called on by the very Anglos who had worked so vehemently to defeat their moderate efforts at civic participation in the 1950s and early 1960s, to join with the Anglo middle class in 1965 after being rebuffed by Los Cinco. Perhaps class was more important to some MACC members than race. Walter Smith, "Mexicano Resistance," 216–17.

92. Delgado, "Fraternization," 6.

93. Jesus Salas, interview, July 27, 1992.

94. Guzman interview. Los Cinco won this election, yet they were voted out of office by 1965 due to the fact that they lacked the organization and discipline to overcome Anglo harassment and the difficulty of governing. For my purposes, it is the community mobilization on the part of Mexican American youth that is central here, not the fact that those elected were soon out of office. On this and the related history of Crystal City, see Shockley, *Chicano Revolt*; Ignacio García, *United We Win*; and Navarro, *Mexican American Youth Organization* and *La Raza Unida Party*.

95. Salas, interview, July 27, 1992.

96. Ignacio Garcia, *Viva Kennedy*, 146–56.

Chapter 3

1. "Wisconsin Migrants March to Capitol to Protest Pay," *NYT*, Aug. 16, 1966; "Twenty-Six Migrants Conduct 'Respectability' March," *WP*, Aug. 16, 1966. On Chávez's march in California, see "Farm Hands Win Round in California," *MJ*, Apr. 7, 1966; and "Protest March for Farm Labor Gets under Way," *LAT*, Mar. 18, 1966. And for the Texas march, see "Texas Farm Laborers March to Protest Pay," *LAT*, July 12, 1966; "Texas Farm Hands Start Protest March to Austin," *NYT*, July 12, 1966; Kostyu, *Shadows in the Valley*; and "Leader of Texas March Visits Wautoma," *LVM*, Aug. 4, 1967. On the social changes in Mexican American life, see "Social Ferment Stirs Mexican-Americans," *LAT*, May 8, 1966. The newly formed NFWA, with support from the AFL-CIO, attempted to organize workers in California and South Texas. On the South Texas effort, see Kostyu, *Shadows in the Valley*; and "A Long Struggle with La Casita," *Texas Observer*, June 24, 1966. On California, see Ferriss and Sandoval, *Fight in the Fields*, 117–23.

2. Quoted in Erenburg, "*Obreros Unidos* in Wisconsin," 20; see also Valdés, *Al Norte*, 190; "Migrant Workers to March on Madison," *APC*, Aug. 12, 1966; Salvador Sanchez, "Migrant Stream"; "Wautoma in Spotlight for Migrant March to Madison," *LVM*, Aug. 18, 1966; "Migrant Workers End Pay-Rise Hike,"

NYT, Aug. 20, 1966; and Rosenbaum, "Success in Organizing: Case of Pickle Workers."

3. "Unions on the Farm," *NYT*, Sept. 3, 1966. In fact, the AFL-CIO's George Meany hoped that the NFWA, when chartered as the United Farm Workers Organizing Committee (UFWOC) in September 1966, would focus primarily on the unionization of workers in California yet also begin efforts in the Southwest, Florida, Wisconsin, Michigan, and the eastern states.

4. "Farm Workers Slate Food-Collecting Trek," *LAT*, July 29, 1966, notes that the members of the NFWA laid off by DiGiorno were "mostly from Texas."

5. Alberto Avila, interview; Juanita Ortiz, interview; Menefee, *Mexican Migratory Workers*; Valdés, *Al Norte*, 137–38; Wisconsin Governor's Commission on Human Rights, *Migratory Agricultural Workers*; Raushenbush, *Study of Migratory Workers*; Barker, "In Crystal City," 6; "Migrants Start Trek North" and "Here and There," *ZCS*, May 24, 1957; "Minutes, Oct. 21, 1966, Fact Sheet, Migratory Workers in Wisconsin, 1966," folder 11, Records of the Governor's Committee on Migratory Labor, Wisconsin Historical Society, Madison. These networks functioned in ways similar to those of Mexican workers in California, as detailed in Devra Weber's *Dark Sweat, White Gold*, 63–65.

6. Quoted in Don Olesen, "Jesus Salas: Voice of Wisconsin's Migrants," *MJ*, Sept. 7, 1969, 8. See also Obreros Unidos, "Activities and Plans," 1–2.

7. Salvador Sanchez, interview, July 17, 2000.

8. For more on the many relationships that tied the primarily family-based networks of migrants in Wisconsin to one another across the various migrant streams feeding into the Wisconsin harvest, see Provinzano, "Chicano Migrant Farm Workers."

9. Jesus Salas, interview by Michael Gordon, July 24, 1997.

10. "Manuel Salas," State of Texas, Assessment of Property in Zavala County Owned and Rendered for Taxation, 1960 (Austin, 1960), 118, Genealogy Collection, Texas State Library, Austin, Tex.; listing for "Salas Café," Crystal City, Tex., telephone directory, July 1958; Jesus Salas, interview, July 27, 1992.

11. On several occasions, Manuel Salas Sr. settled his family temporarily in Wisconsin before finally settling there permanently in the late 1950s. In many ways, he was the hub on which the wheel of migrant labor in Wisconsin turned, as he was the labor contractor for the Waushara County–based Libby's. Jesus Salas, interview by the author, July 27, 1992.

12. David Giffey, interview.

13. Jesus Salas, recorded remarks made at the Wisconsin Historical Society, Madison, July 16, 1998.

14. Jesus Salas, interview by Michael Gordon, July 24, 1997.

15. Jesus Salas, recorded remarks made at the Wisconsin Historical Society, Madison, July 16, 1998.

16. See "Labor Legislation" in Commons, *History of Labor*. A lot of ink has been spilled attacking the "Commons School" of labor history when no such school existed. Commons and his students wrote their history not to reveal the

lives of workers but to understand the nature of labor relations and propose models for reforms. They wanted to understand the history of labor relations so that they could create legal reform models. Most of these "historians" were trained economists who spent most of their lives working with government, labor unions, and at universities to create model and actual labor and social welfare laws.

17. Wisconsin Governor's Commission on Human Rights, *Migratory Agricultural Workers*; Wisconsin Governor's Committee on Migratory Labor, *Report for 1966 and 1967*.

18. Her views are covered in Elizabeth Brandeis Raushenbush, "Migrant Labor Problems: Unfinished Business in Labor Legislation—Both in Research and Action," Nov. 1, 1960, box 3, folder 6, Raushenbush Papers, Wisconsin Historical Society, Madison.

19. Mark Erenburg, interview.

20. "Cuatros Jóvenes Tienen un Gran Proyecto," *LVM*, Aug. 6, 1964. The University of Wisconsin graduate students included Gene Armstrong, Peter Hoeffel, Charles Meisner, and Mark Erenburg.

21. Milton Taylor, *Approach to the Migratory Labor Problem*, 40. This study, written by Taylor while a student under Professor Edwin E. Witte, suggested that migrant workers would benefit from a mix of new legislation and enforcement of current laws pertaining to wages and hours, child welfare, housing, health, workmen's compensation, social security, and labor relations, yet warned that "unless the public attitude is stimulated to the point that it promotes and supports needed legislation and effective enforcement, little can be expected."

22. Jesus Salas, interview by Michael Gordon, July 24, 1997; Erenburg, interview; Wisconsin Governor's Committee on Migratory Labor, *Report to the Governor, 1964*. Raushenbush had Salas appointed to the Governor's Committee on Migratory Labor and told Erenburg to contact Salas.

23. Both Hoeffel and Erenburg would later work for *LVM*. Erenburg reported that he and his wife wrote for *LVM* as well. Mark Erenburg, pers. comm. to the author, Dec. 3, 2003.

24. Manuel Laurence Salas, "The Times Are Changing," *LVM*, July 15, 1965; "Aguilas Del Valle Triunfan," *LVM*, Aug. 5, 1965.

25. "Beisbol, Beisbol," *LVM*, July 22, 1965.

26. "Attempt to Organize Migrants," *APC*, Aug. 10, 1966; Jesus Salas, interview by Michael Gordon, July 24, 1997; Erenburg, interview.

27. Quoted in "Ordeal of Migrants," *La Crosse Archdiocese Times Review*, Dec. 1967.

28. See "Wisconsin Migrants March to Capitol to Protest Pay," *NYT*, Aug. 16, 1966; "Statement of the Mexican American Political Association Regarding the Situation in the Delano Strike and Farm Worker Activities," Nov. 27, 1965, box 12, folder 1, Ernesto Galarza Papers, Department of Special Collections and University Archives, Stanford University Libraries, Stanford, Calif.

29. See Jenkins, *Politics of Insurgency*, 118–30; Ngai, *Impossible Subjects*, 163–66; and Ganz, "Resources and Resourcefulness." After the march, Dr. Martin Luther King Jr. wrote Chávez: "Our separate struggles are really one—a struggle for freedom, for dignity and for humanity." King quoted in Mantler, "Black, Brown, and Poor," 24. As Mantler points out, King and Chávez never met, and the number of interethnic alliances between African Americans and Mexican Americans in history are few. In a masterful study of the Poor Peoples Campaign, Mantler shows how bias, misunderstanding, and discrimination on both sides of the black/brown divide limited cooperative possibilities in the 1960s.

30. See National Advisory Committee on Farm Labor, *Farm Labor Organizing*, 44–53; and Levy, *Cesar Chávez*. Chávez's social movement unionism ideal, even as the UFW itself waned, continued to inspire labor unions into the twenty-first century as activists from these unions played a role in a revitalized union movement. Shaw, in *Beyond the Fields*, details the impact of the UFW's social movement unionism on the new labor movement of the twenty-first century and the 2008 presidential campaign strategies of Barack Obama.

31. See Manuel Gonzales, *Mexicanos*, 198–99; and generally see Matthiessen, *Sal Si Puedes*; and Levy, *Cesar Chávez*. For a biographical discussion of the history of farm labor organizing linking Texas, Wisconsin, and California within the context of South Texas religious and political life, see Kostyu, *Shadows in the Valley*.

32. Salvador Sanchez, interview, July 17, 2000; Jesus Salas, interview by Michael Gordon, July 24, 1997. Mark Erenburg joined J. T. Johnson, the local publisher of *LVM*, as an editor with his wife, Mary Erenburg, and Jane Elliot to run the paper in 1966. See *LVM*, Aug. 4, 1966.

33. Jesus Salas, interview by Michael Gordon, Aug. 18, 1997; "Migrant Workers to March on Madison," *APC*, Aug. 12, 1966; "Meeting Scheduled on Demands of Migrants," *APC*, Aug. 13, 1966; "Migrants Will March despite State Efforts," *MJ*, Aug. 14, 1966.

34. Giffey and Salas, *Struggle for Justice*.

35. "Marchers Rest, Leaders, State Officials Meet," *APC*, Aug. 16, 1966; "Migrants March Despite State Efforts," "Comentarios," and "200 Attend Rally at Wautoma El Domingo Pasado," *LVM*, Aug. 19, 1966.

36. Quoted in "Marchers Rest, Leaders, State Officials Meet," *APC*, Aug. 16, 1966. Interestingly, despite the fact that the records of the supportive unions and Chávez's own union records as well as the activists themselves fail to credit California "organizers," the *Milwaukee Journal*, incorrectly perhaps, reported that an "organizing committee" was sent to Wisconsin by Chávez. See "Leader Pleased," *MJ*, Aug. 16, 1966.

37. Obreros Unidos, "Activities and Plans," 4; "Workers Favor NFWA Demands," *LVM*, Aug. 19, 1966; "State Assurance on Demands Fails to Halt Migrant March," *MJ*, Aug. 16, 1966.

38. "Weary Migrants Find Kindness along Route of Protest March," *MJ*, Aug. 16, 1966; "State Officials Say Migrants Won Goal in 'March to Respectability,'" *APC*, Aug. 20, 1966.

39. "Migrant Committee Meeting Misses Real Communication," *Madison Capital Times*, Aug. 24, 1966.

40. "Workers Favor NFWA Demands," *LVM*, Aug. 19, 1966; César Chávez to Governor Warren P. Knowles, Aug. 13, 1966, box 14, folder 23, NFWA Collection, Archives of Labor and Urban Affairs, Walter P. Reuther Library, Wayne State University, Detroit, Mich.

41. Bill Smith, remarks made at the Wisconsin Historical Society, July 16, 1998. Smith said, "[The] keynote speaker was Charlie Heymanns, who was the first trade unionist that I think I had ever really seen or really listened to. Charlie Heymanns was a hero, was a part of the AFL-CIO at the time here in Wisconsin, and was one of the survivors and heroes of the strike in Kohler, Wisconsin, years back. And he was a magical orator, a great German Catholic; he talked about God, and bread, and workers and justice. And I loved him whenever he was here." "Migrant Workers Pleas Presented," *La Crosse Tribune*, Aug. 20, 1966. Although the AFL-CIO was present, in Wisconsin, unlike Starr County, Texas, the organizers and leaders like Salas were not NFWA employees or organizers prior to the activism. In fact, the AFL-CIO sent investigators to report on the march.

42. "Majority Feel Migrants Happy with Conditions," *APC*, Aug. 21, 1966; "Editorial" and "Letters," *Waushara Argus*, Aug. 25, 1966; "Ministers Deplore March of Migrants" and "Wash Line," *Waushara Argus*, Sept. 1, 1966.

43. "Peoples Forum," *APC*, Aug. 21, 1966. In this letters section of the paper, readers speculate as to whether or not Salas and the marchers represent "responsible" migrant workers.

44. "Meeting Set at Wautoma," *Oshkosh Daily Northwestern*, Sept. 2, 1966.

45. "Growers Speak Out on Migrant Workers Issue," *Oshkosh Daily Northwestern*, Sept. 3, 1966.

46. "Three Pickle Harvester Machines Being Tested in Waushara County," *Waushara Argus*, Aug. 18, 1966.

47. Comments of Richard Matthews of Wautoma, researcher for the Central Wisconsin Growers Cooperative and Wisconsin Potato and Vegetable Growers Association, quoted in "Growers Speak Out on Migrant Workers Issue," *Oshkosh Daily Northwestern*, Sept. 3, 1966.

48. Obreros Unidos, "Activities and Plans," 4; Kerry Napuk, "Report on Potato Shed Operations, Plainfield and Almond, Wisconsin (Portage County)," Sept. 30, 1966, p. 2, box 23, folder 9, William Kircher Papers, Archives of Labor and Urban Affairs, Walter P. Reuther Library, Wayne State University, Detroit, Mich.

49. Bill Smith, interview.

50. Obreros Unidos, "Official Report of Obreros Unidos: The Migrant Workers Strike in Almond, Wis.," pp. 1–2, box 23, folder 9, Kircher Papers; Valdés, *Al Norte*, 190–91.

51. Mark Erenburg, interview.

52. Jesus Salas, recorded remarks made at the Wisconsin Historical Society, July 16, 1998.

53. Bill Smith, recorded remarks made at the Wisconsin Historical Society, July 16, 1998.

54. Napuk, "Report on Potato Shed Operations," 4, Kircher Papers; "Migrants' Strike: What Happened?" *MJ*, Oct. 16, 1966; Erenburg, "Obreros Unidos in Wisconsin," 22. In fact, Erenburg wrote that Crystal City residents "formed the core of Obreros Unidos."

55. Napuk, "Report on Potato Shed Operations," 5–6, Kircher Papers.

56. Obreros Unidos, "Official Report," 2, Kircher Papers; Miscellaneous notes marked "341-1617," Oct. 4, 1966, box 11, folder 15, Charles Heymanns Papers, Milwaukee Area Research Center, Golda Meir Library, University of Wisconsin–Milwaukee.

57. Obreros Unidos, "Official Report," 2, Kircher Papers.

58. Notes, phone conversation with Father Finucan, Oct. 7, 1966, box 11, folder 15, Heymanns Papers; "Charge Filed against Firm by Migrants," *MJ*, Nov. 11, 1966.

59. Obreros Unidos, "Official Report," 3, Kircher Papers. The other processing plants began to negotiate, one raising wages, yet did not properly recognize the union. According to Charles Heymanns, after Burns decided to fight the union, Central Sands "flatly refused" to support an election despite the fact that they appeared to be in the process of allowing a union vote. Charles Heymanns to Ed S. Haines, Director of Organizing Department, AFL-CIO, Oct. 25, 1966, box 23, folder 9, Kircher Papers.

60. "The Strike Issue at Burns Plant," *Waushara Argus*, Oct. 13, 1966.

61. Obreros Unidos, "Official Report," 4–5, Kircher Papers; "Migrants Stand Firm, Refuse to Return to Work at Almond," *MJ*, Oct. 13, 1966; "Migrants, Potato Firm Refuse to Negotiate," *Wisconsin State Journal*, Oct. 9, 1966; *Obreros Unidos v. James Burns & Sons Farm, Inc.*, Wisconsin Employment Relations Board Decision no. 7842 (Dec. 1966).

62. "John Schmidt to Take over AFL-CIO," *Stevens Point Daily Journal*, Oct. 7, 1966; Jesus Salas, remarks made at the Wisconsin Historical Society, July 16, 1998.

63. "Wisconsin AFL-CIO," *Stevens Point Daily Journal*, Oct. 14, 1966.

64. "AFL-CIO Backs Migrants with $2,525," *MJ*, Oct. 13, 1966.

65. Obreros Unidos, "Official Report," 5, Kircher Papers.

66. Ibid., 6; "Migrants to Quit Jobs," *MJ*, Oct. 14, 1966; "Migrant Strike, What Happened" and "Tough Target Chosen for First Migrant Strike," *MJ*, Oct. 16, 1966; "Poor Timing, New Workers Break Strike of Migrants," *MS*, Oct. 15, 1966.

67. *Obreros Unidos v. James Burns & Sons Farm, Inc.*, WERB Decision no. 7842, The WERB held that Burns's use of employee interrogation concerning their union activity amounted to unlawful interference and an unfair labor practice.

68. "Striking Migrants, Firm Look to State," *MJ*, Oct. 11, 1966.

69. *Obreros Unidos v. James Burns & Sons Farm, Inc.*

70. See Forbath, *Law and the Labor Movement.*

71. César Chávez to Charles Heymanns, Dec. 21, 1966, and Charles Heymanns to William L. Kircher, Dec. 13, 1967, box 11, folder 15, Milwaukee Urban Archives, University of Wisconsin–Milwaukee.

72. Mark Erenburg to Marc Rodriguez, Aug. 30, 1999.

73. Smith, interview.

74. Charles Heymanns to William L. Kircher, Jan. 16, 1967, box 11, folder 15, Milwaukee Urban Archives.

75. Erenburg to Marc Rodriguez, Aug. 30, 1999; Napuk, "Report on Potato Shed Operations," Kircher Papers. This report, conducted by United Packinghouse, Food and Allied Workers (UPFAWU), suggested that Libby would be the best target for future organizing by Obreros Unidos.

76. Erenberg to Marc Rodriguez, Aug. 30, 1999. Moreover, as early as September 1966, Jesus Salas had informed representatives from the Chicago AFL-CIO organizing offices that he sent letters to Libby, the Chicago Pickle Company, and Green Giant to "invite them to sit down jointly with him and his committee to negotiate." Miguel Arias to Heymanns, Sept. 1, 1966, box 11, folder 15, Heymanns Papers, University of Wisconsin–Milwaukee.

77. Erenburg, interview.

78. Erenburg to Marc Rodriguez, Aug. 30, 1999. Initially, Charles Heymanns was concerned that "a realistic program" for support on the part of Obreros Unidos in January 1967 would be "much less than the current plans and visions of some of our brave but less realistic Wisconsin Farm Workers' leaders." Heymanns to William L. Kircher, Jan. 16, 1967, box 11, folder 15, Heymanns Papers.

79. Heymanns to William L. Kircher, Jan. 16, 1967, box 11, folder 15, Heymanns Papers.

80. Jesus Salas, interview by Michael Gordon, Aug. 18, 1997.

81. Erenburg, interview.

82. "Income Statement for Obreros Unidos," box 23, folder 9, Kircher Papers; Clarus Backes, "The Migrant's Union Comes to Pickle Country," *Chicago Tribune Sunday Magazine*, Oct. 20, 1968.

83. Jesus Salas, interview by Michael Gordon, Aug. 18, 1997.

84. "Jesus Salas of Wautoma Explains Ordeal of Migrants" and "Farm Workers Leader Describes Harassment by Power Structure but Non-Violence Pays Dividends," *La Crosse Times-Review*, Apr. 25, 1967; "Obreros Unidos Summer Calendar," *LVM*, Sept. 7, 1967; Jesus Salas, interview by Michael Gordon, Aug. 18, 1997.

85. Jesus Salas, interview by Michael Gordon, Aug. 18, 1997; "Help for Migrants Pledged by Unions," *MJ*, Aug. 9, 1967.

86. David Giffey, interview.

87. John W. Schmitt, President, Wisconsin State AFL-CIO, to Robert Durkin, July 19, 1967, box 23, folder 11, Kircher Papers; "Salas to Resume Union Efforts,"

MJ, June 14, 1967; "Salas Resumes Efforts to Unionize Migrants," *Madison Capital Times*, June 14, 1967.

88. Charles Heymanns, Director, AFL-CIO, Region 12, to Edward S. Haines, July 24, 1967, box 23, folder 11, Kircher Papers. This letter to Haines reiterated the fact that the workers at Libby are "covered" employees under Wisconsin law.

89. Jesus Salas, interview by Michael Gordon, Aug. 18, 1997.

90. Giffey, interview; Erenburg, interview.

91. Salvador Sanchez, interview, July 17, 2000; "Obreros Unidos Juega con Equipo Local" and "Obreros Unidos Faces Tough Baseball Foes," *LVM*, July 28, 1967.

92. Giffey, interview; Erenburg, interview.

93. "Obreros Unidos Summer Calendar," *LVM*, Sept. 7, 1967.

94. "Leyes: Las Companias Son Responsible por $1.25," *LVM*, July 28, 1967; In "Volunteer Lawyers Commended for Work in Waushara," *LVM*, Sept. 1, 1967, the newspaper noted that Frank D. Hamilton, president of the Wisconsin State Bar Association, commended the attorneys of the Lawyers Committee as "truly possessed of the virtue of charity."

95. "Farm Worker Camps Furnished with Mattresses from Dump," *LVM*, July 28, 1967.

96. Jesus Salas, interview by Michael Gordon, Aug. 18, 1997.

97. Ibid.; Giffey, interview; "Migrants Complain of Code Violations," *MJ*, July 26, 1967; "Migrant Leader Appeals for Help," *MS*, July 27, 1967.

98. "Milwaukee Attorneys Offer Free Aid to Farm Workers," *LVM*, July 28, 1967.

99. Hon. Frederick Kessler, remarks made at the Wisconsin Historical Society, July 16, 1998; "Volunteer Attorneys Find Full Legal Calendar" and "Abogados de Union Ayudan a Trabajadores," *LVM*, Aug. 4, 1967.

100. Hon. Frederick Kessler, remarks made at the Wisconsin Historical Society, July 16, 1998; "Attorneys Say Benefit Was Success" and "Ayuda en Milwaukee," *LVM*, Aug. 4, 1967.

101. Loeffler, "Working within the 'System,'" 11.

102. Frederick Kessler, interview; "10 Attorneys Will Offer Legal Aid to Migrants," *MJ*, July 23, 1967; "Judge Reynolds Stops Mexicans' Deportation," *MJ*, Sept. 23, 1967.

103. "Milwaukee Attorneys Offer Free Aid to Farm Workers," *LVM*, July 28, 1967.

104. "Trabajadores Unen con Obreros Unidos," "Trabajador Acusa a Compania," and "La Voz Comentarios," *LVM*, Aug. 18, 1967, were dedicated to the union organizing effort.

105. "Wisconsin Labor Leaders Meet in Wautoma Office," and "Jefes de Union en Wautoma," *LVM*, Aug. 18, 1967; "State Hiring Linguists to Aid Migrants," *MJ*, Aug. 9, 1967. Representatives of the United Auto Workers, Meat and Allied Food Workers, Brewers, Stevens Point Labor Council, Paper Workers, and state AFL-

CIO leaders all attended the Wautoma meeting pledging support for Obreros Unidos.

106. Jesus Salas, interview by Michael Gordon, Aug. 18, 1997; Giffey, interview.

107. "Salas Demanda Contrato para Union," "Salas Demands Recognition for Union," "Recruiters Promises Don't Come True," "Open Letter to Lopez, Schramek," and "Huelga," all in *LVM*, Aug. 25, 1967; "Migrant Union Seeks Recognition by Libby," *MJ*, Aug. 20, 1967.

108. *Obreros Unidos v. Libby, McNeill & Libby*, Wisconsin Employment Relations Commission, Decision No. 8163 (Aug. 29, 1967), 2; Rosenbaum, "Success in Organizing: Case of Pickle Workers," 11–12; Erenburg, interview. Mark Erenburg knew of a seldom-used provision of Wisconsin labor law that provided for "emergency hearings" in case a "perishable" crop was at risk of spoilage. One of the WERB commissioners, a former professor of Erenburg's, informed him of this special provision applicable to labor disputes involving cucumbers.

109. Quoted in Erenburg, "Obreros Unidos in Wisconsin," 2; *Obreros Unidos v. Libby, McNeill & Libby*, Wisconsin Employment Relations Commission, Decision No. 8163 (Aug. 29, 1967) 2; "Campesinos Votan Por Union," "Workers Vote for Union," and "La Voz Comentarios," *LVM*, Sept. 1, 1967; "Union Gana, 405 Campesinos Votan 'Si,'" *LVM*, Sept. 7, 1967.

110. *Obreros Unidos v. Libby, McNeill & Libby*, Wisconsin Employment Relations Commission, Decision No. 8163 (Aug. 29, 1967), 2–5.

111. Ibid.

112. *Libby, McNeill & Libby v. Wis. Employment Relations Commission and Obreros Unidos (United Workers)*, 179 N.W. 2d 805, 807 (1970).

113. Ibid.

114. *Obreros Unidos v. Libby, McNeill & Libby*, Wisconsin Employment Relations Commission, Decision No. 8616 (July 16, 1968), 8–25.

115. "World Boycott Aimed at California Grapes," *LAT*, May 28, 1968; "Massive Boycott Mounted against State's Grapes," *LAT*, Aug. 12, 1968; "Grape Boycott Pushed," Aug. 15, 1968; "Farm Union's Grape Boycott Drive Nearing Make-or-Break Point," *WSJ*, Aug. 27, 1968; "Grape Issue Stirs Berkeley Crisis," *NYT*, Oct. 20, 1968.

116. Kircher to George Meany, President, AFL-CIO, Jan. 10, 1968; Kircher to Salas, Jan. 12, 1968; Kircher to Chávez, Jan. 12, 1968; Chávez to Kircher, Jan. 20, 1968, all in folder 7; and John W. Schmitt to Kircher, Apr. 30, 1969, folder 12, box 23, Kircher Papers. In the exchange between Kircher and Chávez, both expressed concern about the fact that Salas now worked under the direction of Chávez and had to know that Chávez was in charge. According to Kircher, they needed to be "blunt" so that Salas "understands the need for cooperation and discipline in this . . . type of organizing." Chávez chimed in that "there should not be any misunderstandings in the very definite directions . . . given." Keeping Salas focused on the UFWOC's needs as opposed to those of Obreros Unidos seems to have been the main unspoken issue here.

117. "Bill Smith and Jesus Gathered" (yellow notebook pages), box 18, folder 4; and Kircher to Salas, Oct. 4, 1968, box 68, folder 15, both in Office of the President, United Farm Workers of America (UFWA) Collection, Archives of Labor and Urban Affairs, Walter P. Reuther Library, Wayne State University, Detroit.

118. "A Message to the Small Growers from Jesus Salas of Obreros Unidos," *LVM*, July 27, 1968.

119. Salas to Chávez, Feb. 20, 1968, box 51, folder 20, UFWA Collection.

120. Biweekly report of Jesus Salas for Mar. 16, 1968, box 51, folder 20, Office of the President, UFWA Collection.

121. Handwritten letter, Jesus Salas to César Chávez, summer (1968?), box 51, folder 20, Office of the President, UFWA Collection; biweekly report of Jesus Salas for Nov. 9, 1968, box 68, folder 15, Office of the President, UFWA Collection.

122. "Judge Strikes Down Migrant Pay System," *MJ*, June 28, 1968; "Attorneys Broaden Service to Migrants," *MJ*, July 17, 1968; attorney Allen Samson quoted in "Volunteer Lawyers Will Meet Union Member's Legal Needs," *LVM*, Aug. 3, 1968; "New Social Services at Union Office," "Wautoma Health Clinic Serves All Farm Workers," and "Interfaith Center," *LVM*, July 27, 1968; Clarus Backes, "The Migrants' Union Comes to Pickle Country," *Chicago Tribune Sunday Magazine*, Oct. 20, 1968.

123. Biweekly report of Jesus Salas for July 20, 1968, box 51, folder 20, Office of the President, UFWA Collection; handwritten letter, Jesus Salas to Chávez, box 51, folder 20, Office of the President, UFWA Collection.

124. Backus, "The Migrants' Union Comes to Pickle Country," *Chicago Tribune Sunday Magazine*, Oct. 20, 1968, 37.

125. Handwritten letter, Jesus Salas to Chávez, summer (1968?), box 51, folder 20, Chávez Papers.

126. "Wautoma Ignores Call for Justice" and "Boycott in Wautoma," Aug. 3, 1968; "Obreros Tienen Junta," Aug. 17, 1968; "The Boycott Gathers Tem" and "Chávez: A Leader for Our Times," Aug. 31, 1968; "Wisconsin Boycott Reaches New Peak," July 11, 1969; "La Follette Pickets against Grapes," Aug. 10, 1968, all in *LVM*. "Rally Protests Sale of Grapes," *MJ*, Oct. 9, 1968; "La Follette, Reuss Push Grape Boycott," *MJ*, Oct. 26, 1968; "Special Mass Held for Grape Boycotters," *MS*, Nov. 28, 1968.

127. "Migrants Plan Bias Complaint," *MJ*, Aug. 28, 1969. In the first volley of jurisdictional challenge, migrants under the direction of OU walked off the job at the Fall River Canning Company to protest wage discrimination.

128. Chávez to Manuel Salas, Jan. 23, 1970, box 68, folder 17, Chávez Papers. In 1969, OU, under the direction of Manuel Salas, held significant fund-raisers that also made the case for the UFWOC grape boycott, yet these were targeted efforts organized by the Lawyers Committee of OU to pay the outstanding fees of the farm workers' legal defense effort. See "Group Gives Cheers for Court Fees," *MJ*, June 25, 1969.

129. Jesus Salas to César Chávez, Feb. 25, 1969, box 68, folder 16, Chávez Papers.

130. Ibid.

131. Chávez to Salas, Mar. 9, 1969, box 68, folder 16, Chávez Papers.

132. Ibid.

133. "Workers Protest Discrimination," *LVM*, Sept. 9, 1969; "Hartford Contract is Unfair," *LVM*, Sept. 29, 1969; "Union Vote," *LVM*, Nov. 19, 1969; AFL-CIO Memorandum to William L. Kircher, box 23, folder 13, Kircher Papers. The union was organizing in several canneries across the state in conflict with the Teamsters, and mention is made of another canning facility in Clymon, Wisconsin, which was in conflict with the AMC union. The AFL-CIO union wanted Salas to back off due to interunion jurisdictional agreements.

134. "El Boycoteo Sigue Su Marcha" and "Diez Laboreros se Reunen con UFWOC," July 11; "Boycott Hits Grape Growers," July 18; "Hundreds Attend Boycott Dinner" and "New Target in Milwaukee," July 25; "Boycott Weekend," Aug. 11; "Wisconsin Boycott Ranks High in Nation" and "Chávez Visits Milwaukee," Nov. 19, all in *LVM*, 1969.

135. Jesus Salas to Chávez, May 12, 1970, box 23, folder 13, Kircher Papers; "Canning Plant to Cease Hiring Migrants," *MJ*, May 23, 1970.

136. Memo: Potential United Farm Workers Organizing Committee Activity in Wisconsin, May 15, 1970, box 23, folder 13, Kircher Papers.

137. Handwritten note by Larry (Itliong) to "Nora" on memo from Manuel Salas to César Chávez, May 7, 1970, box 26, folder 22, Chávez Papers.

138. Jesus Salas to Chávez, June 29, 1970, box 68, folder 17, Chávez Papers.

139. *Libby, McNeill & Libby v. Wis. Employment Relations Commission and Obreros Unidos (United Workers)* 42 Wis. 2d. 272 (Oct. 9, 1970); President's Commission on Migratory Labor, *Migratory Labor*, 115.

140. For this view, see Rosenbaum, "Success in Organizing: Case of Pickle Workers." Rosenbaum correctly points out that the organizing success of Obreros Unidos did not lead to a contract that would have sustained the union. While attentive to the larger structural features of the agricultural industry, Rosenbaum's limited conclusion considers only the contract-negotiating phase of what was a broader social movement. Moreover, his analysis ignores the changing social conditions that brought benefits to workers outside the area of union recognition and collective bargaining. He makes much the same argument in "Success in Organizing: Case of Tomato Workers."

141. Jon Wilcox quoted in "Family Wins Justice," *LVM*, Aug. 17, 1968.

142. La Follette quoted in "La Follette Sees Camp Conditions," *LVM*, Aug. 17, 1968.

143. "Wisconsin Boycott Reaches New Peak," July 11; "Black Leaders Support Boycott," July 18, both in *LVM*, 1969. African American elected officials from Milwaukee and Madison attended a rally in support of the grape boycott, where Alderwoman Vel Phillips of Milwaukee called for unity between African Americans and Mexican Americans.

144. On FLOC generally, see Rosenbaum, "Success in Organizing: Case of To-mato Workers"; Farm Labor Organizing Committee, *FLOC: 25 Years of Struggle*; Krass, "Strikers and Ohio Churches"; Barger and Reza, *Farm Labor Movement in the Midwest*. On the continued success of FLOC see O'Neill, "WHERE NO UNION HAS GONE BEFORE." On the role played by OU in inspiring Baldemar Velasquez to establish FLOC, see Mantler, "Black, Brown, and Poor," 174.

Chapter 4

1. On the variety of militant efforts to establish community control in the late 1960s and 1970s, see Lilia Fernandez, "From the Near West Side to 18th Street"; and "Little Village Group Organizes to Fight Community Poverty," *Chicago Tribune*, Sept. 11, 1969. In the Puerto Rican and Mexican American cases, sometimes the effort for community control pitted them against African American agencies or administrators in New York and Los Angeles. See "Puerto Rican–Afro-American Squabble Growing in the Bronx," *New York Amsterdam News*, Jan. 27, 1968; and "EYOA Adopts Plan to Set Ethnic Ratios," *LAT*, Nov. 30, 1971. On other efforts see generally Clayson, *Freedom Is Not Enough*; Bauman, *Race and the War on Poverty*; Kiffmeyer, *Reformers to Radicals*; and Cobb, *Native Activism*.

2. "UMOS in Real Dialogue," *El Cosechador*, Nov. 26, 1968, 1–2; "Staff Short-ages: Debate Goes On," *El Cosechador*, Christmas 1968, 2–3.

3. LAUCR, founded by Ernesto Chacon together with Roberto Hernandez, publisher of the newspaper *La Guardia*, drew activists mainly from within the Tejano milieu. Its membership was also drawn from Puerto Rican and Latin American graduate students and the broader Mexican-ancestry community who embraced the term "Latin American." There was also significant overlap with membership of the Brown Berets.

4. See, for example, such nationally focused works as Matusow, *Unraveling of America*, 255; Patterson, *America's Struggle against Poverty*; Chafe, *Unfinished Journey*, 230–37; and the work of social scientists of the period, including among others Moynihan, *Maximum Feasible Misunderstanding*; and Levitan, *Great Society's Poor Law*. Of course, some of these works do not intend to study the CAP at the grassroots level, but most tend to see it as one of the War on Pov-erty's failures and detail the way various administrations dealt with the political problems and case-specific scandals of some CAP agencies.

5. For recent local studies, see Cobb, "'Us Indians Understand the Basics,'" 41; and Clayson, "'Barrios and Ghettos,'" 158. For perhaps the most focused study of a similar (though nonmigrant) community action service organization serving an urban Mexican American community, see John Chavez, *Eastside Landmark*.

6. Robert Lampman quoted in Bernstein, *Guns or Butter*, 93.

7. Levitan, *Great Society's Poor Law*, 13–14; Bernstein, *Guns or Butter*, 95–113; Shesol, *Mutual Contempt*, 166–71. For more on the development of community action programs before 1964 and popular investigations into poverty, see Lamp-man, *Low Income Population*; Lampman, *Ends and Means*; Murrow, *Harvest of*

Shame; Harrington, *Other Americans*; and MacDonald, "Our Invisible Poor," *New Yorker*, Jan. 19, 1963.

8. Pycior, *LBJ and Mexican Americans*, 20–22, 141.

9. P.L. 88-452, Eighty-eighth Cong., 2nd sess. (Aug. 20, 1964), 516 (emphasis added).

10. Ibid. Soon after passage, the OEO created guidelines for creating programs to assist migrants. See Office of Economic Opportunity, *Migrant and Economic Opportunity Act*.

11. The "Chicano movement" lacked the viable national institutions found in the African American civil rights movement of the period, such as the Congress of Racial Equality or the Southern Christian Leadership Conference. As others have pointed out, the Chicano movement can best be seen as several related, like-minded local civil rights efforts that originated within the ethnic Mexican community, often led by U.S. citizens. The broader Texas-Wisconsin civil rights activism that developed across this migrant network is discussed in my article "Cristaleño Consciousness." Also, it appears that in the late 1960s, the term "Latin American" was used when an organization included and served the interests of people considered "Latinos" in the early twenty-first century. In Milwaukee, the primary groups were Mexican Americans, including Tejanos, and Puerto Ricans. There were several, often well-educated Central and South American natives active in this pan–Latin American activism. Local activists began to label such activism and activists "Latino" or "Latina" in local publications beginning in late 1968.

12. While the panethnicity described is multilayered, there were two layers of cultural unity, which emerged in Milwaukee. The first was a Tejano panethnicity, which mediated hometown rivalries and bias in the name of a broader Tejano identity. The second was a Latino (or Latin American) panethnicity, which allowed Spanish-speaking people to come together as a single group at the political and cultural levels in activist and other organizations. These moments of panethnicity were durable, yet broke down over issues of intraethnic division in some cases. On Latino/a panethnicity from a social science perspective, see Ricourt and Danta, *Hispanas de Queens*; and Fraga et al., *Latino Lives in America*, 145–76.

13. "Parade, Fete Scheduled by Aztec Mutual Society," *MJ*, May 5, 1949; "Cultures Blend, Evolve on the South Side," *MJ*, May 7, 2000. On Mexican and Mexican American Milwaukee, see Gurda, *Latin Community*; Fenton, *Mexicans in Milwaukee*; WMVS Public Television, *I Remember*, episode 254; and Valdez, "Social and Occupational Integration."

14. On Puerto Rican Milwaukee, see Berry-Cabán, *Puerto Rican Community*; Berry-Cabán, "Puerto Rican Strategies"; and Avelardo Valdez, "Social and Occupational Integration." On later panethnic movements to bring greater social, educational, and cultural programming to Milwaukee Latinos see "Spanish Dissatisfied with Klotsche Efforts," *MJ*, Sept. 9, 1970; "Latin Groups Hope to Combine Efforts," *MJ*, Nov. 22, 1970; "Complaints Voiced by Latins," *MJ*, July 12,

1974; "TV Program Bolsters Latin Pride," *MJ*, Dec. 9, 1974; and "Mexican Fiesta Has Roots in Activism," *MJ*, Aug. 21, 2002.

15. Orum, *City Building in America*; Gibson, "Population of 100 Largest Cities"; Gurda, *Latin Community*; Gary Pokorny, "The History of Hispanic Ministry in the Archdiocese of Milwaukee, 1920–1985," 1985, unpublished research paper, University of Wisconsin–Milwaukee, Golda Meir Library, Milwaukee Area Research Center; Joseph Rodriguez et al., *Nuestro Milwaukee*.

16. The moniker "Selma of the North" might have been an overstatement, but Milwaukee was a national center of civil rights protest for much of the period between 1964 and the mid-1970s. Far more diverse in its leadership than in other cities, the Black Power movement in Milwaukee included Italian American Catholic priest James Groppi as a key activist force. See David Llorens, "Miracle in Milwaukee," *Ebony*, Nov. 1967; Jones, "'Not a Color'"; Dougherty, *More than One Struggle*; McGreevy, *Parish Boundaries*, 197–205; and United Migrant Opportunity Services, *Helping People*.

17. "Dow Protest Becomes Disruptive," *UWM Post*, Feb. 27, 1968; "WISCONSIN FACES PROTESTS ON WAR: Radicals Choose Milwaukee as Symbol of Movement," *NYT*, Sep. 29, 1968; "Convict 12 in Burning of Draft Board Files," *Chicago Tribune*, May 27, 1969; "Nixon Warned Not to Ignore Strong Anti-War Feeling," *UWM Post*, Oct. 17, 1969; "Nine Arrested in ROTC Disruption," *UWM Post*, Nov. 14, 1969. For an insightful and provocative treatment of the antiwar protests in Madison, see Maraniss, *They Marched into Sunlight*.

18. "Propose Migrant Aid Plan," *Hartford Times-Press*, May 13, 1965; "Highlight Memorandum: Application for Grant under Title 111-B," box 516, folder "United Migrant Opp. Services, Wisconsin," Records of the Community Services Administration (CSA), RG 381, National Archives, College Park, Md.

19. Alberto Avila, interview.

20. Minutes, Southwestern Wisconsin Migrant Health Committee, Dec. 18, 1963, box 6, folder 7, Migrant Health Program (MHP) Records, Wisconsin Bureau of Community Health and Prevention, Wisconsin Historical Society, Madison. This meeting considered applying for federal funds to operate a "pilot program" and the creation of a "non-profit organization."

21. "1965 Operation," box 6, folder 7, MHP Records. For information on the broad-based effort by UMOS to assist migrants, see "Propose Migrant Aid Plan," *Hartford Times-Press*, May 13, 1965; and "Secretary's phone call notes, Mrs. Margaret Salick, State Economic Opportunity office, to Dr. James L. Wardlaw, Jr., May 5, 1965," box 6, folder 7, MHP Records.

22. "Draft of Statement to be included with the UMOS proposal to OEO and to be given the summer staff: The purpose of UMOS operated pre school day care centers," box 7, folder 9, MHP Records.

23. Jesus Salas, interview by the author, Apr. 20, 2000. According to Salas, children did not play in the fields, as many growers told the public, but rather were important workers in their own right, bringing sacks and baskets for picking, and, if old enough, working as laborers themselves, regardless of laws re-

garding mandatory school attendance or maximum hours of work that applied to them.

24. Robert Holzhauer, Chairman Advisory Committee, to Carl N. Neupert, MD, Sept. 17, 1966, box 6, folder 7, MHP Records; John R. Maurice to Joseph C. Fagan, Commissioner, Nov. 3, 1966, box 121, folder "Governor's Committee on Migratory Labor," Commissioner's Subject Files, Wisconsin Department of Industry, Labor, and Human Relations (DILHR) Records.

25. "A Report on Programs, October 25, 1967," box 24, folder "S24 UMOS General, 1968/1969," Administrative Subject Files, Economic Opportunity Section, Wisconsin Division of Economic Assistance (DEA) Records; "Milwaukee, Wisconsin (Migrant)," June 27, 1966, box 516, folder "United Migrant Opp. Services, Wisconsin," entry 42, CSA Records.

26. United Migrant Opportunity Services, *Helping People*, 3, 59.

27. "United Migrant Opportunity Services, Inc., Proposal Title III-B, Economic Opportunity Act, May 1966–May 1967," box 7, folder 10, MHP Records.

28. Smith, interview. Smith, a graduate student in history, became the Madison-based coordinator for the march on Madison.

29. Raushenbush, *Study of Migratory Workers*.

30. "United Migrant Opportunity Services, Inc., Proposal Title III-B," MHP Records.

31. Ibid., 6.

32. Jesus Salas, interview by the author, Apr. 20, 2000.

33. Parra, "United Migrant Opportunity Services," 56.

34. United Migrant Opportunity Services, Inc., Bylaws (1966), 502 (a)–(f), 509, box 7, folder 10, MHP Records. It appears as if this "migrant advisory committee" did not operate in 1966 or 1967. No minutes of meetings are available, and there is no mention made of it outside the OEO grant and UMOS bylaws.

35. "Relationship of Local Communities to UMOS," box 7, folder 9, MHP Records.

36. Noel H. Klores, Director, Office of Special Field Programs, Community Action Program, OEO Washington Headquarters, to Rev. John A. Maurice, President, UMOS, Aug. 30, 1967 (emphasis added), box 151, folder "United Migrant Opportunity Services, Inc.," DILHR Records.

37. "Five Policy and Personnel Resolutions Recommended by the Executive Committee, 1967" (emphasis added), box 151, folder "United Migrant Opportunity Services, Inc," DILHR Records; "Highlight Memorandum: Application for Grant under Title 11-A, May 24, 1967," CSA Records.

38. Smith, interview. For more on the union, see Rosenbaum, "Success in Organizing: Case of Pickle Workers."

39. "Felicidad, Already, Fiesta Marks First Year of Spanish Center Classes," *MJ*, Dec. 11, 1967; "US to Probe Charges of Bias against Latins," *MJ*, Aug. 25, 1968; "County Panel Stalls Job Fund Proposal," *MJ*, July 12, 1968; "CEP Put 1,971 on Job During 1st Year Here," *MJ*, Oct. 23, 1969.

40. Lalo Valdez, "Narrative History"; "Allen-Bradley Union Silent on Meeting," *MS*, Aug. 13, 1968; "No Progress Evident in A-B Talks," *MJ*, Aug. 13, 1968; "Demonstrators Turn Spotlight on Allen-Bradley Co.," *MS*, Aug. 15, 1968; "Milwaukee Firm May Lose US Work," *Christian Science Monitor*, Jan. 14, 1969.

41. Avelardo Valdez, "Selective Determinants"; Jesus Salas, interview by the author, Apr. 20, 2000; Smith, interview. This crosstown coalition, according to Valdez, did not hold for very long, as the three communities focused mainly on local needs.

42. Avelardo Valdez, "Selective Determinants"; Lalo Valdez, "Narrative History"; *Chicano Civil Rights Struggle*; "A Long Campaign," *MJ*, Oct. 9, 1969; "25 Local Latins to Attend Kansas City Forum," *MJ*, Nov. 17, 1969; "Back Then, a Newspaper Stirred Up Pride in Latino Community," *MJS*, Oct. 2, 2005. In Milwaukee, the LAUCR and the Brown Berets were essentially the same organization.

43. "Poverty Officials Out after Heated Debate," *MJ*, Jan. 31, 1969.

44. William G. Kruse, Executive Director, UMOS, to Board Members, July 20, 1967, and "Minutes, UMOS Board of Directors, July 26, 1967," box 151, folder "United Migrant Opportunity Services, Inc.," DILHR Papers.

45. Jesus Salas, interview by the author, Apr. 20, 2000.

46. Ibid.

47. Ibid.

48. "Poverty Officials Out after Heated Debate," *MJ*, Jan. 31, 1969.

49. OEO Instruction 6005-1, "Participation of the Poor in the Planning, Conduct, and Evaluation of Community Action Programs," Dec. 1, 1968.

50. OEO, *Participation of the Poor*, 2.

51. United Migrant Opportunity Services, *Annual Report* (Milwaukee, Wisc., 1968), 1–9; William R. Bechtel, Staff Director, Senate Subcommittee on Employment, Manpower, and Poverty, to Mrs. Helen Bruner, Center for Community Leadership Development, University of Wisconsin Extension, May 28, 1969, and Margaret Salick to Salvador Sanchez, May 21, 1969, in box 24, folder "S24 UMOS General, 69/69," DEA Records.

52. United Migrant Opportunity Services, *Annual Report*, 1.

53. Ibid.; United Migrant Opportunity Services, *Helping People*, 3–4; Parra, "United Migrant Opportunity Services," 56.

54. Memo: Margaret Salick to Robert Neil Smith, telephone conversation with Bill Koch about Migrant Grievances, Dec. 5, 1968, box 24, folder "S24 UMOS General 1968/1969," DEA Records. Koch was new to the job, having worked for the University of Wisconsin, and so perhaps his actions startled the UMOS management. See "Madison Man Heads Migrant Service Unit," *Waukesha Freeman*, Oct. 2, 1968; and "UMOS Board Will Accept Resignations of 5 Directors," *Madison Capitol Times*, Feb. 4, 1969.

55. This move drew criticism from some UMOS Advisory Committee members who felt that the "en masse resignations" had the effect of "dealing a serious

blow to the UMOS organization." Memo, Helen Bruner, Secretary, Madison UMOS Advisory Committee, to C. L. Creiber, Arthur Kurtz, Bronson LaFollette, Stephan Reilly, Frank Walsh, Melvin Velhulst, Jan. 17, 1969, box 151, folder "United Migrant Opportunity Service, UMOS," DILHR Records; "Five Administrators Quit Migrant Services Program," *MS*, Jan. 16, 1969; "Five Who Quit Migrant Unit Start Own Consulting Firm," *MS*, Feb. 17, 1969; "OEO to Run Migrant Unit 'Temporarily,'" *MS*, Feb. 8, 1969; "US Advises Changes in Migrant Program," *MJ*, Feb. 21, 1969.

56. Memo, Bruner to Creiber et al., Jan. 17, 1969, DILHR Records. Also see Margaret Salick to Larry Powell, Analyst, Chicago OEO, Apr. 25, 1969; Senator Gaylord Nelson to Donald Rumsfeld, OEO, June 12, 1969; and Senator Gaylord Nelson to Helen Bruner, UW Extension, Center for Leadership Development, all in box 24, folder "S24 UMOS 68/69," DEA Records; and "Wautoma Chamber to Seek Removal of Migrant Center," *Oshkosh Daily Northwestern*, Dec. 4, 1968.

57. In "Salas Poorly Qualified," *Waushara Argus*, Apr. 3, 1969, a rural newspaper reprinted a letter that attacked Salas written by Wautoma resident Donald M. Weyenberg and addressed to Wisconsin senator William Proxmire. Wilcox went on the offensive as a legislator, pushing for an amendment to the state's antitrespass statute to bar entry to migrant camps and keep groups like UMOS from "stirring up trouble." "Wilcox 'Anti-Trespass' Bill Can Slam Gates to Migrant Worker Aid," *Madison Capitol Times*, July 29, 1969. Salas also drew fire from Central Wisconsin over his concern that funds for migrant children's school programs were benefiting nonmigrant children. See Jesus Salas to Grace Lensmire, May 27, 1969; Beverly Seekamp to Grace Lensmire, Central Wisconsin Economic Opportunity Committee, Inc., July 10, 1969; and Grace Lensmire to Jesus Salas, July 17, 1969, all in box 24, folder "S24 UMOS General, 69/69," DEA Records.

58. Robert Neal Smith, Director, Wisconsin Division of Economic Assistance, Economic Opportunity Division, to Noel Klores, OEO, Mar. 4, 1969; Salick to Powell, Apr. 25, 1969; Nelson to Rumsfeld, June 12, 1969; and US Representative Robert W. Kastenmeir to Donald Rumsfeld, Director, OEO, June 20, 1969, all in box 24, folder "S24 UMOS General, 69/69," DEA Records.

59. "Migrants React to Grant," *APC*, July 3, 1969. See "Flap #2, June 25, 1969," "Statement of CAP Grant, CG-8514, June 1, 1969," and "Field Representative Assessment of CAA performance," CSA Records. Although informed of the controversy, the OEO considered that some Republicans were "mad" at Salas but that the board's choice of Salas was a "local thing and . . . [the OEO] had no reason to object to it." The OEO field assessment of the organization commented that UMOS operated as "an effective voice for the farmworkers working and attempting to settle in Wisconsin."

60. "Caravan Protests Aid Cuts" and "Confrontation Produces Results for Minorities, 3 Activists Say," *MJ*, Apr. 22, 1969; "Protest to Aid Cuts Called Success, More Promised," *MJ*, Apr. 23, 1969; Mrs. Margaret Salick to Chuck Hill, Nov. 4, 1969, box 24, folder "S24 UMOS General 1968/1969," DEA Records; "Migrant

Project Fears Loss of Federal Funds," *MJ*, June 27, 1969; "US Forces Migrants Into Welfare: Salas," *MJ*, Dec. 5, 1969. News reports noted the great degree of interethnic cooperation between African Americans and Latinos. These protests would continue as multiethnic, cross-community affairs well into the 1970s. Father Groppi, Ernesto Chacon, and members of the LAUCR and UMOS staff, despite countless arrests, continued to protest on behalf of Welfare funding. See "Latins Vow to Push for Pair's Clemency," *MJ*, Mar. 5, 1971; and "Lucey Grants Latins Conditional Pardon," *MJ*, Apr. 7, 1971.

61. Mrs. Denis Rupnow, resident of Ixonia, Wisconsin, to Attorney General Robert Warren, Oct. 1, 1969; Mrs. Margaret Salick to Robert Neal Smith, Oct. 9, 1969; Robert Neal Smith to Mrs. Denis Rupnow, Oct. 17, 1969; and Mrs. Margaret Salick to Chuck Hill, Nov. 4, 1969, all in box 24, folder "S24 UMOS General 1968/1969," DEA Records.

62. "Migrants Could Suffer from Salas' Part in Capitol Protest," *APC*, Feb. 15, 1970. The article cites a federal spokesperson for the OEO stating that "the right of legal protest is the right of every citizen, and we do not deny our employees that." The article then, without citing a source, reported that UMOS's funds could be in jeopardy.

63. "Home at Last," *Wisconsin State Journal*, Mar. 23, 1969. This article describes the UMOS settlement program operating in Madison.

64. United Migrant Opportunity, Inc., Program Coordinator's Report, Oct. 30, 1969, box 24, folder "S24 UMOS General 1968/1969," DEA Records.

65. Jesus Salas, "To All Board and Staff Members" (June 1970), box 24, folder "S-24, UMOS General 1970," DEA Records; "Salas Quits UMOS," *La Guardia*, June 1970.

66. Jesus Salas, "To All Board and Staff Members" (June 1970), box 24, folder "S-24, UMOS General 1970," DEA Records.

67. Margaret Salick to Salvador Sanchez, Nov. 3, 1970, box 24, folder "UMOS General 1970," DEA Records.

68. Salvador Sanchez, interview, July 19, 2000.

69. "Courses Brought to Migrants," *Elkhorn Independent*, Sept. 23, 1971.

70. United Migrant Opportunity Services, *Helping People*, 18.

71. Salvador Sanchez to Thomas Dale, Administrator, Equal Rights Division, Department of Industry Labor and Human Relations, Aug. 20, 1971, series 2419, 1971–77, box 155, folder 16, Patrick J. Lucey Gubernatorial Papers, Wisconsin Historical Society, Madison.

72. Development Associates Inc., *An Evaluation of United Migrant Opportunity Services, Inc. (UMOS), Milwaukee, Wisconsin, Submitted to the Office of Economic Opportunity, Migrant Division, Under Contract Number BIC-5275; SBA0958.8 (a) 71* (Washington, D.C., Nov. 1971), box 24, folder "UMOS 1972," DEA Records.

73. Minutes, United Migrant Opportunity Services, Inc., Special Committee Meeting, Jan. 20, 1972, box 24, folder "UMOS 1972," DEA Records.

74. "Migrant Head Steps Down," *MJ*, May 29, 1974. Despite his years of activism, Sanchez was a reformer, not a revolutionary. He claimed that heading

UMOS had worn him out and that more militant Chicanos sought to destroy "the system." Sanchez commented that the system "shouldn't be destroyed."

75. "Martinez to Head Migrant Agency," *MJ*, Sept. 9, 1974; "The Latin Corner," *MJ*, May 26, 1975; "Migrant Job-Training Program Gets Off to a Successful Start," *MS*, Mar. 17, 1984; "Cinco de Mayo Events Set Sunday at Mitchell Park," *MJS*, May 5, 1990; "Cinco de Mayo Festival Plans Set," *MJS*, May 6, 2005. Even Salas and Chacon entered the mainstream. See "Latinos Gain Political Clout," *MJS*, Sept. 20, 2003; "UW regent helped farmworkers assert their rights," *MJS*, Feb. 9, 2006.

76. For some examples of this new perspective on the War on Poverty and the CAP, see Orleck, *Storming Caesar's Palace*; Ashmore, *Carry It On*; Bauman, *Race and the War on Poverty*; Germany, *New Orleans after the Promises*; Kiffmeyer, *Reformers to Radicals*.

Chapter 5

1. The connection of migrants to the story of political activism in Crystal City after 1969 builds significantly on Armando Navarro's research into the activism at Crystal City after 1963 by including the central migrant component. Many of the Crystal City activists detailed in Navarro's work participated in efforts to organize an independent migrant labor union, built migrant and Latino service organizations, and led the state-level grape boycott in Wisconsin. See Navarro, *Cristal Experiment*, 55.

2. "Militants Denounce Traditional Stands at Chicano Parley," *LAT*, Mar. 31, 1969; "Anglo 'Integration' Rejected by Chicanos," *LAT*, Apr. 7, 1969; "Brown Berets Hail 'La Raza' and Scorn the Establishment," *LAT*, June 16, 1969.

3. For an insightful comparative analysis of the possibilities and limits of such nationalism, see Klor de Alva, "Aztlán, Boriquen and Hispanic Nationalism." For a view that downplays Chicano nationalism when set in comparative perspective, see Wiebe, *Who We Are*.

4. "Accused New Mexico Raid Leader Seized," *LAT*, June 11, 1967; "5 Sentenced in N.M. Raids on Courthouse," *LAT*, Dec. 16, 1967; "Legend Emerging in New Mexico," *LAT*, February 5, 1968. On Tijerina generally, see Tijerina, *They Called Me "King Tiger"*; Nabokov, *Tijerina and the Courthouse Raid*; Busto, *King Tiger*.

5. On the Crusade for Justice and Rodolfo "Corky" Gonzales, see "Chicano Must Be Nationalist to Last in U.S.," *LAT*, Apr. 18, 1969; Juan Quiñones, *Chicano Politics*, 112–14; and Limón, *Mexican Ballads, Chicano Poems*, 115–30. On Gonzales and the Crusade for Justice generally, see Vigil, *Crusade for Justice*; and Rodolfo Gonzales, *Message to Aztlán*.

6. On the general growth of MAYO see Navarro, *Mexican American Youth Organization*; Sepúlveda, *Life and Times of Willie Velásquez*; and José Gutiérrez, *Making of a Chicano Militant*.

7. On the role of Aztlán in the Chicano movement, see the various essays in Anaya and Lomeli, *Aztlán*, as well as Barrera, *Beyond Aztlán*; and John Chavez, *Lost Land*.

8. See examples in Cashion, *Pigskin Pulpit*; and Bissinger, *Friday Night Lights*.

9. Shockley, *Chicano Revolt*, 118–19.

10. See the *Crystal City High School Javelin* for 1962, 1963, and 1970. In the yearbooks for 1962 and 1963, Anglos are the socially dominant group, despite the fact that Mexican Americans accounted for the largest group of enrolled students. Pompom squad and other student groups were Anglo-dominated, with only token Mexican American representation. José Angel Gutiérrez and Francisco Rodriguez were two of the Mexican American students whose families seem to have focused on education: both participated in various Anglo-dominated student activities like debate and honor society.

11. De La Fuente, interview.

12. "Students Air Grievances," *ZCS*, May 1, 1969. After the boycott, Palacios went on to become senior class president and the captain of the cheer squad. She later would work as a legal secretary for a Crystal City law firm before becoming Crystal City's city manager in 2003.

13. Quoted in Shockley, *Chicano Revolt*, 273 n. 33.

14. The community-level mobilization is covered in Navarro, "El Partido de La Raza Unida," 187–304; and Miller, "Conflict and Change," which presents a discussion of these events in "Farmington," a pseudonym for Crystal City, Texas.

15. De La Fuente, interview; Shockley, *Chicano Revolt*, 120; Navarro, *Mexican American Youth Organization*, 133; *ZCS*, May 1, 1969.

16. "A Challenge to Build a New Society," *NYT*, Apr. 20, 1969; "A New Mexican-American Militancy," *NYT*, Apr. 20, 1969; "A Family Fight Embitters Chicanos," *WP*, May 25, 1969.

17. For the development of MAYO and the San Antonio chapter of the Brown Berets and the internal tensions these developments revealed in Mexican American politics, see, generally, Montejano, *Quixote's Soldiers*.

18. Navarro, *Mexican American Youth Organization*, 133–34; Shockley, *Chicano Revolt*, 126–27; José Gutiérrez, *Making of a Chicano Militant*, 129–30; Reed Harp, "Interview with Gutiérrez," *Texas Observer*, Jan. 2, 1970. Armando Navarro perhaps credits Gutiérrez with too great a role in this early student activism, since Gutiérrez did not arrive in Crystal City until June 1969. He certainly counseled the students, but the students had their own ideas about protest in the spring of 1969. Yet it is clear that, as Navarro asserts, it was Gutiérrez who helped them define, channel, and organize these efforts the following fall semester. Gutiérrez's 1968 master's thesis was later republished as *La Raza and Revolution*.

19. See *ZCS*, May 1, 1969; Navarro, "El Partido de La Raza Unida," 134; Shockley, *Chicano Revolt*, 120; José Gutiérrez, "Toward a Theory."

20. De La Fuente, interview.

21. On the long-standing connections between migrant Tejanos and the San Jose region, as well as the Great Lakes, see Pitti, *Devil in Silicon Valley*, 93–94, 106–7, 124–25; Rodriguez, "Movement of Young Mexican Americans." For in-

formation on the developing "Chicano" protests in California, see "Chicanos Told to Fight Like Blacks for Respect," *LAT*, Apr. 9, 1969.

22. See "Homecoming Activities Moved," *ZCS*, Nov. 20, 1969; and Navarro, *Mexican American Youth Organization*, 135.

23. Navarro, *Mexican American Youth Organization*, 136; Reed Harp, "Walkout in Crystal City," *Texas Observer*, Jan. 2, 1970.

24. The mention of "violence" may have been a result of supposed statements made by Gutiérrez on Apr. 10, 1969, in San Antonio, Texas, in which he was quoted as saying that he would "kill" gringos, and also perhaps to a specific editorial published in the *San Antonio Express* on Apr. 12, 1969, which characterized the MAYO, then active in San Antonio, as a "handful of apparently frustrated young men" and Gutiérrez as a "violent young man." For nearly a month after his remarks in San Antonio, critics such as representative Henry B. Gonzalez, editorial writers, and others attacked Gutiérrez for his actions, rhetoric, and youthfulness in letters to the newspaper. In these letters, editorials, and commentary pieces, various writers branded Gutiérrez a "boy," "baby face," and "a young juvenile with a tamale on his shoulder." See *Dallas Morning News*, Apr. 12, 1969; and *San Antonio Express*, Apr. 12, 16, 20, 1969.

25. "Letter to the Editor, Larry C. Volz," *ZCS*, Nov. 20, 1969. This charity thesis regarding public education was a quite common refrain across the Southwest during the period of Mexican American civil rights activism. According to its logic, since large landowners and middle-class Anglos paid more in local taxes, Mexicans were somehow indebted to Anglos for public school education. What these criticisms fail to mention is that Anglo schools benefited directly from the presence of Mexican children in school districts, since Texas determined the amount of funding granted to local districts based on a census of school-age children reported each year. Districts counted all the Mexican children, yet they maintained schools that aimed to educate Anglo students through high school graduation, while providing few opportunities for Mexican American children to advance beyond the elementary grades.

26. Letters to the editor, *ZCS*, Nov. 27, 1969.

27. De La Fuente, interview. In an anonymous letter to the *ZCS* published on November 20, 1969, the writer calculated that over 26 percent of Crystal City High School graduates old enough to have a daughter try out for the court were Mexican American yet did not provide information on how many actually had a daughter in the high school. It seems as if the single-student figure is accurate.

28. "Homecoming Court Presented" and "Jim Byrd Heads Ex-Students," *ZCS*, Nov. 27, 1969.

29. Parker, "Power-in-Conflict," 31; "Teach-in Starts for Students," *ZCS*, Dec. 18, 1969. The students named the group the "Youth Association," but it also seems that some referred to it as MAYO, since its membership was entirely Mexican American.

30. Shockley, *Chicano Revolt*, 133.

31. "U.S. to Investigate High School Boycott in Texas," *NYT*, Dec. 19, 1969; "News of the Day; The Nation," *LAT*, Jan. 5, 1970; Shockley, "La Raza Unida," 318.

32. "U.S. to Investigate High School Boycott in Texas," *NYT*, Dec. 19, 1969.

33. José Gutiérrez, *Making of a Chicano Militant*, 142–76; "The Barker," *ZCS*, Dec. 11, 1969; "School Boycott in Second Week," *ZCS*, Dec. 18, 1969.

34. On the Black Panther and Young Lords protests in New York City, see "Boycott Keeps 1,450 Out of School in Harlem," *NYT*, Mar. 14, 1967; and "Puerto Rican Group Seizes Church in East Harlem in Demand for Space," *NYT*, Dec. 29, 1969.

35. "Teach-In Starts for Students," *ZCS*, Dec. 18, 1969; Navarro, *Mexican American Youth Organization*, 142–43. For detailed coverage of these events, see Shockley, *Chicano Revolt*, 131–39.

36. "Students Return to Classes," *ZCS*, Jan. 1, 1970; Miller and Preston, "Vertical Ties"; Calvin Trillin, "U.S. Journal: Crystal City, Texas," *New Yorker*, Apr. 17, 1971, 102–5.

37. Journalists were also trying to define the term "Chicano" and explore what this now national movement stood for. For examples of these discussions after Crystal City, see "The Chicanos Want In," *WP*, Jan. 11, 1970; "Texas Mexicans Win New Rights," *NYT*, Jan. 11, 1970; "Who Is a Chicano? And What Is It the Chicanos Want?" *LAT*, Feb. 7, 1970; Navarro, "El Partido de La Raza Unida," 143. Other similar "blowouts" occurred in Texas and Southern California, although the results were less dramatic. See Weinberg, *Chance to Learn*, 171.

38. "Who Is a Chicano?," *LAT*, Feb. 7, 1970.

39. Gutiérrez, interview, Apr. 18, 1995.

40. De La Fuente, interview; Navarro, "El Partido de La Raza Unida," 141. My focus is on the linkages between Texas and Wisconsin rather than a retelling of this well-documented political movement. For narrative social science histories of these events, see Shockley, *Chicano Revolt*; and Navarro, *Cristal Experiment*.

41. Parker, "Power-in-Conflict," 277.

42. Ibid., 36.

43. Richard A. Shaffer, "Brown Power," *WSJ*, Sept. 5, 1975. Shaffer also referred to Crystal City as a "test tube" for the Chicano movement, with CU serving as the "backbone" of the party. On the development of the party and its early history, see José Gutiérrez, *Making of a Chicano Militant*, 186–87; and oral memoir of José Angel Gutiérrez, 97, Mexican American Project, Institute for Oral History, Baylor University, Waco, Tex.

44. "Gutiérrez Slate Wins in Crystal City," *San Antonio Express*, Apr. 5, 1970.

45. Gonzalez, interview.

46. United Migrant Opportunity Services, *Helping People*, 9; Shockley, *Chicano Revolt*, 188–89. Gutiérrez visited friends in Milwaukee, primarily Francisco Rodríguez, in the taverns; lobbied for support back in Crystal City; and provided assistance in mobilization in Milwaukee.

47. Raul Rodriguez, interview.

48. Lazcano, interview.

49. "Primary in Texas Pits Old and New," *NYT*, Apr. 27, 1970; "Chicanos in Texas Bid for Key Political Role," *NYT*, Aug. 2, 1970; "Chicano Group Seeks Control of South Texas," *LAT*, Aug. 23, 1970; Ignacio Garcia, *United We Win*, 57.

50. Antonio Camejo, "How La Raza Unida Party Is Changing Crystal City," *La Guardia*, May 1970.

51. See early editions of *La Verdad*, especially those published in 1970. Available editions reference earlier editions yet are currently unavailable. For one example of Tejano diasporic linkages, see "Nuevos Centros De Niños," *La Verdad*, Nov. 20, 1970.

52. Gonzalez, interview; Shockley, *Chicano Revolt*, 189; "Mexican Americans Win," *NYT*, Apr. 7, 1971; "La Raza Unida Party Survives Texas Elections," *La Guardia*, Dec. 1970.

53. "Students Walk-Out," *La Guardia*, Sept. 1970.

54. "Chicanos in Texas Bid for Key Political Role," *NYT*, Aug. 2, 1970; "The Politics of Change: Cotulla Texas," *WP*, Aug. 18, 1970; "Chicano Group Seeks Control of South Texas," *LAT*, Aug. 23, 1970.

55. Ignacio Garcia, *United We Win*, 63–71; *La Raza Unida Party v. Harold J. Dean, Judge et al.* (462 S.W.2d 570).

56. "La Raza Unida Party Survives Texas Elections."

57. Ibid.; "Commentario Sobre Las Elecciones," *La Verdad*, Nov. 20, 1970; "The Nation," *LAT*, Sept. 20, 1970.

58. United Migrant Opportunity Services, *Helping People*, 9; José Gutiérrez, oral memoir, 13–14, Baylor University, Waco, Tex.; "Mexican American Hostility Deepens in Tense East Los Angeles," *NYT*, Sept. 4, 1970; "Chicano Political Party Foretold by Spokesman," *LAT*, May 9, 1971. In Wisconsin, according to Gutiérrez, the RUP candidate ran as a Democrat, and in California in 1971, Bert Corona, serving as a representative for the party, announced that the RUP California was seeking ballot status.

59. José Gutiérrez, *Making of a Chicano Militant*, 212; Francisco Rodriguez, interview, July 28, 1998. Rodriguez was of the belief that an activist should not seek to become a permanent fixture in a job post and therefore entered Crystal City intent on resignation within a few years in order to provide another Chicano with the opportunity to gain experience in governmental affairs.

60. Navarro, *Cristal Experiment*, 76. Carlos Reyes left Crystal City in the late 1970s and in Wisconsin first joined UMOS, then later the University of Wisconsin, Chicano Studies Department, a campus department, and later a program founded by Jesus Salas and student activists at UW-Madison. MAYO founder Mario Compean also followed this stream to UMOS and UW-Madison and then to the Northwest, again following the Crystal City migrant stream.

61. For frank discussions of the role of women in the RUP in Crystal City, see "Oral Memoir of Martha P. Cotera," Mexican American Project, Institute for Oral History, Baylor University, Waco, Tex.; Cotera, *Diosa y Hembra*; José Angel

Gutiérrez, Oral History Interview with Lidia Serrata (1997), no. 107, and Oral History Interview with Viviana (Santiago) Cavada (1998), no. 66, Center for Mexican American Studies, Bell Library, University of Texas at Arlington.

62. "Latin Groups Fight 'Anglo Integration,'" *LAT*, Feb. 23, 1968; "Wiggins Confers with Mexican-Americans in Washington," *LAT*, June 17, 1968; "Mexican-Americans to Hold Youth Conference," *LAT*, Mar. 23, 1969; "Chicanos Must Be Nationalist to Last in U.S., Leader Says," *LAT*, Apr. 18, 1969.

63. "3000 Chicanos Parley in Denver," *La Guardia*, May 1970; "Chicanos Gather for Liberation Meeting," *LAT*, Mar. 28, 1970; "Time Arrives for Talk of Third Party," *LAT*, Apr. 18, 1971.

64. "Chicanos Gain Power in Texas," *Chicago Tribune*, Feb. 13, 1972; "Mexican-American Politics to Bloom over Labor Day," *WP*, Aug. 27, 1972; "Chicanos: A Power in Texas Politics," *NYT*, Sept. 3, 1972; Navarro, *Cristal Experiment*, 107–12.

65. "Four-Day Convention Ends: Raza Party Drafts Political Goals," *Chicago Tribune*, Sept. 5, 1972; Juan Quiñones, *Chicano Politics*, 128–38; Acuña, *Occupied America*, 34–341. Gutiérrez's personal notes from the convention are located in box 24, "Raza Unida Party," José Angel Gutiérrez Papers, Benson Latin American Collection, University of Texas at Austin.

66. Salazar memo, p. 2, box 24, Gutiérrez Papers.

67. Ignacio Garcia, *United We Win*, 103–16; José Gutiérrez, *Making of a Chicano Militant*, 230; Salazar memo, p. 2, box 24, Gutiérrez Papers; Tony Castro, "Chicano Party Elects Texan as Chairman," *WP*, Sept. 5, 1972; Martin Waldron, "Chicanos Reject Two Old Parties, Then Formally Found a Third One," *NYT*, Sept. 5, 1972.

68. Gutiérrez, interview, Apr. 19, 1995.

69. Parker, "Power-in-Conflict," 280.

70. Gutiérrez, interview, Apr. 18, 1995.

71. See, for example, Shockley, *Chicano Revolt*; Ignacio Garcia, *United We Win*; Navarro, *Mexican American Youth Organization*; and Navarro, *Cristal Experiment*, all focused primarily on the birth of La Raza Unida Party in 1969.

72. "Chicano Split," *WP*, Oct. 22, 1972.

73. Ibid.; "Two Militant Negro, Latin American Groups Plan Cooperation Pact," *LAT*, Oct. 13, 1967; "Denver Man Killed, 6 Wounded in Gunfight at Chicano Building," *NYT*, Mar. 18, 1973; "Chicano Is Slain and 6 Wounded in Chicano Gun Battle," *WP*, Mar. 18, 1973; United Migrant Opportunity Services, *Helping People*, 9; "Raza Unida Party," Wisconsin folder, box 24, Gutiérrez Papers.

74. "Raza Unida Party," Wisconsin folder, Correspondence, 1974, box 24, Gutiérrez Papers. Gutiérrez, from as early as 1969, had directly recruited several of his classmates from Crystal City High School then living in Milwaukee to return and assist his efforts in Crystal City.

75. "Raza Unida Party," Wisconsin folder, Correspondence, 1973, box 24, Gutiérrez Papers.

76. Reyes, interview. After leaving jobs in Crystal City, several La Raza Unida party members sought and found work in migrant programs in Wisconsin by

traveling the migrant stream. Once in Wisconsin, however, people like Reyes and Rodriguez kept each other abreast of developments.

77. Salas, interview by the author, Mar. 22, 1995; Miguel Delgado, interview, Feb. 8, 1997; Nieri, interview; José Gutiérrez, "Oral Memoir of José Angel Gutiérrez," 94. Each of these men worked for federally supported community-based organizations in Milwaukee, Wisconsin. Gutiérrez recruited them because of their experience in grant writing and grant management to come to Crystal City and write the grant for and take over management of the heretofore unsuccessful economic development program. The Milwaukee activists formed the Zavala County Economic Development Corporation at Crystal City, which unlike past efforts received a large federal grant. Navarro, *Cristal Experiment*, 270–71.

78. Gutiérrez, interview, Apr. 19, 1995; Castro, *La Causa Politica*, 169. Tony Castro viewed the Crystal City political scene under Raza Unida as "the old politics of ward campaigning disguised as new Chicano politics." In many ways, this was true, but the nature of family organization also tied the local to the translocal community.

79. Jesus Salas, interview by the author, July 27, 1992.

80. The micro-historical details of the fall of RUP in Crystal City are covered well in Navarro, *Cristal Experiment*, 172–81; and José Gutiérrez, *Making of a Chicano Militant*, 198–201.

81. See Navarro, *Cristal Experiment*, 172–81.

82. "Natural Gas Cutoff of Town in Texas Delayed by a Justice," *WSJ*, Sept. 2, 1977; "Coastal States Gas Unit Cleared to Cut Off Gas to Crystal City, Texas," *WSJ*, Sept. 6, 1977; "Crystal City, Texas, Is Learning to Live without Gas Supply," *WSJ*, Sept. 26, 1977; Bill Curry, "Crystal City: Second Day without Gas," *WP*, Sept. 25, 1977; "U.S. Aid Valve Opens for Gasless Texas City," *WP*, Sept. 28, 1977; Nicholas C. Chriss, "1978 Prospects Looking Bleak in 'Gasless' Texas Community," *WP*, Jan. 4, 1978; "Follow Up," *Chicago Tribune*, Jan. 30, 1978.

83. Edward Walsh, "President Weighs Claim of Executive Privilege," *WP*, Mar. 15, 1978; Edward Walsh, "Judge Backs President on Executive Privilege," *WP*, Apr. 8, 1978; "Transcripts of the President's News Conference on Foreign and Domestic Matters," *NYT*, June 15, 1978.

84. Navarro, *Cristal Experiment*, 319–25.

85. Ibid., 331; José Gutiérrez, *Making of a Chicano Militant*, 198–201. For a summary of many of the problems faced by the RUP in Crystal City in its final years, see Tom Curtis, "Raza Desunida," *Texas Monthly*, Feb. 1977.

Bibliography

Manuscript Collections

Arlington, Tex.
    University of Texas at Arlington Library
        Center for Mexican American Studies
            Tejano Voices Oral History Collection
Austin, Tex.
    Lyndon Baines Johnson Presidential Library
        Papers of John B. Connally
        James Gaither Papers
        White House Central Files
    Texas State Library
        Genealogy Collection
        Texas Good Neighbor Commission, Records, 1943–87
    University of Texas at Austin
        General Libraries
            Center for American History
                Crystal City Clipping File
            Benson Latin American Collection
                José Angel Gutiérrez Papers
College Park, Md.
    National Archives
        RG 381, Records of the Community Services Administration
Corpus Christi, Tex.
    Texas A&M University
        Special Collections, Mary and Jeff Bell Library
            Dr. Hector Perez Garcia Papers, 1913–96
Crystal City, Tex.
    Crystal City Festival Association, press release, "The City of Crystal City
        Proudly Celebrates Its Seventy-fifth Anniversary, 1907–1982"

Office of the City Manager, Application to the Department of Housing
and Urban Development for a Grant to Plan a Comprehensive
City Demonstration Program, Apr. 11, 1967
Office of the Superintendent, Crystal City Independent School District,
School Board Minutes, 1948–55
Detroit, Mich.
Wayne State University
Archives of Labor and Urban Affairs, Walter P. Reuther Library
César Chávez Papers
William Kircher Papers
National Farm Workers of America Collection
United Farm Workers of America Collection
Madison, Wisc.
Wisconsin Historical Society
Records of the Governor's Committee on Migratory Labor
Patrick J. Lucey Gubernatorial Papers
Paul A. and Elizabeth Brandeis Raushenbush Papers
Wisconsin Bureau of Community Health and Prevention,
Migrant Health Program Records
Wisconsin Department of Industry, Labor, and Human Relations,
Commissioner's Subject Files
Wisconsin Division of Economic Assistance, Economic Opportunity
Section, Administrative Subject Files (unprocessed collection)
Milwaukee, Wisc.
University of Wisconsin–Milwaukee
Milwaukee Area Research Center, Golda Meir Library
Charles Heymanns Papers
Milwaukee Urban Archives
Riverside, Calif.
Special Collections and Archives, University of California
Riverside Libraries
Tomás Rivera Archive, Collection 253
Stanford, Calif.
Department of Special Collections and University Archives,
Stanford University Libraries
Ernesto Galarza Papers, 1936–84, Collection M0224
Waco, Tex.
Baylor University
Institute for Oral History, Mexican American Project
Oral memoir of José Angel Gutiérrez
Zavala County, Tex.
Zavala County Judges Criminal Docket, Books 5–6, 1952–64

Periodicals

Appleton Post-Crescent
Austin Observer
Chicago Tribune Sunday Magazine
Christian Science Monitor
Crystal City High School Javelin
Dallas Morning News
Ebony
El Cosechador
Elkhorn Independent
Esperanze
Hartford Times-Press
La Crosse Archdiocese Times Review
La Crosse Tribune
La Guardia
Latin Times (Chicago)
La Verdad
La Voz Mexicana
Look
Los Angeles Times
Madison Capital Times
Milwaukee Journal

Milwaukee Journal-Sentinel
Milwaukee Sentinel
National Observer
Newsweek
New York Amsterdam News
New Yorker
New York Times
Oshkosh Daily Northwestern
San Antonio Express
Stevens Point Daily Journal
Texas Monthly
Texas Observer
Time
UWM Post
Wall Street Journal
Washington Post
Waukesha Freeman
Waushara Argus
Wisconsin State Journal
Zavala County Sentinel

Interviews

All interviews are by the author unless otherwise specified.

Aguillar, Amalia. Crystal City, Tex., Feb. 10, 1997.

Arrambide-Cervera, Eva. Milwaukee, Wisc., June 23, 1999.

Avila, Alberto. Milwaukee, Wisc., Aug. 18, 2002.

Cervera, Oscar. Milwaukee, Wisc., June 21, 23, 1999.

Cornejo, Juan. Crystal City, Tex., Feb. 24, 1997.

Cuellar, Gloria. Crystal City, Tex., Feb. 6, 1997.

De La Fuente, Severita Lara. Crystal City, Tex., Feb. 15, 1997.

Delgado, Miguel. Crystal City, Tex., Feb. 4, 8, 10, 12, 20, 1997.

Delgado, Victor H. Milwaukee, Wisc., July 13, 1992.

Erenburg, Mark. Evanston, Ill., July 22, 1999.

Gatica, Mercedes. Dallas, Tex., Dec. 23, 1995.

Giffey, David. Madison, Wisc., Aug. 27, 1999.

Gonzalez, Arturo. Crystal City, Tex., Feb. 22, 1997.

Guajardo, Jose. Dallas, Tex., Apr. 11, 1996.

Gutiérrez, José Angel. Arlington, Tex., Apr. 19, 1995; July 2, 1996;
    Sept. 26, 2003.

Guzman, Ezequiel. Crystal City, Tex., Feb. 19, 1997.

Hererra, Jose. Crystal City, Tex., Feb. 13, 1997.

Hill, T. C. Crystal City, Tex., Feb. 12, 1997.

Kessler, Frederick. Milwaukee, Wisc., June 4, 1999.

Lazcano, Geraldo. Milwaukee, Wisc., Aug. 10, 1992.

Ledesma, Jose Guadalupe and Marta M., Cudahy, Wisc., May 6, 2006.

Leeper, Bernard. Crystal City, Tex., Feb. 14, 1997.

Loeffler, David. Milwaukee, Wisc., July 19, 1999.

Martinez, Rosa. Crystal City, Tex., Feb. 20, 1997.

Nieri, Alejandro. Madison, Wisc., July 14, 1999.

Ortiz, Juanita. Crystal City, Tex., Aug. 29, 2002.

Reyes, Carlos. Madison, Wisc., July 14, 1999.

Rodriguez, Francisco. Madison, Wisc., July 25, 28, 1998; July 29, 2000.

Rodriguez, Guadalupe. Milwaukee, Wisc., May 22, 1999.

Rodriguez, Raul. Milwaukee, Wisc., July 16, 1992.

Salas, Jesus. Milwaukee, Wisc., July 27, Aug. 27, 1992; Mar. 22, 1995; Feb. 9, 1998; Apr. 20, 2000.

Salas, Jesus. Interview by Michael Gordon, Milwaukee, Wisc., July 24, Aug. 18, 1997. Tapes in author's possession.

Saldana, Geraldo. Phone interview by author, San Antonio, Tex., June 17, 2006.

Sanchez, Alberto. Crystal City, Tex., Feb. 22, 1997.

Sanchez, Salvador. Milwaukee, Wisc., July 17, 19, 2000.

Smith, Bill. Milwaukee, Wisc., Aug. 23, 2000.

Other Works

Acuña, Rodolfo. *Occupied America: The Chicanos Struggle toward Liberation.* San Francisco: Canfield Press, 1972.

———. *Occupied America: A History of Chicanos.* New York: Harper and Row, 1988.

Alamillo, José M. *Making Lemonade out of Lemons: Mexican American Labor and Leisure in a California Town, 1880–1960.* Urbana: University of Illinois Press, 2006.

Allsup, Carl. *The American G.I. Forum: Origins and Evolution.* Austin: University of Texas Press, 1982.

Almaguer, Tomas. *Racial Fault Lines: The Historical Origins of White Supremacy in California.* Berkeley: University of California Press, 1994.

———. "Toward the Study of Chicano Colonialism." *Aztlán* 2 (1971): 7–22.

Alvarez, Luis. "The Power of the Zoot: Race, Community and Resistance in American Youth Culture, 1940–1945." Ph.D. diss., University of Texas, Austin, 2001.

Alway, Lazalle D. *Will You Make a School?* New York: National Child Labor Committee, 1957.

American G.I. Forum of Texas and Texas State Federation of Labor. *What Price Wetbacks?* Austin: G.I. Forum, 1953.

American Me. Dir. Edward James Olmos. Los Angeles: Universal Home Video, 1992. Videocassette.

Anaya, Rudolfo A., and Francisco Lomelí, eds. *Aztlán: Essays on the Chicano Homeland*. Albuquerque: University of New Mexico Press, 1989.

Anders, Evan. *Boss Rule in South Texas: The Progressive Era*. Austin: University of Texas Press, 1982.

Araiza, Lauren. "For the Freedom of Other Men: Civil Rights, Black Power, and the United Farm Workers, 1965–1973." Ph.D. diss., University of California–Berkeley, 2006.

Arredondo, Gabriela F., Aida Hurtado, Norma Klahn, Olga Najera-Ramirez, and Patricia Zavella, eds. *Chicana Feminisms: A Critical Reader*. Durham: Duke University Press, 2003.

Arreola, Daniel D. *Tejano South Texas: A Mexican American Cultural Province*. Austin: University of Texas Press, 2002.

Ashmore, Susan Youngblood. *Carry It On: The War on Poverty and the Civil Rights Movement in Alabama, 1964–1972*. Athens: University of Georgia Press, 2008.

Baca Zinn, Maxine. "Urban Kinship and Midwest Chicano Families: Evidence in Support of Revision." *De Colores* 6, no. 1–2 (1982): 85–98.

Banks, James A., and Cherry A. McGee Banks, eds. *Handbook of Research on Multicultural Education*. 2nd ed. New York: Macmillan, 2004.

Barger, Walter K., and Ernesto M. Reza. *The Farm Labor Movement in the Midwest: Social Change and Adaptation among Migrant Farmworkers*. Austin: University of Texas Press, 1994.

Barker, M. Dale. "In Crystal City: The Problem of Migratory Labor." *Sun and Soil*, Apr. 1957.

Barrera, Mario. *Beyond Aztlán: Ethnic Autonomy in Comparative Perspective*. Notre Dame: University of Notre Dame Press, 1990.

———. *Race and Class in the Southwest: A Theory of Racial Inequality*. Notre Dame: University of Notre Dame Press, 1979.

Bauman, Robert. *Race and the War on Poverty: From Watts to East L.A.* Norman: University of Oklahoma Press, 2008.

Bellah, Robert, Richard Madsen, William M. Sullivan, Ann Swidler, and Steven M. Tipton. *Habits of the Heart: Individualism and Commitment in American Life*. Berkeley: University of California Press, 1985.

Berkowitz, Peter. *Virtue and the Making of Modern Liberalism*. Princeton: Princeton University Press, 1999.

Bernstein, Irving. *Guns or Butter: The Presidency of Lyndon Johnson*. New York: Oxford University Press, 1996.

Berry-Cabán, Cristóbal S. "Puerto Rican Strategies for Survival: Work and Kinship among Esperanceños in Milwaukee." Ph.D. diss., University of Wisconsin–Milwaukee, 1981.

———. *A Survey of the Puerto Rican Community on Milwaukee's Northeast Side in 1976*. Milwaukee: Milwaukee Urban Observatory, University of Wisconsin–Milwaukee, 1976.

Bertrand, Michael T. *Race, Rock, and Elvis*. Urbana: University of Illinois Press, 2000.

Best, Wallace D. *Passionately Human, No Less Divine: Religion and Culture in Black Chicago, 1915–1952*. Princeton: Princeton University Press, 2005.

Bhabha, Homi K. *The Location of Culture*. London: Routledge, 1994.

Bissinger, H. G. *Friday Night Lights: A Town, a Team, and a Dream*. Reading, Mass.: Addison-Wesley, 1990.

The Black Public Sphere, ed. *The Black Public Sphere Collective*. Chicago: University of Chicago Press, 1995.

Blackwell, Maylei. "Contested Histories: Las Hijas de Cuauhtémoc, Chicana Feminisms, and Print Culture in the Chicano Movement, 1968–1973." In *Chicana Feminisms: A Critical Reader*, ed. Gabriela F. Arredondo, Aida Hurtado, Norma Klahn, Olga Najera-Ramirez, and Patricia Zavella, 59–89. Durham: Duke University Press, 2003.

Blanton, Carlos Kevin. "The Citizenship Sacrifice: Mexican Americans, the Saunders-Leonard Report, and the Politics of Immigration, 1951–1952." *Western Historical Quarterly* 40, no. 3 (2009): 299–320.

———. "George I. Sanchez, Ideology, and Whiteness in the Making of the Mexican American Civil Rights Movement: 1930–1960." *Journal of Social History* 72, no. 3 (2006): 569–604.

———. *The Strange Career of Bilingual Education in Texas, 1836–1981*. College Station: Texas A&M University Press, 2004.

Blauner, Robert. *Racial Oppression in America*. New York: Harper and Row, 1972.

Boyer, Paul. *Promises to Keep: The United States since World War II*. Lexington, Mass.: D. C. Heath, 1995.

Braziel, Jana Evans, and Anita Mannur. *Theorizing Diaspora: A Reader*. New York: Blackwell, 2003.

Braznell, William. *California's Finest: The History of the Del Monte Corporation and the Del Monte Brand*. San Francisco: Del Monte Corporation, 1982.

Brilliant, Mark. *Color Lines: Civil Rights Struggles on America's "Racial Frontier," 1945–1975*. Oxford: Oxford University Press, 2008.

Brown, William E. "Crystal City: New City Council Names Teamster Mayor." *International Teamster*, May 1963, 16–21.

———. "Crystal City: Symbol of Hope." *Labor Today* 2 (Dec. 1963–Jan. 1964): 16–20.

Busto, Rudy V. *King Tiger: The Religious Vision of Reies López Tijerina*. Albuquerque: University of New Mexico Press, 2005.

Calavita, Kitty. *Inside the State: The Bracero Program, Immigration, and the I.N.S.* New York: Routledge, 1992.

Camarillo, Albert M. *Chicanos in a Changing Society: From Mexican Pueblos to American Barrios in Santa Barbara and Southern California, 1848–1930*. Cambridge, Mass.: Harvard University Press, 1979.

Cardenas, Gilbert. "*Los Desarraigados*: Chicanos in the Midwestern Region of the United States." *Aztlán* 7, no. 2 (1976): 153–85.

———. "Who Are the Midwestern Chicanos? Implications for Chicano Studies." *Aztlán* 7, no. 2 (1976): 141–52.

Carrigan, William D. *The Making of a Lynching Culture: Violence and Vigilantism in Central Texas, 1836–1916*. Urbana: University of Illinois Press, 2004.

Carroll, Patrick J. "Tejano Living and Educational Conditions in World War II South Texas." *South Texas Studies*, no. 5 (1994): 82–103.

Carroll, Peter J. *Felix Longoria's Wake: Bereavement, Racism, and the Rise of Mexican American Activism*. Austin: University of Texas Press, 2003.

Cashion, Ty. *Pigskin Pulpit: A Social History of Texas High School Football Coaches*. Austin: Texas State Historical Association, 1998.

Castro, Tony. *Chicano Power: The Emergence of Mexican America*. New York: Saturday Review Press, 1974.

Chafe, William H. *The Unfinished Journey: America since World War II*. New York: Oxford University Press, 2003.

Chavez, Ernesto. *"¡Mi Raza Primero!" (My People First!): Nationalism, Identity, and Insurgency in the Chicano Movement in Los Angeles, 1966–1968*. Berkeley: University of California Press, 2002.

Chavez, John R. *Eastside Landmark: A History of the East Los Angeles Community Union*. Stanford: Stanford University Press, 1998.

———. *The Lost Land: The Chicano Image of the Southwest*. Albuquerque: University of New Mexico Press, 1984.

The Chicano Civil Rights Struggle in Wisconsin: Interview with Ernesto Chacon, Irma Guerra, and Maria Flores. Chicano Studies Program, University of Wisconsin–Madison, May 1989. Videocassette.

Chicano!: History of the Mexican American Civil Rights Movement. Vol. 4, *Fighting for Political Power*. Los Angeles: National Latino Communications Center Educational Media, 1996. Videotape.

Christian, Carole E. "Joining the American Mainstream: Texas's Mexican Americans during World War I." *Southwestern Historical Quarterly* 92, no. 4 (Apr. 1989): 559–95.

Clayson, William. "'The Barrios and the Ghettos Have Organized!': Community Action, Political Acrimony, and the War on Poverty in San Antonio." *Journal of Urban History* 28, no. 2 (Jan. 2002): 158–83.

———. *Freedom Is Not Enough: The War on Poverty and the Civil Rights Movement in Texas*. Austin: University of Texas Press, 2010.

Cobb, Daniel M. *Native Activism in Cold War America: The Struggle for Sovereignty*. Lawrence: University Press of Kansas, 2008.

———. "'Us Indians Understand the Basics': Oklahoma Indians and the Politics of Community Action, 1964–1970." *Western Historical Quarterly* 33, no. 1 (Spring 2002): 41–66.

Cohen, Robin. *Global Diasporas: An Introduction.* Seattle: University of Washington Press, 1997.

Commons, John R. *History of Labor in the United States, 1896–1932.* New York: Macmillan, 1918.

Copeland-Carson, Jacqueline. *Creating Africa in America: Translocal Identity in an Emerging World City.* Philadelphia: University of Pennsylvania Press, 2004.

Copp, Nelson Gage. *"Wetbacks" and Braceros: Mexican Migrant Laborers and American Immigration Policy, 1930–1960.* San Francisco: R&E Research Associates, 1971.

Cotera, Martha P. *Diosa y Hembra: The History and Heritage of Chicanas in the U.S.* Austin: Information Systems Development, 1976.

Cox, Patrick L. "Land Commissioner Bascom Giles and the Texas Veterans Land Board Scandals." M.A. thesis, University of Texas at Austin, 1988.

Cuellar, Robert A. "Social and Political History of the Mexican American Population, 1929–1963." Master's thesis, North Texas State University, 1969.

Cummings, Laura L. "Cloth-Wrapped People, Trouble, and Power: Pachuco Culture in the Greater Southwest." *Journal of the Southwest* 45, no. 3 (2003): 329–48.

Curtis, Tom. "Raza Desunida." *Texas Monthly*, Feb. 1977, 102–60.

Darder, Antonia, Rodolfo D. Torres, and Henry Gutierrez, eds. *Latinos and Education: A Critical Reader.* New York: Routledge, 1997.

De la Garza, Beatriz. *A Law for the Lion: A Tale of Crime and Injustice in the Borderlands.* Austin: University of Texas Press, 2003.

De la Torre, Adela, and Beatriz M. Pesquera, eds. *Building with Our Hands: New Directions in Chicana Studies.* Berkeley: University of California Press, 1993.

Del Castillo, Richard Griswold. *The Los Angeles Barrio, 1850–1890: A Social History.* Berkeley: University of California Press, 1979.

De León, Arnoldo. *They Called Them Greasers: Anglo Attitudes toward Mexicans in Texas, 1821–1900.* Austin: University of Texas Press, 1983.

Delgadillo, Theresa. "Exiles, Migrants, Settlers, and Natives: Literary Representations of Chicano/as and Mexicans in the Midwest." *Midwestern Miscellany*, no. 30 (Fall 2002): 27–45.

Delgado, Miguel A. "The Fraternization of the Pachuco and the Chicano." Unpublished manuscript, dated Sept. 20, 1972, in author's possession.

Denning, Michael. *The Cultural Front: The Laboring of American Culture in the Twentieth Century.* New York: Verso, 1996.

Dittmer, John. *Local People: The Struggle for Civil Rights in Mississippi.* Urbana: University of Illinois Press, 1995.

Donato, Ruben. *The Other Struggle for Equal Schools: Mexican Americans during the Civil Rights Era.* Albany: State University of New York Press, 1997.

Dougherty, Jack. *More than One Struggle: The Evolution of Black School Reform in Milwaukee.* Chapel Hill: University of North Carolina Press, 2004.

Dublin, Thomas. *Women at Work: The Transformation of Work and Community in Lowell, Massachusetts, 1826–1860.* New York: Columbia University Press, 1981.

Dudziak, Mary L. *Cold War Civil Rights: Race and the Image of American Democracy.* Princeton: Princeton University Press, 2000.

Eames, Alfred W., and Richard G. Landis. *The Business of Feeding People: The Story of Del Monte Corporation.* New York: Newcomen Society in North America, 1974.

Erenburg, Mark. "*Obreros Unidos* in Wisconsin." *Monthly Labor Review* 91, no. 6 (June 1968): 17–23.

———. "A Study of the Potential Relocation of Texas-Mexican Migratory Farm Workers to Wisconsin." Ph.D. diss., University of Wisconsin, Madison, 1969.

Estrada, Daniel, and Richard Santillán. "Chicanos in the Northwest and the Midwest United States: A History of Cultural and Political Commonality." *Perspectives in Mexican American Studies* 6 (1997): 195–228.

Farm Labor Organizing Committee. *FLOC: 25 Years of Struggle.* Toledo, Ohio: The Committee, 1992.

Fass, Paula S. *The Damned and the Beautiful: American Youth in the 1920s.* New York: Oxford University Press, 1977.

Fenton, Agnes M. *The Mexicans in the City of Milwaukee, Wisconsin.* Milwaukee: YWCA International Institute, 1930.

Fernandez, Johanna L. "Radicals in the Late 1960s: A History of the Young Lords Party in New York City, 1969–1974." Ph.D. diss., Columbia University, 2004.

Fernandez, Lilia. "From the Near West Side to 18th Street: Mexican Community Formation and Activism in Mid-twentieth Century Chicago." *Journal of the Illinois State Historical Society* 98, no. 3 (2005): 162–83.

Ferriss, Susan, and Ricardo Sandoval. *The Fight in the Fields: Cesar Chavez and the Farmworkers Movement.* New York: Harcourt Brace, 1997.

Flores, William V., and Rina Benmayor, eds. *Latino Cultural Citizenship: Claiming Identity, Space, and Rights.* Boston: Beacon, 1998.

Foley, Douglas E. *From Peones to Politicos: Class and Ethnicity in a Small Texas Town, 1900–1987.* Austin: University of Texas Press, 1988.

———. *Learning Capitalist Culture: Deep in the Heart of Tejas.* Philadelphia: University of Pennsylvania Press, 1990.

———. "The Transition of Early South Texas Society from 1930 to 1960." Washington, D.C.: U.S. Department of Health, Education and Welfare, 1974.

Foley, Douglas, Clarice Mota, and Ignacio Lozano. *Early South Texas Society and Schools from 1900 to 1930.* Austin: University of Texas Press, 1974.

Foley, Neil. "Becoming Hispanic: Mexican Americans and the Faustian Pact with Whiteness." In *Reflexiones: New Directions in Mexican American Studies*, ed. Neil Foley, 53–70. Austin: Center for Mexican American Studies University of Texas at Austin, 1998.

———. Quest for Equality: The Failed Promise of Black-Brown Solidarity. Cambridge: Harvard University Press, 2010.

———. *The White Scourge: Mexicans, Blacks, and Poor Whites in Texas Cotton Culture.* Berkeley: University of California Press, 1999.

———, ed. *Reflexiones: New Directions in Mexican American Studies.* Austin: Center for Mexican American Studies, University of Texas at Austin, 1997.

Forbath, William E. *Law and the Shaping of the American Labor Movement.* Cambridge, Mass.: Harvard University Press, 1991.

Fraga, Luis R., John A. Garcia, Rodney E. Hero, Michael Jones-Correa, Valerie Martinez-Ebers, and Gary Segura. *Latino Lives in America: Making It Home.* Philadelphia: Temple University Press, 2010.

Gabaccia, Donna R. *Italy's Many Diasporas.* Seattle: University of Washington Press, 2000.

———. *Militants and Migrants: Rural Sicilians Become American Workers.* New Brunswick: Rutgers University Press, 1988.

Ganz, Marshall. "Resources and Resourcefulness: Strategic Capacity in the Unionization of California Agriculture, 1959–1966." *American Journal of Sociology* 105, no. 4 (2000): 1003–62.

Garcia, Alma M. *Chicana Feminist Thought: The Basic Historical Writings.* New York: Routledge, 1997.

Garcia, F. Chris. *Latinos and the Political System.* Notre Dame: University of Notre Dame Press, 1988.

———, ed. *La Causa Politica: A Chicano Politics Reader.* Notre Dame: University of Notre Dame Press, 1974.

Garcia, Ignacio M. *Chicanismo: The Forging of a Militant Ethos among Mexican Americans.* Tucson: University of Arizona Press, 1997.

———. *United We Win: The Rise and Fall of La Raza Unida Party.* Tucson: University of Arizona Press, 1989.

———. *Viva Kennedy: Mexican Americans in Search of Camelot.* College Station: Texas A&M University Press, 2000.

Garcia, Mario T. *Mexican Americans: Leadership, Ideology, and Identity, 1930–1960.* New Haven: Yale University Press, 1991.

Garcia, Matt. *A World of Its Own: Race, Labor, and Citrus in the Making of Greater Los Angeles, 1900–1970.* Chapel Hill: University of North Carolina Press, 2001.

Garcia, Richard A. *Rise of the Mexican American Middle Class, San Antonio, 1919–1941.* College Station: Texas A&M University Press, 1991.

Garcia y Griego, Larry Manuel. "The Bracero Policy Experiment: U.S.-Mexican Responses to Mexican Labor Migration, 1942–1955." Ph.D. diss., University of California–Los Angeles, 1988.

Germany, Kent B. *New Orleans after the Promises: Poverty, Citizenship, and the Search for the Great Society.* Athens: University of Georgia Press, 2007.

Gerstle, Gary. "The Crucial Decade: The 1940s and Beyond." *Journal of American History* 92, no. 4 (Mar. 2006): 1292–99.

———. *Working-Class Americanism: The Politics of Labor in a Textile City, 1914–1960.* 2nd ed. Princeton: Princeton University Press, 2002.

Gibson, Campbell. "Population of the 100 Largest Cities and Other Urban Places in the United States: 1790 to 1990." Population Division Working Paper, no. 27. Washington, D.C.: Population Division, U.S. Bureau of the Census, June 1998.

Giffey, David, and Jesus Salas. *Struggle for Justice: The Migrant Farm Worker Labor Movement in Wisconsin.* Madison: Wisconsin Labor Historical Society, 1998.

Gilmer-Aikin Committee on Education. *To Have What We Must: A Digest of Proposals to Improve Public Education in Texas.* Austin: Texas Legislature, Gilmer-Aikin Committee on Education, 1948.

Gleason, Phillip. "American Identity and Americanization." In *Harvard Encyclopedia of American Ethnic Groups,* ed. Stephen Thernstrom, 39–41. Cambridge, Mass.: Harvard University Press, 1980.

Goldman, Shifra M. "The Iconography of Chicano Self-Determination: Race, Ethnicity and Class." *Art Journal* 49, no. 2 (Summer 1990): 167–73.

Gonzales, Gilbert G. *Chicano Education in the Era of Segregation.* Philadelphia: Balch Institute Press, 1990.

———. *Labor and Community: Mexican Citrus Worker Villages in a Southern California County, 1900–1950.* Urbana: University of Illinois Press, 1994.

Gonzales, Manuel G. *Mexicanos: A History of Mexicans in the United States.* Bloomington: Indiana University Press, 2009.

Gonzales, Rodolfo. *Message to Aztlán: Selected Writings of Rodolfo "Corky" Gonzales.* Houston: Arte Público, 2001.

Grebler, Leo, Joan W. Moore, and Ralph Guzman. *The Mexican-American People: The Nation's Second Largest Minority.* New York: Free Press, 1970.

Gregory, James N. *The Southern Diaspora: How the Great Migrations of Black and White Southerners Transformed America.* Chapel Hill: University of North Carolina Press, 2006.

Grimm, Agnes G. "Texas History Seldom Told." *Texas Outlook* 41, no. 7 (July 1957): 12–14.

Grossman, James R. *Land of Hope: Chicago, Black Southerners, and the Great Migration.* Chicago: University of Chicago Press, 1989.

Guglielmo, Thomas. "Fighting for Caucasian Rights: Mexicans, Mexican Americans, and the Transnational Struggle for Civil Rights in World War II Texas." *Journal of American History* 92, no. 4 (2006): 1212–37.

Guinier, Lani, and Gerald Torres. *The Miner's Canary: Enlisting Race, Resisting Power, Transforming Democracy.* Cambridge, Mass.: Harvard University Press, 2002.

Gurda, John. *The Latin Community of Milwaukee's Near South Side.* Milwaukee: Milwaukee Urban Observatory, University of Wisconsin–Milwaukee, 1976.

Gutiérrez, David G. "An Ethnic Consensus?: Mexican American Political Activism since the Great Depression." *Reviews in American History* 19, no. 2 (June 1991): 289–95.

———. "Globalization, Labor Migration, and the Demographic Revolution: Ethnic Mexicans in the Late Twentieth Century." In *The Columbia History of Latinos in the United States since 1960*, ed. David G. Gutiérrez, 1–42. New York: Columbia University Press, 2004.

———. "Migration, Emergent Ethnicity, and the 'Third Space': The Shifting Politics of Nationalism in Greater Mexico." *Journal of American History* 86, no. 2 (1999): 481–517.

———. *Walls and Mirrors: Mexican Americans, Mexican Immigrants, and the Politics of Ethnicity*. Berkeley: University of California Press, 1995.

———, ed. *The Columbia History of Latinos in the United States since 1960*. New York: Columbia University Press, 2004.

Gutiérrez, José Angel. "La Raza and Revolution: The Empirical Conditions of Revolution in Four South Texas Counties." Master's thesis, Saint Mary's University, 1968.

———. *La Raza and Revolution: The Empirical Conditions of Revolution in Four South Texas Counties*. San Francisco: R&E Research Associates, 1972.

———. *The Making of a Chicano Militant: Lessons from Cristal*. Madison: University of Wisconsin Press, 1998.

———. "Toward a Theory of Community Organization in a Mexican American Community in South Texas." Ph.D. diss., University of Texas–Austin, 1977.

Gutiérrez, Ramón. "Aztlán, Montezuma, and New Mexico: The Political Uses of American Indian Mythology." In *Aztlán: Essays on the Chicano Homeland*, ed. Rudolfo A. Anaya and Francisco Lomelí, 172–90. Albuquerque: University of New Mexico Press, 1989.

———. "Community, Patriarchy and Individualism: The Politics of Chicano History." *American Quarterly* 45, no. 1 (Mar. 1993): 44–72.

———. "Internal Colonialism: The History of a Theory." *Du Bois Review: Social Science Research on Race* 1, no. 2 (Summer 2004): 281–96.

Gutmann, Amy, ed. *Freedom of Association*. Princeton: Princeton University Press, 1998.

Guzman, Ralph C. *The Political Socialization of the Mexican-American People*. New York: Arno, 1976.

Handbook of Texas Online, s.v. "Aldrete, Cristóbal (1924–1991)," ⟨http://www.tsha.utexas.edu/handbook/online/articles/AA/falwl.html⟩. Accessed July 2, 2006.

———. s.v. "Allee, Alfred Young," ⟨http://www.tsha.utexas.edu/handbook/online/articles/AA/fal97.html⟩. Accessed July 16, 2006.

Harding, Bill. "Migrant Pupils." *Texas Outlook* 39, no. 5 (July 1955): 6–13.

Harrington, Michael. *The Other Americans*. New York: Macmillan, 1962.

Hendrickson, Kenneth E., Michael L. Collins, and Patrick Cox, eds. *Profiles in Power: Twentieth-Century Texans in Washington*. Austin: University of Texas Press, 2004.

Hernandez v. Driscoll Consolidated Independent School Dist., 2 Race Rel. L. Reptr. 329 (S.D. Tex. Jan. 11, 1957).

Hill, Wallace C., and Paul T. Vickers. "Sorry, No Hablo Español." *Texas Outlook* 41, no. 12 (Dec. 1957): 20–22.

Hinojosa, Gilberto Miguel. *A Borderlands Town in Transition: Laredo, 1755–1870.* College Station: Texas A&M University Press, 1983.

Hobsbawm, Eric. *The Age of Extremes: A History of the World, 1914–1991.* New York: Vintage, 1994.

Holdsworth, Ernest, Sr. *A History of Zavala County.* Crystal City: Mimeography, 1940.

Jackson, H. Joaquin, with David Marion Wilkinson. *One Ranger: A Memoir.* Austin: University of Texas Press, 2005.

Jenkins, J. Craig. *The Politics of Insurgency: The Farm Worker Movement in the 1960s.* New York: Columbia University Press, 1985.

Jesus Salvatierra v. Inhabitants of Del Rio Independent School District, 33 S.W.2d 790. Tex. Civ. App., 1930.

Johnson, Benjamin Heber. *Revolution in Texas: How a Forgotten Rebellion and Its Bloody Suppression Turned Mexicans into Americans.* New Haven: Yale University Press, 2003.

Jones, Patrick. "'Not a Color, but an Attitude': Father James Groppi and Black Power Politics in Milwaukee." In *Groundwork: Local Black Freedom Movements in America,* ed. Jeanne Theoharis and Komozi Woodard, 259–81. New York: New York University Press, 2005.

———. *The Selma of the North: Civil Rights Insurgency in Milwaukee.* Cambridge, Mass.: Harvard University Press, 2009.

Kaplowitz, Craig A. *LULAC: Mexican Americans and National Policy.* College Station: Texas A&M University Press, 2005.

Kelley, Robin D. G. *Race Rebels: Culture, Politics, and the Black Working Class.* New York: Free Press, 1994.

Kibbe, Pauline R. *Latin Americans in Texas.* Albuquerque: University of New Mexico Press, 1946.

Kiffmeyer, Thomas. *Reformers to Radicals: The Appalachian Volunteers and the War on Poverty.* Lexington: University Press of Kentucky, 2008.

Kingrea, Nellie W. *History of the First Ten Years of the Texas Good Neighbor Commission.* Forth Worth: Texas Christian University Press, 1954.

Klor de Alva, J. Jorge. "Aztlán, Boriquen and Hispanic Nationalism in the United States." In *Aztlán: Essays on the Chicano Homeland,* ed. Rudolfo A. Anaya and Francisco Lomeli, 135–71. Albuquerque: Academia/El Norte Publications, 1989.

Kostyu, Frank A. *Shadows in the Valley: The Story of One Man's Struggle for Justice.* Garden City, N.Y.: Doubleday, 1970.

Krass, Alfred. "Strikers and Ohio Churches: In the Soup." *Christian Century* 97 (Aug. 13–20, 1980): 796–98.

Kreneck, Thomas K. *Mexican American Odyssey: Felix Tijerina, Entrepreneur and Civic Leader, 1905–1965.* College Station: Texas A&M University Press, 2001.

Kymlicka, Will. "Ethnic Associations and Democratic Citizenship." In *Freedom of Association*, ed. Amy Gutmann, 177–213. Princeton: Princeton University Press, 1998.

———. *Multicultural Citizenship: A Liberal Theory of Minority Rights*. New York: Oxford University Press, 1995.

———. *Politics in the Vernacular: Nationalism, Multiculturalism, and Citizenship*. New York: Oxford University Press, 2001.

Lampman, Robert J. *Ends and Means in the War against Poverty*. Madison: University of Wisconsin Institute for Research on Poverty, 1966.

———. *The Low Income Population and Economic Growth*. Washington, D.C.: U.S. Government Printing Office, 1959.

Levitan, Sar A. *The Great Society's Poor Law: A New Approach to Poverty*. Baltimore: Johns Hopkins University Press, 1969.

Levy, Jacques E. *Cesar Chavez: Autobiography of La Causa*. Minneapolis: University of Minnesota Press, 2007.

Lieberson, Stanley. *A Piece of the Pie: Blacks and White Immigrants since 1880*. Berkeley: University of California Press, 1981.

Limón, José E. *American Encounters: Greater Mexico, the United States, and the Erotics of Culture*. Boston: Beacon, 1999.

———. *Mexican Ballads, Chicano Poems: History and Influence in Mexican-American Social Poetry*. Berkeley: University of California Press, 1992.

Lipsitz, George. *Time Passages: Collective Memory and American Popular Culture*. Minneapolis: University of Minnesota Press, 1990.

Little, George R., Jr. "A Study of the Texas Good Neighbor Commission." Master's thesis, University of Houston, 1953.

Loeffler, David. "Working within the 'System': The Progress of United Farm Workers (Obreros Unidos) under Wisconsin Law." *Newsletter of the Wisconsin Psychiatric Institute* 2 (1968): 11–15.

Lucas, Colin, ed. *The French Revolution and the Creation of Modern Political Culture*. New York: Perganon, 1987.

Macedo, Stephen. *Liberal Virtues: Citizenship, Virtue, and Community in Liberal Constitutionalism*. New York: Oxford University Press, 1990.

Magruder, Calvert. "A Half Century of Legal Influence upon the Development of Collective Bargaining." *Harvard Law Review* 50 (1937): 1071.

Mansbridge, Jane. "The Making of Oppositional Consciousness." In *Oppositional Consciousness: The Subjective Roots of Social Protest*, ed. Jane Mansbridge and Aldon Morris, 1–19. Chicago: University of Chicago Press, 2001.

Mansbridge, Jane, and Aldon Morris, eds. *Oppositional Consciousness: The Subjective Roots of Social Protest*. Chicago: University of Chicago Press, 2001.

Mantler, Gordon. "Black, Brown, and Poor: Martin Luther King Jr., the Poor People's Campaign, and Its Legacies." Ph.D. diss., Duke University, 2008.

Manuel, Herschel T. *The Educational Problem Presented by the Spanish-Speaking Child of the Southwest*. New York: Scientific Press, 1934.

————. *The Education of Mexican and Spanish-Speaking Children in Texas.*
Austin: Fund for Research in the Social Sciences, University of Texas, 1930.
————. "Progress in Inter-American Education and Plans in Prospect." *Texas Outlook* 29 (Mar. 1945): 13–15.
————. *Spanish-Speaking Children of the Southwest: Their Education and the Public Welfare.* Austin: University of Texas Press, 1965.

Maraniss, David. *They Marched into Sunlight: War and Peace in Vietnam and America, October 1967.* New York: Simon and Schuster, 2003.

Marquez, Benjamin. *Constructing Identities in Mexican American Political Organizations: Choosing Issues, Taking Sides.* Austin: University of Texas Press, 2003.

Martin, Philip, Manolo Abella, and Christiane Kuptsch. *Managing Labor Migration in the Twenty-first Century.* New Haven: Yale University Press, 2006.

Martinez, George A. "The Legal Construction of Race: Mexican-Americans and Whiteness." *Harvard Latino Law Review* 2 (1997): 321–47.
————. "Legal Indeterminacy, Judicial Discretion and the Mexican-American Litigation Experience, 1930–1980." *University of California at Davis Law Review* 27 (1994): 555–618.

Martinez, Manuel Luis. *Countering the Counterculture: Rereading Postwar American Dissent from Jack Kerouac to Tomás Rivera.* Madison: University of Wisconsin Press, 2003.

Matthiessen, Peter. *Sal Si Puedes: Cesar Chavez and the New American Revolution.* New York: Random House, 1969.

Matusow, Allen J. *The Unraveling of America: A History of Liberalism in the 1960s.* New York: Perennial, 1984.

May, Lary, ed. *Recasting America: Culture and Politics in the Age of Cold War.* Chicago: University of Chicago Press, 1989.

McGreevy, John T. *Parish Boundaries: The Catholic Encounter with Race in the Twentieth-Century Urban North.* Chicago: University of Chicago Press, 1998.

McWilliams, Carey. *Ill Fares the Land: Migrants and Migratory Labor in the United States.* Boston: Little, Brown, 1942.

Meier, Matt S., and Margo Gutierrez. *Encyclopedia of the Mexican American Civil Rights Movement.* Westport: Greenwood Press, 2000.

Mellenbruch, Julia. "Let's Teach Spanish to Spanish Speaking Pupils." *Texas Outlook* 39, no. 7 (July 1955): 14–15.

Menchaca, Martha. *The Mexican Outsiders: A Community History of Marginalization and Discrimination in California.* Austin: University of Texas Press, 1995.
————. *Recovering History, Constructing Race: The Indian, Black, and White Roots of Mexican Americans.* Austin: University of Texas Press, 2002.

Menefee, Seldon Cowles. *Mexican Migratory Workers of South Texas.* Washington, D.C.: U.S. Government Printing Office, 1941.

Miller, Michael. "Conflict and Change in a Bifurcated Community: Anglo-Mexican-American Political Relations in a South Texas Town." Master's thesis, Texas A&M University, 1971.

Miller, Michael V., and James D. Preston. "Vertical Ties and the Redistribution of Power in Crystal City." *Social Science Quarterly* 53, no. 4 (Mar. 1973): 772–84.

Missouri Pacific Railroad Company. *South Texas and the Winter Garden District.* Houston: Missouri Pacific Lines, 1930.

Montejano, David. *Anglos and Mexicans in the Making of Texas, 1836–1986.* Austin: University of Texas Press, 1987.

———. *Quixote's Soldiers: A Local History of the Chicano Movement, 1966–1981.* Austin: University of Texas Press, 2010.

Moore, Joan W. "Colonialism: The Case of Mexican-Americans." *Social Problems* 17 (1970): 463–71.

Moynihan, Daniel Patrick. *Maximum Feasible Misunderstanding: Community Action in the War on Poverty.* New York: Free Press, 1969.

Munoz, Carlos, Jr. *Youth, Identity, Power: The Chicano Movement.* New York: Verso, 1989.

Murrow, Edward R., dir. *Harvest of Shame.* CBS Video, 1991. Videocassette.

Nabokov, Peter. *Tijerina and the Courthouse Raid.* Albuquerque: University of New Mexico Press, 1969.

National Advisory Committee on Farm Labor. *Farm Labor Organizing, 1905–1967.* New York: National Advisory Committee on Farm Labor, 1967.

National Latino Communications Center. *Chicano!: The History of the Mexican American Civil Rights Movement.* Vol. 4, *Fighting for Political Power.* Los Angeles: National Latino Communications Center, NLCC Educational Media, 1996. Videocassette.

Navarro, Armando. *The Cristal Experiment: A Chicano Struggle for Community Control.* Madison: University of Wisconsin Press, 1998.

———. "El Partido de La Raza Unida in Crystal City: A Peaceful Revolution." Ph.D. diss., University of California–Riverside, 1974.

———. *La Raza Unida Party: A Chicano Challenge to the U.S. Two-Party Dictatorship.* Philadelphia: Temple University Press, 2000.

———. *Mexican American Youth Organization: Avant-Garde of the Chicano Movement in Texas.* Austin: University of Texas Press, 1995.

———. *Mexicano Political Experience in Occupied Aztlán: Struggles and Change.* Walnut Creek, Calif.: Altamira, 2004.

Neal, Mark Anthony. *What the Music Said: Black Popular Music and Black Popular Culture.* London: Routledge, 1999.

Nederveen Pieterse, Jan. *Globalization and Culture: Global Mélange.* Lanham, Md.: Rowan and Littlefield, 2003.

Ngai, Mae N. "Braceros, 'Wetbacks,' and the National Boundaries of Class." In *Repositioning North American Migration History: New Directions in Modern*

Continental Migration, Citizenship, and Community, ed. Marc S. Rodriguez, 206–83. Rochester: University of Rochester Press, 2004.

———. *Impossible Subjects: Illegal Aliens and the Making of Modern America, 1924–1965*. Princeton: Princeton University Press, 2004.

Obreros Unidos v. James Burns & Sons Farm, Inc. Wisconsin Employment Relations Board, Decision Number 7842, Dec. 15, 1966.

Obreros Unidos v. Libby, McNeill & Libby. Wisconsin Employment Relations Commission, Decision Number 8163, Aug. 29, 1967.

Obreros Unidos v. Libby, McNeill & Libby. Wisconsin Employment Relations Commission, Decision Number 8616, July 16, 1968.

Office of Economic Opportunity. *The Migrant and the Economic Opportunity Act*. Washington, D.C.: U.S. Government Printing Office, Feb. 1965.

———. *Participation of the Poor in the Community Decision-Making Process*. CAP Mission Guide, OEO Guidance 6005-1 (Aug. 1969).

Olivas, Michael A. *Colored Men and Hombres Aqui: "Hernandez v. Texas" and the Emergence of Mexican American Lawyering*. Houston: Arte Público, 2006.

Olneck, Michael R. "Americanization and the Education of Immigrants, 1900–1925: An Analysis of Symbolic Action." *American Journal of Education* 97, no. 4 (Aug. 1989): 398–423.

———. "Immigrants and Education in the United States." In *Handbook of Research on Multicultural Education*, 2nd ed., ed. J. Banks, 381–403. New York: Macmillan, 2004.

O'Neill, Patrick. "Where No Union Has Gone Before: Baldemar Velasquez Settles in for the Long Haul on Behalf of Cucumber Pickers in the South." *Sojourners Magazine* 27, no. 5 (1998): 42–43.

Orleck, Annelise. *Storming Caesar's Palace: How Black Mothers Fought Their Own War on Poverty*. Boston: Beacon Press, 2006.

Oropeza, Lorena. *¡Raza Sí! ¡Guerra No!: Chicano Protest and Patriotism during the Viet Nam War Era*. Berkeley: University of California Press, 2005.

Ortner, Sherry B. "Burned like a Tattoo: High School Social Categories and 'American Culture.'" *Ethnography* 3, no. 2 (2003): 115–48.

———. *New Jersey Dreaming: Capital, Culture, and the Class of '58*. Durham: Duke University Press, 2003.

Orum, Anthony M. *City-Building in America*. Boulder: Westview, 1995.

Pagan, Eduardo Obregón. *Murder at the Sleepy Lagoon: Zoot Suits, Race, and Riot in Wartime L.A.* Chapel Hill: University of North Carolina Press, 2003.

Parker, Benny L. "Power-in-Conflict: A Chicano Political Party's Definition of Social Disequilibrium and Anglo-Chicano Power Relationships Expressed through a Situational Analysis of Public Address in Crystal City, Texas, in 1972." Ph.D. diss., Southern Illinois University, 1975.

Parra, Pilar A. "United Opportunity Services, Inc.: An Historical and Organizational Analysis of Changing Goals." Master's thesis, University of Wisconsin–Madison, 1984.

Parsons, Timothy H. *Race, Resistance, and the Boy Scout Movement in British Colonial Africa*. Athens: Ohio University Press, 2004.

Pastrano, Jose Guillermo. "Industrial Agriculture in the Peripheral South: State, Race, and the Politics of Migrant Labor in Texas, 1890–1930." Ph.D. diss., University of California–Santa Barbara, 2006.

Patterson, James T. *America's Struggle against Poverty, 1900–1994*. Cambridge, Mass.: Harvard University Press, 1994.

———. *Grand Expectations: The United States, 1945–1974*. New York: Oxford University Press, 1996.

Pattillo-McCoy, Mary. *Black Picket Fences: Privilege and Peril among the Black Middle Class*. Chicago: University of Chicago Press, 2000.

Peña, Manuel. *Musica Tejana*. College Station, Tex.: Texas A&M University Press, 1999.

Perea, Juan F. "The Black/White Binary Paradigm of Race: The 'Normal Science' of American Racial Thought. *University of California Law Review* 85 (1997): 1213–58.

Perlman, Joel. *Ethnic Differences: Schooling and Social Structure among the Irish, Italians, Jews, and Blacks in an American City, 1880–1935*. New York: Cambridge University Press, 1989.

Phillips, Michael. *White Metropolis: Race, Ethnicity, and Religion in Dallas, 1841–2001*. Austin: University of Texas Press, 2006.

Pitti, Stephen J. *The Devil in Silicon Valley: Northern California, Race, and Mexican Americans*. Princeton: Princeton University Press, 2003.

Portes, Alejandro, and Min Zhou. "The New Second Generation: Segmented Assimilation and Its Variants." *Annals of the American Academy of Political and Social Science* 530 (Nov. 1993): 74–96.

Portes, Alejandro, and Ruben G. Rumbaut. *Legacies: The Story of the Immigrant Second Generation*. Berkeley: University of California Press, 2001.

Post, Donald E. "Ethnic Competition for Control of Schools in Two South Texas Towns." Ph.D. diss., University of Texas at Austin, 1974.

Post, Donald E., and Walter E. Smith. "Clergy: Outsiders and Adversaries; The Story of Catholic and Protestant Clergy in Three South Texas Towns during the Period of 1945–1975 Who Were Cast in the Midst of Changing Mexicano-Anglo Relations." Saint Edward's University, Library Archives, Austin, Tex., 1976. Photocopy.

Poulos, William T. "They Learn Basic English before School Starts." *Texas Outlook* 43, no. 8 (Aug. 1959): 15–34.

President's Commission on Migratory Labor. *Migratory Labor in American Agriculture*. Washington, D.C.: U.S. Government Printing Office, 1951.

Pridgen, William McKinley. "A Survey and Proposed Plan of Reorganization of the Public Schools in Zavala County, Texas." Master's thesis, University of Texas at Austin, 1939.

Provinzano, James. "Chicano Migrant Farm Workers in a Rural Wisconsin County." Ph.D. diss., University of Minnesota, 1971.

Pycior, Julie Leininger. "Henry B. Gonzales." In *Profiles in Power: Twentieth-Century Texans in Washington*, ed. Kenneth E. Hendrickson, Michael L. Collins, and Patrick Cox, 293–308. Austin: University of Texas Press, 2004.

———. *LBJ and Mexican Americans: The Paradox of Power*. Austin: University of Texas Press, 1997.

Quiñones, Juan G. *Chicano Politics: Reality and Promise, 1940–1990*. Albuquerque: University of New Mexico Press, 1990.

Quiñones, Naomi. "Rosita the Riveter: Welding Tradition with Wartime Transformations." In *Mexican Americans and World War II*, ed. Maggie Rivas-Rodriguez, 245–68. Austin: University of Texas Press, 2005.

Ramos, Henry A. J. *The American GI Forum: In Pursuit of the Dream, 1948–1983*. Houston: Arte Público, 1998.

Rangel, Jorge C., and Carlos M. Alcala. "Project Report: De Jure Segregation of Chicanos in Texas Schools." *Harvard Civil Rights–Civil Liberties Law Review* 7 (1972): 307–91.

Raushenbush, Elizabeth Brandeis. *A Study of Migratory Workers in Cucumber Harvesting, Waushara County, Wisconsin, 1964*. Madison: University of Wisconsin, 1966.

"Report of the Governor's Committee on Public School Education, Research Report Volume V, Public Education in Texas, Financing the System." Austin: Governor's Committee on Public School Education, 1969.

Reyes, David, and Tom Waldman. *Land of a Thousand Dances: Chicano Rock 'n' Roll from Southern California*. Albuquerque: University of New Mexico Press, 1998.

Ricourt, Milagros, and Ruby Danta. *Hispanas de Queens: Latino Panethnicity in a New York City Neighborhood*. Ithaca: Cornell University Press, 2003.

Rios-Bustamante, Antonio, and Pedro Castillo. *An Illustrated History of Mexican Los Angeles, 1781–1985*. Los Angeles: University of California, Chicano Studies Research Center, 1986.

Rivas-Rodriguez, Maggie, ed. *Mexican Americans and World War II*. Austin: University of Texas Press, 2005.

Rivera, Tomás. *And the Earth Did Not Part*. Berkeley: Quinto Sol, 1971.

———. *And the Earth Did Not Part*. Bilingual edition. Houston: Arte Público, 1992.

Rodriguez, Joseph A., Sara Filzen, Susan Hunter, Dana Nix, and Marc Rodriguez. *Nuestro Milwaukee: The Making of the United Community Center*. Milwaukee: Wisconsin Humanities Council and United Community Center, 2000.

Rodriguez, Marc S. "Cristaleño Consciousness: Mexican-American Activism between Crystal City, Texas and Wisconsin, 1963–1980." In *Oppositional Consciousness: The Subjective Roots of Social Protest*, ed. Jane Mansbridge and Aldon Morris, 146–69. Chicago: University of Chicago Press, 2001.

———. "A Movement of 'Young Mexican Americans Seeking Change': Critical Citizenship, Migration, and the Chicano Movement in Texas and Wisconsin, 1960–1975." *Western Historical Quarterly* 34, no. 3 (Autumn 2003): 274–99.

———. "MUSIC and the Making of a Northern Civil Rights Movement." Master's thesis, Northwestern University, 1994.

———, ed. *Repositioning North American Migration History: New Directions in Modern Continental Migration, Citizenship, and Community*. Rochester: University of Rochester Press, 2004.

Rojas, David. "The Making of Zoot Suiters in 1940s Mexican Los Angeles." Ph.D. diss., University of California–Berkeley, 2001.

Romo, Ricardo. *East Los Angeles: History of a Barrio*. Austin: University of Texas Press, 1983.

Rosaldo, Renato, Robert A. Calvert, and Gustav L. Seligmann, eds. *Chicano: The Beginnings of Bronze Power*. Minneapolis: Winston, 1973.

———. *Chicano: The Evolution of People*. New York: William Morrow, 1974.

Rosaldo, Renato, and William V. Flores. "Identity, Conflict, and Evolving Latino Communities: Cultural Citizenship in San Jose, California." In *Latino Cultural Citizenship: Claiming Identity, Space, and Rights*, ed. William V. Flores and Rina Benmayor, 57–96. Boston: Beacon Press, 1997.

Rosenbaum, Rene Perez. "Success in Organizing, Failure in Collective Bargaining: The Case of Pickle Workers in Wisconsin, 1967–1968." Working Paper Series, no. 11. East Lansing: Julian Samora Research Institute, Michigan State University, 1991.

———. "Success in Organizing, Failure in Collective Bargaining: The Case of Tomato Workers in Northwest Ohio, 1967–1968." Working Paper Series, no. 2. East Lansing: Julian Samora Research Institute, Michigan State University, 1991.

Rosenthal, Michael. *The Character Factory: Baden-Powell and the Origins of the Boy Scout Movement*. New York: Pantheon, 1986.

Rubel, Arthur. *Across the Tracks*. Austin: University of Texas Press, 1966.

Ruiz, Vicki L. *Cannery Women, Cannery Lives: Mexican Women, Unionization, and the California Food Processing Industry, 1930–1950*. Albuquerque: University of New Mexico Press, 1987.

———. *From Out of the Shadows: Mexican Women in Twentieth-Century America*. New York: Oxford University Press, 1998.

Ryan, Susan M. *Grammar of Good Intentions: Race and the Antebellum Culture of Benevolence*. Ithaca: Cornell University Press, 2005.

Samford, Van P. "The Gilmer-Aikin Committee: Its Proposals and Subsequent Effects on Texas Public Schools." Master's thesis, Stephen F. Austin State College, 1949.

Samora, Julian, Joe Bernal, and Albert Peña. *Gunpowder Justice: A Reassessment of the Texas Rangers*. Notre Dame: University of Notre Dame Press, 1979.

Sanchez, George J. *Becoming Mexican American: Ethnicity, Culture, and Identity in Chicano Los Angeles, 1900–1945*. New York: Oxford University Press, 1993.

Sanchez, Salvador. "The Migrant Stream." *Newsletter of the Wisconsin Psychiatric Institute* 2 (1968): 9–10.

Sanjek, Roger, and Steven Gregory, eds. *Race*. New Brunswick: Rutgers University Press, 1994.

San Miguel, Guadalupe, Jr. *"Let All of Them Take Heed": Mexican Americans and the Campaign for Educational Equality in Texas, 1910–1981*. Austin: University of Texas Press, 1987.

———. "Roused from Our Slumbers." In *Latinos and Education: A Critical Reader*, ed. Antonia Darder, Rodolfo D. Torres, and Henry Gutierrez, 135–57. New York: Routledge, 1997.

Sepúlveda, Juan. *The Life and Times of Willie Velásquez: Su Voto Es Su Voz*. Houston: Arte Público, 2003.

Sewell, William. "Le Citoyen/La Citoyenne: Activity, Passivity and the Revolutionary Concept of Citizenship." In *The French Revolution and the Creation of Modern Political Culture*, vol. 2, ed. Colin Lucas, 105–23. New York: Pergamon, 1988.

Shaw, Randy. *Beyond the Fields: Cesar Chavez, the UFW, and the Struggle for Justice in the 21st Century*. Berkeley: University of California Press, 2008.

Sherry, Michael S. *In the Shadow of War: The United States since the 1930s*. New Haven: Yale University Press, 1995.

Shesol, Jeff. *Mutual Contempt: Lyndon Johnson, Robert Kennedy, and the Feud that Defined a Decade*. New York: W. W. Norton, 1997.

Shockley, John S. *Chicano Revolt in a Texas Town*. Notre Dame: University of Notre Dame Press, 1974.

———. "Crystal City: La Raza Unida and the Second Revolt." In *Chicano: The Evolution of a People*, ed. Renato Rosaldo, Robert A. Calvert, and Gustav L. Seligmann, 314–26. Minneapolis: Winston, 1973.

———. "Crystal City, Texas: Mexican Americans and Political Change." Ph.D. diss., University of Wisconsin–Madison, 1972.

Simmons, Ozzie. "Anglo-Americans and Mexican-Americans in South Texas." Ph.D. diss., Harvard University, 1952.

Simmons, Thomas E. "The Citizen Factories: The Americanization of Mexican Students in Texas Public Schools, 1920–1945." Ph.D. diss., Texas A&M University, 1976.

Smith, Michael M. "Beyond the Borderlands: Mexican Labor in the Central Plains." *Great Plains Quarterly* 1, no. 4 (1981): 239–51.

Smith, Robert Courtney. *Mexican New York: Transnational Lives of New Immigrants*. Berkeley: University of California Press, 2005.

Smith, Walter Elwood. "Mexicano Resistance to Schooled Ethnicity: Ethnic Student Power in South Texas, 1930–1970." Ph.D. diss., University of Texas at Austin, 1978.

Smith, Walter Elwood, and Douglas E. Foley. *The Transition of Multiethnic Schooling in Model Town, Texas, 1930–1969*. Washington, D.C.: U.S. Department of Health, Education, and Welfare, 1975.

Sugrue, Thomas J. *Sweet Land of Liberty: The Forgotten Struggle for Civil Rights in the North*. New York: Random House, 2008.

Takaki, Ronald. *Double Victory: A Multicultural History of America in World War II*. Boston: Little, Brown, 2000.

Tate, R. C. "History of Zavala County, Texas." Master's thesis, Southwest Texas State College, 1942.

Taylor, Milton C. *An Approach to the Migratory Labor Problem through Legislation*. Madison: Wisconsin Governor's Commission on Human Rights, 1950.

Taylor, Paul S. *Mexican Labor in the United States*. New York: Arno, 1970.

———. *Mexican Labor in the United States: Dimmit County, Winter Garden District, South Texas*. Berkeley: University of California Publications in Economics, 1930.

Texas Education Agency. "Report of Pupils in Texas Public Schools Having Spanish Surnames, 1955–56." Austin: Texas Education Agency, Division of Research, 1957.

———. *Texas Public Schools: Sesquicentennial Handbook*. Austin: Texas Education Agency, 2004.

Theoharis, Jeanne, and Kmozi Woodard, eds. *Groundwork: Local Black Freedom Movements in America*. New York: New York University Press, 2005.

Thernstrom, Stephan. *The Other Bostonians: Poverty and Progress in the American Metropolis, 1880–1970*. Cambridge, Mass.: Harvard University Press, 1973.

———, ed. *Harvard Encyclopedia of American Ethnic Groups*. Cambridge, Mass.: Harvard University Press, 1980.

Thomas, Lorrin. *Puerto Rican Citizen: History and Political Identity in Twentieth-Century New York City*. Chicago: University of Chicago Press, 2010.

Thomas, Mary Eloise. "A Study of the Causes and Consequences of the Economic Status of Migratory Farm Workers in Illinois, Michigan, and Wisconsin, 1940–1958." Ph.D. diss., University of Notre Dame, 1960.

Tijerina, Reies. *They Called Me "King Tiger": My Struggle for the Land and Our Rights*. Houston: Arte Público, 2000.

Tiller, James W., Jr. "Some Economic Aspects of Commercial Cool Season Vegetable Production in the Texas Winter Garden." Ph.D. diss., University of Oklahoma, 1969.

———. *The Texas Winter Garden: Commercial Cool-Season Vegetable Production*. Austin: University of Texas Bureau of Business Monographs, 1971.

Torres, Gerald. Prologue to *The Miner's Canary: Enlisting Race, Resisting Power, Transforming Democracy*, by Lani Guinier and Gerald Torres, 1–10. Cambridge, Mass.: Harvard University Press, 2002.

Trujillo, Armando L. "Community Empowerment and Bilingual/Bicultural Education: A Study of the *Movimiento* in a South Texas Community." Ph.D. diss., University of Texas at Austin, 1993.

Tushnet, Mark V. *Making Civil Rights Law: Thurgood Marshall and the Supreme Court, 1936–1961*. New York: Oxford University Press, 2004.

United Migrant Opportunity Services, Inc. *Annual Report*. Milwaukee: United Migrant Opportunity Services, 1968.

———. *Helping People Help Themselves: United Migrant Opportunity Services, Inc. Celebrating 20 Years of Service*. Milwaukee: United Migrant Opportunity Services, 1985.

United States Congress. Senate. Subcommittee on Migratory Labor of the Committee on Labor and Public Welfare. *The Migrant Farm Worker in America: Background Data on the Migrant Worker Situation in the United States Today*. 88th Cong., 2nd sess., 1960.

———. Committee on Commerce. *Federal Trade Commission Oversight*. 93rd Cong., 2nd sess., Mar. 1, 7, and 14, and May 9, 1974.

———. Senate. Hearings before the Special Committee on Bilingual Education of the Committee on Labor and Public Welfare. 90th Cong., 1st sess., part 2. June 24, and July 21, 1967.

United States President's Commission on Migratory Labor. *Migratory Labor in American Agriculture*. Washington, D.C.: Government Printing Office, 1951.

Valdés, Dennis Nodin. *Al Norte: Agricultural Workers in the Great Lakes Region, 1917–1970*. Austin: University of Texas Press, 1991.

———. *Barrios Norteños: St. Paul and Midwestern Mexican Communities in the Twentieth Century*. Austin: University of Texas Press, 2000.

Valdez, Avelardo. "Selective Determinants in Maintaining Social Movement Organizations: Three Case Studies from the Chicano Community." In *Latinos and the Political System*, ed. F. Chris Garcia, 236–54. Notre Dame: University of Notre Dame Press, 1988.

———. "The Social and Occupational Integration of Mexican and Puerto Rican Ethnics in an Urban Industrial Society." Ph.D. diss., University of California–Los Angeles, 1980.

Valdez, Lalo. "A Narrative History of the Latin Community since 1968, Part 1." *La Guardia*, Nov. 1974.

Valdéz, Luis. *Zoot Suit and Other Plays*. Houston: Arte Público, 1992.

Van der Linden, Marcel. *Transnational Labour History*. London: Ashgate, 2003.

Vargas, Zaragosa. "Armies in the Fields and Factories: The Mexican Working Classes in the Midwest in the 1920s." *Mexican Studies–Estudios Mexicanos* 7, no. 1 (1991): 47–71.

———. *Labor Rights Are Civil Rights: Mexican American Workers in Twentieth-Century America*. Princeton: Princeton University Press, 2004.

Vigil, Ernesto B. *The Crusade for Justice: Chicano Militancy and the Government's War on Dissent*. Madison: University of Wisconsin Press, 1999.

Villarreal, Mary Ann. "*Cantantes y Cantineras*: Tejana Musicians and the Mapping of Public Space." Ph.D. diss., Arizona State University, 2003.

Weber, Devra. *Dark Sweat, White Gold: California Farm Workers, Cotton, and the New Deal*. Berkeley: University of California Press, 1994.

Weinberg, Meyer. *A Chance to Learn: A History of Race and Education in the United States*. New York: Cambridge University Press, 1977.

Werbner, Pnina, and Nira Yuval-Davis. *Women, Citizenship, and Difference*. New York: Zed, 1999.

West, Stanley A., and June Macklin, eds. *The Chicano Experience*. Boulder: Westview, 1979.

Westminster School District v. Mendez. 161 F.2d 774. 9th Cir., 1947.

Whalen, Carmen Theresa, and Víctor Vazquez-Hernandez. *The Puerto Rican Diaspora: Historical Perspectives*. Philadelphia: Temple University Press, 2005.

Wiebe, Robert H. *Who We Are: A History of Popular Nationalism*. Princeton: Princeton University Press, 2002.

Wilson, Stephen H. "Brown over 'Other White': Mexican Americans' Legal Arguments and Litigation Strategy in School Desegregation Lawsuits." *Law and History Review* 21, no. 1 (Spring 2003): 145–94.

Wisconsin Governor's Commission on Human Rights. *Migratory Agricultural Workers in Wisconsin: A Problem in Human Rights*. Madison: Governor's Commission on Human Rights, 1950.

Wisconsin Governor's Committee on Migratory Labor. *Report to the Governor, 1964*. Madison: Governor's Commission on Human Rights, 1964.

———. *Report for 1966 and 1967 with a Summary of Earlier Developments, by Elizabeth Brandeis Raushenbush, Chairman*. Madison: Equal Rights Division, Department of Industry, Labor and Human Relations, 1968.

WMVS Public Television. *I Remember: Hispanic Heritage*. Episode no. 254. Milwaukee: Video Recording, 1999.

Works, George A. *Texas Educational Survey Report*. Vol. 3, *General Report*. Austin: Texas Educational Survey Commission, 1925.

Yamashita, Shinji. "Introduction: 'Glocalizing' Southeast Asia." In *Globalization in Southeast Asia: Local, National, and Transnational Perspectives*, ed. Shinji Yamashita and J. S. Eades, 1–18. New York: Berghahn, 2002.

Yamashita, Shinji, and J. S. Eades, eds. *Globalization in Southeast Asia: Local, National, and Transnational Perspectives*. New York: Berghahn, 2002.

Zavala County Historical Commission. *Now and Then in Zavala County: A History of Zavala County, Texas, Written by the People of Zavala*. Crystal City, Tex.: Shelton Press, 1985.

Zolov, Eric. *Refried Elvis: The Rise of the Mexican Counter Culture*. Berkeley: University of California Press, 1999.

Index

Black Power, 106, 193 (n. 16)

Bracero Program, 16, 40; AGIF and, 25, 30, 171 (n. 55); Crystal City and, 24–25, 30, 168 (nn. 35–36), 169 (nn. 37–38); end of, 66, 67; migrant farmworkers and, 24–25, 30, 56, 66

Brandeis, Louis D., 65

Briscoe, Dolph, 151

Brown Berets, 115, 140, 142, 146, 191 (n. 3), 195 (n. 42)

Brown v. Board of Education, 28–29

California, 3, 15, 59, 168 (n. 35); Chicano movement and, 8, 127, 133, 144, 146, 147; Community Service Organization and, 28, 49, 68; grape boycott and, 87–88, 92, 94, 95, 99, 106, 115, 124, 142; Mexican American education and, 38, 174 (n. 15); migrant farmworker activism and, 2, 12, 60, 67–68, 71, 78, 83; NFWA and, 62, 67–68, 180 (n. 1), 181 (nn. 3–4); Raza Unida Party and, 13, 143, 144, 147, 149, 151, 152, 202 (n. 58); Tejano migrants and, 2, 4, 20, 34, 42, 62, 126, 133, 162 (n. 4), 165 (n. 2), 181 (nn. 4–5); UFW and, 9–10, 12, 95, 183 (n. 30); UFWOC and, 80, 87, 88, 90, 91, 92, 93, 94, 97, 181 (n. 3)

Cal-Pak. *See* Del Monte Corporation

Carrizo Springs, Tex., 29, 53, 139, 143, 154, 171 (n. 56)

Carter, Jimmy, 151

Catholic Church, 23, 56, 68, 69, 75, 92, 117

Central Sands Produce, 75, 185 (n. 59)

Certantes, Neno, 21

Cervera, Oscar, 21, 167 (n. 18)

Chacon, Ernesto, 89, 99, 102, 115, 116, 140, 146, 147, 155, 191 (n. 3)

Chafe, William, 100

Chávez, César, 12, 67, 68, 71, 78, 87, 128, 129, 183 (nn. 29–30, 36); Obreros Unidos and, 61, 80–81, 88, 90, 91, 92–93, 94, 95, 188 (n. 116)

Chicago, 12, 104, 146

Chicago Tribune, 92

Chicano America, 145–46

Chicano Moratorium, 144

Chicano movement, 127–29, 137, 145–46, 149, 157–58, 201 (n. 37); Americanism and, 9, 10, 153; in California, 8, 127, 133, 144, 146, 147; civil rights activism and, 8, 192 (n. 11); in Crystal City, 50, 129, 134, 152–53, 158, 201 (n. 43), 204 (n. 78); Mexican Americanism and, 6, 8, 59, 127, 152; in Milwaukee, 101, 113, 123

Chicano Youth Liberation Conferences, 128, 145–46

Citizens Association Serving All Americans (CASA), 57

Ciudadanos Unidos (Citizens United, CU), 138, 139, 145, 150, 201 (n. 43)

Civil rights: for African Americans, 1, 11, 15, 28–29, 68, 92, 127; African Americans vs. Mexican Americans, 96–97, 191 (n. 1), 192 (n. 11); AGIF and Mexican Americans, 15–16, 28, 30, 37, 171 (n. 60); Chicano movement and, 8, 192 (n. 11); in Crystal City, 16, 27, 35–37, 38, 56, 127, 136, 152; for Mexican Americans, 10–11, 13, 27–29, 62, 72, 91, 101, 126, 132, 181 (n. 5), 200 (n. 25); Milwaukee and, 9, 92, 99, 101, 106, 112–14, 115, 119, 121, 164 (n. 19), 193 (n. 16), 195 (n. 41), 196–97 (n. 60). *See also* Latin American Union for Civil Rights

Commons, John R., 12, 65, 181–82 (n. 16)

Community Action Agencies (CAAs), 101, 117, 124

Community Action Program (CAP), 98, 100, 101, 117, 124, 191 (n. 4)

Community Service Administration (CSA), 149, 150, 151

Compean, Mario, 149, 153, 155, 202 (n. 60)

Comprehensive Employment and Training Act, 123

Congress of Racial Equality (CORE), 106

Connally, John, 53, 54, 55, 179 (n. 77)

Cornejo, Juan, 1, 47, 48, 51, 52, 53, 54, 57, 59, 176 (n. 39), 177 (n. 43), 178 (n. 62)

Corona, Bert, 144, 202 (n. 58)

Cortinas, Guadalupe, 150, 152

166 (n. 15), 168 (nn. 35–36), 169 (nn. 37–38); veterans, 26, 27, 30, 32, 33, 34, 35; voter registration and, 47, 48, 49–50, 51, 64, 132, 145; women, 22, 23, 50, 74, 108, 145; young activists, 10–12, 13, 39, 47–48, 49, 50–51, 58, 60–61, 92, 94. *See also* American GI Forum; Crystal City High School; Los Cinco

Crystal City School Board, 31, 32, 34, 35, 36, 48, 134, 172–73 (n. 76)

Cucumber harvesting, 62, 63, 118; conditions for harvesters, 65, 66, 83, 110; labor activism and, 60, 72, 73, 75; labor unions and, 77–79, 80, 82, 83, 84–87, 91–92, 186 (nn. 75–76, 78), 188 (n. 108); mechanized picking, 72, 86, 87, 91–92, 95

Cuellar, Gloria, 20, 21

Dallas Morning News, 49

Delano, Calif., 60, 67, 68, 88, 93, 97, 147

De La Rosa, Frank, 32

Delgado, Miguel, 58, 149, 151, 169 (n. 38)

Delgado v. Bastrop Independent School District, 36

Del Monte Corporation, 24, 25, 47, 48–49, 53, 168 (n. 32)

Del Rio Independent School District v. Salvatierra, 35, 36

Democratic Party, 143, 151, 156

Denver, Colo., 128, 129, 137, 141, 143, 146, 147, 148–49

Dickens, Andrew, 48

Dimmit County, 17, 143, 174 (n. 12)

Economic Opportunity Act (EOA), 101, 103, 108, 112, 115, 116, 124, 192 (n. 10)

El movimiento. See Civil rights

El Paso, Tex., 146

Erenburg, Mark, 66, 73, 75, 78, 79–80, 82, 182 (n. 23), 183 (n. 32), 188 (n. 108)

Fagan, Joseph C., 69, 71, 72

Farm Labor Organizing Committee (FLOC), 97

Foley, Douglas, 30

Forbath, William, 77

Fourteenth Amendment, 28

Galvan, Salvador G., 52

Galvan family, 25

Gamez, Jesse, 134, 152

Gamez, Roberto, 142

Garcia, Hector P., 15, 29, 31, 35, 55, 171 (n. 56)

Garcia, Ignacio, 8

Garrigan, Michael, 69

Garrison, Homer, 55

Giffey, David, 64, 70, 80, 81, 82, 89, 102, 114

Giles, Bascom, 33

Gilmer, Claud, 40

Gonzales, Luis, 135

Gonzales, Rodolfo "Corky," 128, 129, 141, 143, 146, 147, 148

Gonzalez, Antonio, 60

Gonzalez, Arturo, 21, 138–39, 142, 150, 151

Gonzalez, Enrique, 141

Gonzalez, Henry B., 28–29, 56, 132, 200 (n. 24)

Good Neighbor Commission, 40

Good Neighbor Policy, 39

Governor's Committee on Migratory Labor (GCML), 65, 72, 182 (n. 22)

Grape boycott, 91, 94, 95, 106; Wisconsin support for, 87–88, 89, 90, 92, 99, 101, 102, 112, 113, 142, 189 (n. 128), 190 (n. 143), 198 (n. 1)

Grape workers, 62, 67, 91

Greene, Jerry, 55

Groppi, James, 106, 115, 119, 193 (n. 16)

Guajardo, Frank, 55

Guevara, Abbie, 31, 32, 34

Gutiérrez, José Angel, 13, 170 (n. 46), 199 (n. 10); Crystal City activism, 1963, 46, 47, 49, 50, 51, 53, 58, 64, 176 (n. 39); Crystal City activism, 1969, 10, 129, 132–33, 134, 135, 136, 137–38, 139, 199 (n. 18), 200 (n. 24), 201 (n. 46), 203 (n. 74), 204 (n. 77); Raza Unida Party and, 139–41, 143, 144, 146, 147–48, 149, 150, 151, 152, 153, 202 (n. 58)

Mothers' March on Madison," 119, 196–97 (n. 60). *See also* University of Wisconsin–Madison

Maldonado, Manuel, 53, 178 (n. 62)

Martinez, Lupe, 123

Martinez, Noelia, 134

Martinez, Rosa, 24

Maschmeier, Ralph, 108

Mata, José, 52

Maurice, John R., 108, 113, 117

McAllen, Tex., 63, 73

McCann, E. Michael, 84

Meany, George, 71, 181 (n. 3)

Medina, Eliseo, 93

Medina, Genevieve, 108

Mendoza, "Jeep," 142

Mexican Americanism, 160, 161–62 (n. 2); Chicano movement and, 6, 8, 59, 127, 152; community control and, 103, 124; in Crystal City, 16, 26–37, 47, 55, 56, 72–73; development of, in Texas and Wisconsin, 6, 11, 13–14, 155; postwar period and, 2, 16; radical nature of, 6, 56, 58–59

Mexican American Legal Defense and Educational Fund (MALDEF), 134, 141

Mexican American Political Associations of California/Texas, 49, 143

Mexican Americans: "cultural" citizenship and, 11, 164–65 (n. 20), 172 (n. 71); education and, 8, 11, 28, 42–43, 58, 127, 200 (n. 25); segregation and, 17, 23–24, 165 (n. 5), 168 (n. 30); segregation in schools and, 40, 42, 173 (n. 5); today, 159–60; traditional historical approach to, 3; veterans, 15, 170 (nn. 45, 48); World War II and, 15, 26, 169 (n. 42). *See also* Civil rights; Crystal City Mexican Americans; Migrant farmworkers; Milwaukee; Tejano migrants; Wisconsin

Mexican American Youth Organization (MAYO), 58, 139, 145, 152, 200 (nn. 24, 29); leadership of, 129, 132, 136, 138, 149, 153, 155, 202 (n. 60)

Mexican Revolution of 1910, 4, 159, 162 (n. 4)

Michigan, 62, 136, 141, 147, 149

Migrant farmworkers: Bracero Program and, 24–25, 30, 56, 66; children and, 41–42, 63, 74, 108–9, 193 (n. 22), 193–94 (n. 23); Del Monte Corporation and, 24, 25, 48–49, 53; education and, 38, 41–42, 44; grape workers, 62, 67, 91; housing conditions, 83, 96; Lawyers Defense Committee and, 83–84; potato processing, 73, 74–77, 78, 79, 185 (nn. 59, 67); spinach and, 17, 23, 24, 47, 48–49, 166 (n. 11); sugar beets and, 62, 141; women, 74. *See also* California; Crystal City Mexican Americans; Cucumber harvesting; Grape boycott; *La Voz Mexicana*; Obreros Unidos; Texas; United Migrant Opportunity Services, Inc.; Wisconsin

Miguel Hidalgo Association, 22

Milwaukee: African Americans and, 9, 92, 105, 106, 113, 115, 118–19, 190 (n. 143); Chicano movement and, 101, 113, 123; civil rights in, 9, 92, 99, 101, 106, 112–14, 115, 119, 121, 164 (n. 19), 193 (n. 16), 195 (n. 41), 196–97 (n. 60); Latino activism, 9, 10, 97, 98, 104, 109, 110, 113–25, 164 (n. 19), 192 (nn. 11–12); Mexican American population of, 103–6, 156–57; Mexican American/Tejano activism in, 9, 10, 12–13, 58, 99–100, 191 (n. 3); migrant farmworker unions and, 75, 76, 80–81, 84; Raza Unida Party and, 140, 141–42, 143, 144, 146, 150, 202 (n. 58), 203 (n. 74), 203–4 (n. 76), 204 (n. 77); Tejano activism and, 98–103, 106, 107, 139, 140, 152, 157, 192 (nn. 11–12), 201 (n. 46), 204 (n. 77); Tejano migrant communities in, 9, 34, 92, 98–100, 101, 103–4, 106, 107–8, 154–55, 156–57, 160, 201 (n. 46), 203 (n. 74); UMOS and, 112–13, 140, 157. *See also* University of Wisconsin–Milwaukee

Milwaukee Christian Center, 113

Montejano, David, 132

Moore, Carlos, 51

Muhammad, Elijah, 148

Rexnord Corporation, 107
Reyes, Carlos, 149, 153, 155, 202 (n. 60), 203–4 (n. 76)
Reyes, Carolina, 74
Ritchie, E. W., Jr., 52
Rivera, Juan, 45, 176 (n. 30)
Rivera, Tomás, 6
Rodriguez, Francisco, 13, 58; activism in Wisconsin, 89, 91, 139, 155, 201 (n. 46); Los Cinco and, 50–51, 64, 176 (n. 39); Raza Unida Party and, 144–45, 149, 201 (n. 46), 202 (n. 59), 203–4 (n. 76); at school, 42, 45, 47, 176 (n. 39), 199 (n. 10)
Rodriguez, Raul, 139
Rodriguez, Tomas M., 55
Roggerson, Chris, 136
Rubio, Trinidad, 135
Rumsfeld, Donald, 118

Salas, Carlos, 110
Salas, Jesus, 13, 58, 139, 155, 202 (n. 60); cucumber processing action and, 78–79, 82, 83, 84, 85, 186 (n. 76); family of, 63, 64; "March on Madison" and, 1–2, 60, 69–73, 110, 184 (nn. 41, 43); migrant farmworker activism and, 64–65, 66, 67, 80–81, 89, 95, 96, 142, 182 (n. 22), 190 (n. 133), 193–94 (n. 23); potato processing action and, 73–74, 75, 76; Raza Unida Party and, 149, 150, 151, 153; at school, 44, 60, 64, 176 (n. 39); UFWOC and, 81, 87, 88, 90–91, 92, 93, 99, 188 (n. 116); UMOS and, 99, 115–16, 118, 119–20, 196 (nn. 57, 59), 197 (n. 62); "Welfare Mothers' March on Madison" and, 118–19
Salas, Julian, 138
Salas, Manuel, Jr., 64, 66, 78, 79, 90, 92–93, 94, 110, 142, 189 (n. 128)
Salas, Manuel, Sr., 21, 63, 64, 73, 79, 181 (n. 11)
Salas, Teophillo, 64
Salas Café, 79
Salas tavern, 24–25, 63
Salazar, Ruben, 137
Salazar, Suzie, 42
Saldana, Geraldo, 35

San Antonio, 16, 47, 54, 158; Mexican Americans of, 3, 12, 28–29; Mexican American Youth Organization and, 58, 129, 132; Raza Unida Party and, 143, 152; Teamsters Union and, 48, 49, 56
Sanchez, George I., 55
Sanchez, Salvador, 63, 66; migrant farmworker activism and, 70, 73, 74, 78–79, 82, 110; UMOS and, 115, 116, 120–21, 123, 197–98 (n. 74)
Santiago, Viviana, 145
Santiestevan, Henry, 76
Schmitt, John, 76, 82, 84
Serna, Diana, 136
Shafer, Ray, 48
Shaw, Barry, 69
Sifuentes, Hermania, 42
Smith, Bill, 69, 73, 74, 75, 78, 94, 95, 102, 142, 184 (n. 41), 194 (n. 28)
Smith, Robert Neal, 119
Southwest Texas Junior College, 47
Spinach, 17; cannery, 24, 47, 48–49, 166 (n. 11); Spinach Festival, 23, 160
Starr County, Tex., 60, 90
Stars and Stripes, 64, 80
Students for a Democratic Society (SDS), 106–7
Sugar beets, 62, 141
Supreme Court of Texas, 143

Talamantez, Jose, 142
Taylor, Irl, 54
Teamsters Union, 80, 90; Del Monte Corporation and, 24, 49, 53; Los Cinco campaign and, 47, 48, 49–50, 51, 53, 177 (n. 40); Los Cinco victory and, 1, 39, 55, 56, 57–58; in Wisconsin, 88, 91, 92, 93, 94, 95, 190 (n. 133)
Tejano migrants: Chicano movement and, 6, 8, 10; seeking seasonal work in north and west, 3–7, 9, 161 (n. 1), 163 (n. 9); social networks and, 62–63, 138–39; Tejano diaspora, defined, 3, 162 (n. 4); urban communities of, 9, 12; young activists and, 2–3, 6, 60–61. *See also* California; Crystal City Mexican Americans; Madison;

Migrant farmworkers; Milwaukee; United Migrant Opportunity Services, Inc.; Wisconsin

Texas: Bracero Program and, 24–25, 30, 40; Chicano movement and, 129, 137, 146, 149; civil rights and, 15–16, 27–29, 56, 132, 136, 200 (n. 25); education and, 8, 11, 27, 28, 38, 39–42, 200 (n. 25); Mexican American activism and, 11–12, 35, 59; Mexican Americanism and, 6, 11, 13–14, 155; Mexican American political process and, 1, 17–18, 153; Mexican American population, 15; Mexican Americans and, 3, 4, 164 (n. 17); Mexican immigrants in, 4, 17, 24–25, 40; migrant farmworkers and, 10, 12, 56, 60, 62, 63, 180 (n. 1); Obreros Unidos and, 79, 90, 93; Raza Unida Party and, 13, 139, 141, 143–45, 149, 151; segregation and, 17, 19–20, 29, 165 (n. 5); segregation in schools and, 27, 28–29, 35–36, 40; veterans and, 32–34. *See also* Austin; Crystal City, Tex.; Crystal City Mexican Americans; San Antonio

Texas Department of Public Safety, 55

Texas Education Agency (TEA), 40, 136

"Texas History Seldom Told" (*Texas Outlook*), 41

Texas Outlook, 41

Texas Rangers, 11, 46, 51, 53, 54, 55, 141, 179 (n. 77)

Texas State Teachers Association, 41

Texas Veterans' Land Act (1946), 32–34

Tijerina, Felix, 42–43

Tijerina, Reies López, 128, 129, 148

To Have What We Must (Texas state legislature), 40

Torres, Antonio, 140

Torres, Mauro, 30

Towery, Ken, 33

Trevino, Mario, 136

Tuberculosis, 20, 108

United Auto Workers (UAW), 68, 71

United Brewery Workers Union, 76, 82

United Electrical, Radio, and Machine Workers, 115

United Farm Workers (UFW), 9–10, 12, 95, 183 (n. 30)

United Farm Workers Organizing Committee (UFWOC), 78, 80, 95, 97, 181 (n. 3); grape boycott and, 87–88, 90, 94, 101, 113, 142, 189 (n. 128); Jesus Salas and, 81, 87, 88, 90–91, 92, 93, 99, 188 (n. 116)

United Migrant Opportunity Services, Inc. (UMOS), 91, 196 (nn. 57, 59), 197 (n. 62), 202 (n. 60); board members for, 98, 111, 112, 117, 118, 119–20, 194 (n. 34), 195 (n. 54), 195–96 (n. 55); day care schools, 108, 111–12, 193 (n. 22); independent review of, 121, 123; lack of political involvement by, 110, 115–16; Latinization of, 117, 118, 195–96 (n. 55); march to Madison, 121, 122; Milwaukee and, 112–13, 140, 157; origins of, 100–101, 108, 193 (n. 20); Raza Unida Party and, 139, 140, 144, 147, 149, 150, 153, 155; recruiting former farmworkers, 101, 109; Tejano activism and, 12–13, 98–100, 103, 104, 112, 115–18, 120–23, 124–25, 196–97 (n. 60), 197–98 (n. 74); Tejano roving counselors, 109, 110–11, 112, 120; work of, 101, 103, 106, 107, 108–9, 120, 121, 123, 157, 197 (n. 63)

United Packinghouse Food and Allied Workers (UPFAWU), 74, 186 (n. 75)

U.S. Department of Health, Education, and Welfare (HEW), 136

U.S. House Education and Labor Committee, 27

University of Texas, 40, 55

University of Wisconsin–Madison, 69, 82, 107, 117, 119, 149, 155, 195 (n. 54); Chicano Studies Department, 153, 202 (n. 60); Institute for Research on Poverty, 65, 66; research on migrant farmworkers, 109–10, 182 (nn. 20–21, 23), 194 (n. 28)

University of Wisconsin–Milwaukee, 92, 107, 144

Uvalde, Tex., 29, 47, 151, 154

Uvalde County, 17